Concepts and Practices in Marketing Research

Concepts and Practices in Marketing Research

Dr. R.P. Sharma

RANDOM

RANDOM PUBLICATIONS
NEW DELHI (INDIA)

Concepts and Practices in Marketing Research

ISBN 978-93-5111-659-2

Published in 2015 in India by

RANDOM PUBLICATIONS

4376-A/4B, Gali Murari Lal, Ansari Road
New Delhi-110 002
Phone : +9111-43580356, 011-23289044, 011-43142548
e-mail: sales@randompublications.com,
info@randompublications.com, randomexports@gmail.com

Reprinted 2026

Type Setting by : Friends Media, Delhi-110089

Preface

Marketing research is "the process or set of processes that links the consumers, customers, and end users to the marketer through information — information used to identify and define marketing opportunities and problems; generate, refine, and evaluate marketing actions; monitor marketing performance; and improve understanding of marketing as a process. Marketing research specifies the information required to address these issues, designs the method for collecting information, manages and implements the data collection process, analyzes the results, and communicates the findings and their implications."

Research, as a general concept, is the process of gathering information to learn about something that is not fully known. Nearly everyone engages in some form of research. From the highly trained geologist investigating newly discovered earthquake faults, to the author of best selling spy novels gaining insight into new surveillance techniques, to the model train hobbyist spending hours hunting down the manufacturer of an old electric engine, each is driven by the quest for information. For marketers, research is not only used for the purpose of learning, it is also a critical component needed to make good decisions. Market research does this by giving marketers a picture of what is occurring (or likely to occur) and, when done well, offers alternative choices that can be made.

Marketing research also collects full information about the competitors. The company uses this information to fight competition. It also helps the marketing manager to take decisions. Marketing research is a special branch and soul of 'Marketing Management'.

It is of recent origin and widely used by manufacturers, exporters, distributors and service organisations. Marketing research is very systematic, scientific, objective and organised. It has a wide scope. It includes product research, consumer research, packaging research, pricing research, etc.

This book attempts to blend marketing research into marketing and sales. The author wishes to create an ideal perspective for market research among marketers, advertisers, sales professionals, consultants and, above all, market researchers.

I would like to thank my team for standing beside me throughout my career and writing this book. My special thanks go to "Random Publications" who have published the book.

– Dr. R.P. Sharma

Contents

1

Introduction

Research is the cornerstone of any science, including both the hard sciences such as chemistry or physics and the social sciences such as psychology, management, or education. It refers to the organized, structured, and purposeful attempt to gain knowledge about a suspected relationship.

Many argue that the structured attempt at gaining knowledge dates back to Aristotle and his identification of deductive reasoning.

Deductive reasoning refers to a structured approach utilizing an accepted premise, a related minor premise, and an obvious cease. This way of gaining knowledge has been called a syllogism, and by following downward from the general to the specific, knowledge can be gained about a particular relationship.

An example of an Aristotelian syllogism might be:

Major Premise:	All students attend school regularly
Minor Premise:	John is a student
Cease:	John attends school regularly

In the early 1600s, Francis Bacon identified a different approach to gaining knowledge. Rather than moving from the general to the specific, Bacon looked at the gathering of specific information in order to make general ceases.

This type of reasoning is called inductive and unlike Aristotelian logic allows new major premises to be determined. Inductive reasoning has been adopted into the sciences as the preferred way to explore new relationships because it allows us to use accepted knowledge as a means to gain new knowledge.

For example:

Specific Premises:	John, Sally, Lenny and Sue attended class regularly
Specific Premises:	John, Sally, Lenny, and Sue received high grades
Cease:	Attending class regularly results in high grades

Researchers combine the powers of deductive and inductive reasoning into what is referred to now as the scientific method. It involves the determination of a major premise and then the analysis of the specific examples that would logically follow. The results might look something like:

Major Premise:	**Attending classes regularly results in high grades**	
Class Attendance: (Suspected Cause)	Group 1:	John, Sally, Lenny and Sue attend classes regularly
	Group 2:	Heather, Lucinda, Ling, and Bob do not attend classes regularly
Grades: (Suspected Effect)	Group 1:	John, Sally Lenny, and Sue received A's and B's
	Group 2:	Heather, Lucinda, Ling, and Bob received C's and D's
Cease:	Attending class regularly results in higher grades when compared with not attending class regularly (the Major Premise or Hypothesis is therefore supported)	

Utilizing the scientific method for gaining new information and testing the validity of a major premise, John Dewey suggested a series of logical steps to follow when attempting to support a theory or hypothesis with actual data.

In other words, he proposed using deductive reasoning to develop a theory followed by inductive reasoning to support it. These steps are:

- Identify and define the problem,
- Determine the hypothesis or reason why the problem exists,
- Collect and analyse data,
- Formulate conclusions,
- Apply conclusion to the original hypothesis.

The steps involved in the research process can vary depending on the type of research being done and the hypothesis being tested.

The most stringent types of research, such as experimental methods, contain the most structured process. Naturalistic observation, surveys, and other non-intrusive studies, are often less structured. A general process guide for doing research, especially laboratory research are:

- Determine your theory or educated guess about a relationship. Involves identifying and defining a problem and reviewing the current literature.

- Operationally define all variables to be involved in the research.
- Develop hypothesis by plugging variables into original theory. A hypothesis is a testable theory with operationally defined variables.
- Standardized the research methods by developing a research protocol to be used with every subject. Include in this step the methods for subject selection and assignment as well as how you will attempt to control for any extraneous variable.
- Select subjects and assign to groups using the protaocol developed in step 4.
- Test subjects using the protocol developed in step 4.
- Analyse results.
- Determine the significance of the results and how these results compare with other studies. Critique your research and suggest needs for further research based on your findings.
- Communicate results through journal publication, book, book chapter, repor, presentation, or any means that will benefit those to whom the research applies.
- Replicate, while part of the research process, this step is most often completed by a different researcher.

DETERMINING OF RESEARCH THEORY

While you may see a theory as an absolute, such as the theory of gravity or the theory of relativity, it is actually a changing phenomenon, especially in the soft or social sciences. Theories are developed based on what is observed or experienced, often times in the real world. In other words, a theory may have no additional backing other than an educated guess or a hunch about a relationship.

For example, while teaching a college course in research, we notice that non-traditional students tend to be more involved in class lectures and perform better on class exams than traditional students. Our theory, then, could be that older students are more dedicated to their education than younger students.

At this point, however, we have noticed only a trend within a single class that may or may not exist. We have developed a theory based on our observations and this theory, at least at this point, has no practical applications. Most theories are less concerned with application and more concerned with explanations.

For example, we could assume, based on our observations, that older students have witnessed the importance of education through their work and interactions with others. With this explanation, we now have a theoretical cause and effect relationship: Students who have had prior experience in the workforce are more dedicated to their education than students who have not had this experience.

This point it is always wise to do a literature review on your topic and areas related to your topic. Results from this search will likely help you determine how to proceed with your research. If, for example, you find that several studies have already been completed on this topic with similar results, doing yet another experiment may add little to what is already known. If this is the case, you would need to rethink your ideas and perhaps replicate the previous research using a different type of subject or a different situation or you may choose to scrap the study all together.

DEFINING VARIABLES

Variables can be defined as any aspect of a theory that can vary or change as part of the interaction within the theory. In other words, variables are anything can effect or change the results of a study. Every study has variables as these are needed in order to understand differences.

In our theory, we have proposed that students exposed to the workforce take a more active role in their education than those who have no exposure. Looking at this theory, you might see that several obvious variables are at play, including 'prior work experience' and 'age of student.' However, other variables may also play a role in or influence what we observed.

It is possible that older students have better social skills causing them to interact more in the classroom.

They may have learned better studying skills, resulting in higher examination grades. They may feel awkward in a classroom of younger students or doubt their ability more and therefore try harder to succeed. All of these potential explanations or variables need to be addressed for the results of research to be valid.

Let's start with the variables that are directly related to the theory. First, the prior work experience is what we are saying has the effect on the classroom performance. We could say that work history is therefore the cause and classroom grades are the effect. In this example, our independent variable, the variable we start with is work experience. Our dependent variable or the variable we end up with is grades.

We could add additional variables to our list to create more complex research. If we also looked at the affect of study skills on grades, study skills would become a second independent variable. If we wanted to measure the length of time to graduation along with grades, this would become a second dependent variable.

There is no limit to the number of variables that can be measured, although the more variables, the more complex the study and the more complex the statistical analysis. The most powerful benefit of increasing our variables, however, is control. If we suspect something might impact our outcome, we need to either include it as a variable or hold it constant between all groups.

If we find a variable that we did not include or hold constant to have an impact on our outcome, the study is said to be confounded. Variables that can confound our results, called confounding variables, are categorized into two groups: extraneous and intervening.

EXTRANEOUS VARIABLES

Extraneous variables can be defined as any variable other than the independent variable that could cause a change in the dependent variable. In our study we might realise that age could play a role in our outcome, as could family history, education of parents or partner, interest in the class topic, or even time of day, preference for the instructor's teaching style or personality. The list, unfortunately, could be quite long and must be dealt with in order to increase the probability of reaching valid and reliable results.

INTERVENING VARIABLES

Intervening variables, like extraneous variables, can alter the results of our research. These variables, however, are much more difficult to control for. Intervening variables include motivation, tiredness, boredom, and any other factor that arises during the course of research. For example, if one group becomes bored with their role in the research more so than the other group, the results may have less to do with our independent variable, and more to do with the boredom of our subjects.

DEVELOPING THE HYPOTHESIS

The hypothesis is directly related to a theory but contains operationally defined variables and is in testable form. Hypotheses allow us to determine, through research, if our theory is correct. In other words, does prior work experience result in better grades? When doing research, we are typically looking for some type of difference or change between two or more groups. In our study, we are testing the difference between having work experience and not having work experience on college grades. Every study has two hypotheses; one stated as a difference between groups and one stated as no difference between groups.

When stated as a difference between groups, our hypothesis would be, "students with prior work experience earn higher grades than students without prior work experience." This is called our research or scientific hypothesis. Because most statistics test for no difference, however, we must also have a null hypothesis. The null hypothesis is always written with the assumption that the groups do not differ. In this study, our null hypothesis would state that, "students with work experience will not receive different grades than students with no work experience."

The null hypothesis is what we test through the use of statistics and is abbreviated H_0. Since we are testing the null, we can assume then that if the null is not true then some alternative to the null must be true. The research hypothesis stated earlier becomes our alternative, abbreviated H_1. In order to make research as specific as possible we typically look for one of two outcomes, either the null or the alternative hypothesis.

To conclude that there is no difference between the two groups means we are accepting our null hypothesis. If we, however, show that the null is not true then we must reject it and therefore conclude that the alternative hypothesis must be true. While there may be a lot of gray area in the research itself, the results must always be stated in black and white.

STANDARDIZATION

Standardization refers to methods used in gathering and treating subjects for a specific study. In order to compare the results of one group to the results of a second group, we must assure that each group receives the same opportunities to succeed. Standardized tests, for instance, painstakingly assure that each student receives the same questions in the same order and is given the same amount of time, the same resources, and the same type of testing environment. Without standardization, we could never adequately compare groups.

For example, imagine that one group of students was given a particular test and allowed four hours to complete it in a quiet and well lit room. A second group was given the same test but only allowed 30 minutes to complete it while sitting in a busy school lunchroom full of laughing and talking children. If group 1 scored higher than group 2 could we truly say that they did better? The answer is obviously 'no.' To make sure we can compare results, we must make everything equal between the two or more groups. Only then could we say that group 1 performed better than group 2.

Standardization of the research methods is often a lengthy process. The same directions must be read to each student, the same questions must be given, and the same amount of time must be assured. All of these factors must be decided before the first subject can be tested. While standardization refers mainly to the testing situation itself, these principles of 'sameness' involve the selection of subjects as well.

SELECTING AND TESTING SUBJECTS

If we want to know if Billy performed better than Sally, or if boys scored higher than girls in our class, or even if Asian children receive higher grades in our school than Caucasian children, the selection of subjects is rather simple. When we are testing the entire population of possible subjects, we are adequately assured that no subject bias has occurred.

A population refers to the entire pool of possible subjects. In a classroom or other setting where the entire population is relatively small, testing all subjects may be simple. However, if we are attempting to understand or gain knowledge related to a large population, such as all third grade children, all depressed adults, or all retail employees, gathering and testing everyone would be relatively impossible. In this situation, we would need to gather a sample of the population, test this sample, and then make inferences aimed at the entire population of which they represent.

When determining which potential subjects from a large population to include in our study there are several approaches to choose from. Each of these sampling techniques have its own strengths and, of course, its own weaknesses. The idea behind adequate sampling, however, remains the same: to gather a sample of subjects that is representative of the greater population. The ideal research sample is therefore often referred to as a representative sample.

SIMPLE RANDOM SAMPLE

To assure that the sample of subjects taken from a known population truly represents the population, we could test every subject in the population and choose only those who fall around the mean of the entire population. This technique is usually pointless because doing so means we could just as easily have tested the entire population on our independent and dependent variables. Therefore in order to make sure all possible subjects have an equal opportunity to be chosen, simple random sampling is most often the selection method used.

To choose a random group of 10 students from a class of 30, for example, we could put everyone's name in a hat and use the first ten names drawn as our sample. In this method, subjects are chosen just as 'B6' is chosen in a game of BINGO. This technique can work well with a small population but can be time consuming and archaic when the population size is large. To choose 30 students from a class of 250 students would be easier utilizing technology and what is referred to as a random number table.

A random number table is a computer generated list of numbers placed in random order. Each of the 250 students would be randomly assigned a number between one and 250. Then the groups would be formed once again using a random number generator.

SYSTEMATIC SAMPLE

When a population is very large, assigning a number to each potential subject could also be tiresome and time consuming. A systematic sample is a random sample compiled in a systematic manner. If you had a list of all licensed teachers, for example, and wanted to mail a survey to 200 of them, systematic sampling might be the sampling method of choice. For this example, a page and a teacher number on that page are determined at random. This would represent the first subject and the starting point for choosing the remaining subjects. A random number would be generated, for example 150. Then every 150th teacher would become a subject until you have selected enough for your study. If you complete the list before selecting enough subjects, you would continue back at the beginning of the list. Once the subjects are selected, the technique of random assignment can be used to assign subjects to particular groups.

STRATIFIED RANDOM SAMPLE

The use of a stratified sample refers to the breaking down of the population into specific subsets before choosing which ones will take part in the study. For example, if you are studying all third grade students in your state, you may want to make sure that every county in your state is represented in your study.

If you used a simple random sampling technique, you could conceivably end up with many subjects from one county and no subjects from other counties. A stratified sample allows you to choose your subject pool randomly from a predetermined set of subsets.

In this example, we may want to choose 10 subjects at random from each county within the state.

Other subsets can also be used, such as age, race, or socioeconomic background.

If you wanted to make sure that there were an equal number of males and females, you could use sex as your subset and then randomly choose the same number of subjects from each subset.

This type of sampling is useful when the population has some known differences that could result in different outcomes.

For instance, if you already know that 80 per cent of the students are male, you may want to select 40 male students and 10 female students so that your sample represents the breakdown of sex within the population.

CLUSTER SAMPLE

Cluster sampling could be considered a more specific type of stratified sample. When this technique is used, potential subsets of subjects are first randomly eliminated and then the remaining subsets are used to randomly select the sample of subjects to be used in the study.

For example, if you are measuring the effect of prior work experience on college grades in a particular state, you may first make a list of all colleges in the state.

Then you would randomly select a number of colleges to either include or eliminate in the selection process. Once you have a subset of colleges, you could use the same technique to randomly include or eliminate the specific classes. From the remaining classes, you would then randomly select a group of students with work experience and a group of students with no work experience to be placed in your two groups.

NON-PROBABILITY SAMPLE

Non-probability refers to a group of subjects chosen based on their availability rather then their degree of represe-ntativeness of the population.

Surveys are often done in this manner. Imagine going to the local mall to gather information about the buying habits of mall shoppers.

Your subject pool does not represent all mall shoppers but rather those mall shoppers who happen to walk by your location on that day. The same would hold true for a survey over the phone or via mail. Those who respond to your questions or return the mailed survey do not necessarily represent the population at large. Instead, they represent the population who was home and was willing to respond to your questions or those who took the time to complete and return the survey.

While at first glance this method seems unprofessional, it allows for the gathering of information in a short amount of time. It is not considered standardized research and would be scrutinized if submitted to a professional journal, but it does have its place.

When watching a news programme you may have not changed channels because you are waiting for the results of a survey that will be reported at the end of the programme. We are highly interested in these 'informal' polls and using a non-probability sample is a quick way to gather large amounts of information in a relatively short amount of time.

TESTING SUBJECTS

Once you determined your variables, applied the concept of standardization, and selected your subjects, you are almost ready to begin the testing process. The concept of testing refers to the application or analysis of your independent and dependent variables. If there is any manipulation of the subjects in your study, it occurs during this phase. Before testing any human subject, however, some type of consent form is necessary. Consent forms basically describe the study, how the results will be used, and any possible negative effects that may occur.

They also give the subject the right to withdrawal from the study at any time without consequence. Your specific hypothesis does not need to be disclosed but each subject must be made aware of any general concerns and be able to ask questions before testing can begin..

If your hypothesis, for example, asked if there is a difference in effectiveness of different treatments for depression, you might assign your subjects to one of several different groups: cognitive therapy, dynamic therapy, humanistic therapy and possibly no therapy.

Each subject would likely be tested prior to the study to determine a baseline for his or her level of depression and would then begin a predetermined and standardized treatment plan. Because you are standardizing your study, each subject should get identical treatment short of the independent variable. In other words, the only thing you want to be different between the groups is the type of therapy received.

The no therapy group would be considered a control group and may participate in some type of non-therapy related activity while the other subjects receive therapy. This group is used to determine if time plays a role in the decrease of depressive symptoms. Without a control group you couldn't say that any particular therapy was more helpful than no therapy because subjects may have improved merely because of some outside factor unrelated to treatment. These factors are called extraneous variables, and control groups, along with randomization, help to keep the impact of these variables to a minimum.

ANALYZING RESULTS

The specific analysis performed on the subjects depends on the type of subjects, the type of questions being asked, and the purpose of the research. When we gathered and tested all possible subjects from a known population we would use descriptive statistics to analyse our results. Descriptive statistics require the testing of everyone in the population and are used to describe the qualities of the population in numerical format. For example, we could say that the mean score on an IQ test for all third graders at Jefferson High School is 102. We could also state that there is no difference between the IQs of boys and girls within our subjects if the data support these ceases.

When we are using a sample of subjects smaller than the entire population, we must make some inferences using what we call inferential statistics. Like any inferences, we also assume a certain degree of error when making determinations about a population based on a sample of that population. Because of this, the results of inferential statistics are often stated within a predetermined level of confidence.

If we found that the mean of one group was 10 points higher than the mean of a second group in our work experience and college grades study, we could not assume that the population means are identical. We could, however, state that the means of the entire population are likely to differ by five to 15 points or that there is a 95 per cent probability that the means of the entire population differs by ten points.

In this sense, we are predicting the scores of the entire population based on the scores of our sample and stating them within a range or a predetermined level of confidence. This allows us to include the likely error that occurs whenever an inference is made.

DETERMINING SIGNIFICANCE OF RESEARCH MARKETING

The term significance when related to research has a very specific role. Significance refers to the level of certainty in the results of a study. We can say that our subjects differed by an average of ten points with 100 per cent certainty because we personally witnessed this difference. To say that the population will differ is another story. To do this, we must determine how valid our results are based on a statistical degree of error. If we find, through the use of inferential statistics, that the grades of those with and without work experience are different me must state the estimated error involved in this inference. While the standard acceptable error is 5 per cent, it can be as high as 20 per cent or as low as 0.1 per cent.

The amount of error to be accepted in any study must be determined prior to beginning the study. In other words, if we want to be 95 per cent confident in our results, we set the significance level at.05. If we want to be 99 per cent confident, our significance level is set at.01. We can then state that there is a difference in the population means at the 95 per cent significance level or at the 99 per cent significance level if our statistics support this statement.

If our statistics estimate that there is 10 per cent error and we said we would accept only 5 per cent, the results of our study would be stated as 'not significant.' When determining significance, we are saying that a difference exists within our acceptable level of error and we must therefore reject the null hypothesis. When results are found to be not significant, the only option available is to accept the null hypothesis.

COMMUNICATING RESULTS

Results of a study are disseminated in many forms. The highest level of communicating results is often in a peer-reviewed professional journal. Peer-reviewed refers to a group of professionals in a particular field who read all submissions and publish only those that meet the highest degree of scrutiny and applicability. When errors are found in the sampling of subjects, the statistical analysis, or the inferences made, the study will often be rejected or returned to the author for revisions. Published substances in peer-reviewed would likely be the best source for research when you begin looking into your theory.

Results of research studies are also disseminated through textbooks, book chapters, conferences, presentations, and newsletters. For example, a study comparing the average salary in a particular county might be published in the local newspaper or in a brochure for the chamber of commerce. Our study of non-traditional students and work experience might be summarized in a board meeting of the college's department of student retention or published in a trade journal such as the "Journal of Higher Education."

Some studies are never released, especially if the results do not add to the already available research. Other studies are meant only to provide direction for larger studies. Our study of college students may be used only to determine if a larger study is likely to result in important findings. If we get significant results then a larger study, including a broader subject pool, may then be conducted. These types of studies are often called pilot studies because the goal is not to gather knowledge about the population, but rather to guide further research in a particular area.

REPLICATION

Replication is the key to the support of any worthwhile theory. Replication involves the process of repeating a study using the same methods, different subjects, and different experimenters. It can also involve applying the theory to new situations in an attempt to determine the generalizability to different age groups, locations, races, or cultures.

For example, our study of non-traditional students may be completed using students from another college or from another state. It may be changed slightly to add additional variables such as age, sex, or race to determine if these variables play any role in our results.

Replication, therefore, is important for a number of reasons, including:

- Assurance that results are valid and reliable;
- Determination of generalizability or the role of extraneous variables;
- Application of results to real world situations; and
- Inspiration of new research combining previous findings from related studies.

PUTTING IT ALL TOGETHER

We asked the question,'do college students with work experience earn better grades than those without work experience.' Knowing the steps involved in doing research and now having a basic understanding of the process, we could design our experiment and with fictional results could determine our ceases and how to report our findings to the world. To do this, lets start with our theory and progress through each of the ten steps.

DETERMINING A THEORY

Theories are developed through our interaction with our environment. For our particular theory, we observed that older college students tend to perform better on classroom tests than younger students.

As we attempt to explain why, we developed our theory that real world work experience creates a motivation in students that allows them to perform better than students without this motivation. Our theory, therefore, states that prior work experience will result in higher grades.

DEFINING VARIABLES

Every experiment has an independent and a dependent variable. The independent variable is what we start with; it refers to the separation of our groups. In our case, we want to look at prior work experience so the presence or absence of this would constitute our experimental groups. We may place those students who have been in the workforce for more than one year in group 1 and those with less than one year in group 2.

Our dependent variable is our outcome measure so in our case we are looking for a difference in class grades. To operationally define the variable grades, we might use the final course average as our outcome measure. If the independent and dependent variable(s) are difficult to determine, you can always complete the following statement to help narrow them down: The goal of this study is to determine what effect ________ (IV) has on ________ (DV). For us, the goal is to determine what effect one year or more of prior work experience has on course average.

DETERMINING HYPOTHESIS

When we plug our variables into our original theory we get our research hypothesis. Simply stated, Students with one or more years of prior work experience will receive higher final course averages than students with less than one year of prior work experience. Since statistical analysis often tests the null hypothesis or the idea that there is no difference between groups, our null hypothesis could be stated as: Final course averages of students with one or more years of prior work experience will not differ from final course averages of students with less than one year of prior work experience.

STANDARDIZATION

To make sure that each subject, no matter which group they belong to, receives the same treatment, we must standardize our research. While this may be difficult in the real world, our goal is to get as close as possible to the ideal.

Therefore, we may choose to gather subjects from a general psychology class since this is a class required of most students and will not be affected by college major. We may further decide to research only those students who have a specific instructor to keep the instruction between the two groups as similar as possible. Remember, our goal is to assure, at least as much as possible, that the only difference between the two groups is the independent variable.

SELECTING SUBJECTS

Because our population consists of all college students, it will be impossible to include everyone in the study. Therefore we need to apply some type of random selection. Since we want to use only those students who have the same instructor, we may ask all of this instructors students, prior to any teaching, how much work experience they have had. Those who report a year or more become the potential subject pool for group 1 and those who have less than one year become the subject pool for group 2.

We could, at this point decide to include all of these subjects or to further reduce the subjects randomly. To reduce the subject pool we could assign each student in each group a random number and then choose, at random, a specific number of students to become subjects in our study. For the purpose of this example, as suggested, randomly choose 20 students in each group to participate in our study.

TESTING SUBJECTS

Since we are not applying any type of treatment to our subjects, this phase in the procession can be omitted. If we were determining if the teaching styles of different instructors played a role in grades, we would randomly assign each student to a teacher. In that case, teaching style would become an independent variable in our study.

ANALYZING RESULTS

Our original question asked if final averages would be different between our two groups. To determine this as suggested, look at the mean of each group. Therefore, as suggested, add up the averages of the 20 subjects in each group and divide each of these by 20.

If, after comparing the means of each group, we find that group 1 has a mean of 88 and group 2 has a mean of 82 then we can descriptively state that there is a six-point difference between the means of the two groups. Based on this statistic, we would then begin to show support for our alternative hypothesis and can progress to the next step.

DETERMINATION OF SIGNIFICANCE

Our goal was not to describe what their averages were, but rather to make inferences about what is likely happening in the entire population. We must therefore apply inferential statistics to our results to determine the significant or lack of significant findings.

As suggested, set our confidence level at 95 per cent and then apply statistical analysis to our results to see if the difference of six points with a sample size of 40 is significant.

Imagine that we did find a significant difference. In this case we could say that with a 95 per cent confidence level, students with one year of more work experience receive higher averages than those with less than one year of work experience.

Since the null hypothesis, which stated that no difference exists between the two groups, was not correct, we must reject it. And by rejecting the null, we automatically accept our alternative hypothesis.

COMMUNICATING RESULTS

When communicating the results of our study we need to do several things. We need to make a case for why we did this research, which is often based on our literature search. We then need to report the process we took in gathering our sample and applying the treatment.

We can then report our results and argue that there is a difference between the two groups and that this difference is significant enough to infer it will be present in the entire population.

Finally, we must evaluate our research in terms of its strengths, weaknesses, applicability, and needs for further study. In terms of strengths, we might include the rigors of gathering subjects and the fact that we used a random sample of students. We may argue that the statistical methods used were ideal for the study or that we considered the recommendations of previously completed studies in this area. Weaknesses might include the small sample size, the limited pool from which our sample was gathered, or the reliance on self-reported work experience.

To discuss applicability and needs for further studies we could suggest that more studies be completed that use a broader base of subjects or different instructors. We could recommend that other variables be investigated such as student age, type and location of college, family educational history, sex, race, or socioeconomic background. We might even suggest that while our findings were significant they are not yet applicable until these other variables are investigated.

REPLICATION

The final step in any research is replication. This can be done by us but is most often completed by other researchers based on their own review of the literature and the recommendations made by previous researchers. If others compete a similar study, or look at different variables and continue to find the same results, our results become stronger.

When ten other studies agree with ours, the chances are greatly improved that our results were accurate.

If ten other studies disagree with our findings then the validity of our study will be, and most certainly should be, called into question. By replicating studies and using previously gained knowledge to search for new answers, our profession continues to move forward.

After all, we used the ideas of other researchers to design our research, and future researchers may incorporate our findings to make recommendations in their research. The cycle is never ending and allows for perpetual seeking of new knowledge.

DEALS IN MARKETING RESEARCH

These terms often are used interchangeably, but technically there is a difference.

Market research deals specifically with the gathering of information about a market's size and trends. *Marketing research* covers a wider range of activities. While it may involve market research, marketing research is a more general systematic process that can be applied to a variety of marketing

PROBLEMS IN VALUE OF INFORMATION

Information can be useful, but what determines its real value to the organization? In general, the value of information is determined by:

- The ability and willingness to performance on the information.
- The accuracy of the information.
- The level of indecisiveness that would exist without the information.
- The amount of variation in the possible results.
- The level of risk aversion.
- The reaction of competitors to any decision improved by the information.
- The cost of the information in terms of time and money.

MARKETING RESEARCH PROCESS

Once the need for marketing research has been established, most marketing research projects involve these steps:

- Define the problem,
- Determine research design,
- Identify data types and sources,
- Design data collection forms and questionnaires,
- Determine sample plan and size,
- Collect the data,
- Analyse and interpret the data,
- Prepare the research report.

PROBLEM DEFINITION

The decision problem faced by management must be translated into a market research problem in the form of questions that define the information that is required to make the decision and how this information can be obtained. Thus, the decision problem is translated into a research problem. For example, a decision problem may be whether to launch a new product.

The corresponding research problem might be to assess whether the market would accept the new product. The objective of the research should be defined clearly.

To ensure that the true decision problem is addressed, it is useful for the researcher to outline possible scenarios of the research results and then for the decision maker to formulate plans of action under each scenario. The use of such scenarios can ensure that the purpose of the research is agreed uponbefore it commences.

RESEARCH DESIGN

Marketing research can classified in one of three categories:

- Exploratory research,

- Descriptive research,
- Causal research.

These classifications are made just as to the objective of the research. In some cases the research will fall into one of these categories, but in other cases different phases of the same research project will fall into different categories.

- *Exploratory research:* Has the goal of formulating problems more precisely, clarifying concepts, gathering explanations, gaining insight, eliminating impractical ideas, and forming hypotheses. Exploratory research can be performed using a literature search, surveying certain people about their experiences, focus groups, and case studies. When surveying people, exploratory research studies would not try to acquire a representative sample, but rather, seek to interview those who are knowledgeable and who might be able to provide insight concerning the relationship among variables. Case studies can include contrasting situations or benchmarking against an organization known for its excellence. Exploratory research may develop hypotheses, but it does not seek to test them. Exploratory research is characterized by its flexibility.
- *Descriptive research:* Is more rigid than exploratory research and seeks to describe users of a product, determine the proportion of the population that uses a product, or predict future demand for a product. As opposed to exploratory research, descriptive research should define questions, people surveyed, and the method of analysis prior to beginning data collection. In other words, the who, what, where, when, why, and how aspects of the research should be defined. Such preparation allows one the opportunity to make any required changes before the costly process of data collection has begun.

  There are two basic types of descriptive research: Longitudinal studies and cross-sectional studies. Longitudinal studies are time series analyses that make repeated measurements of the same individuals, thus allowing one to monitor behaviour such as brand-switching. However, longitudinal studies are not necessarily representative since many people may refuse to participate because of the commitment required. Cross-sectional studies sample the population to make measurements at a specific point in time. A special type of cross-sectional analysis is a cohort analysis, which tracks an aggregate of individuals who experience the same event within the same time interval over time. Cohort analyses are useful for long-term forecasting of product demand.
- *Causal research:* Seeks to find cause and effect relationships between variables. It accomplishes this goal through laboratory and field experiments.

DATA TYPES AND SOURCES

Secondary Data

Before going through the time and expense of collecting primary data, one should check for secondary data that previously may have been collected for other purposes but that can be used in the immediate study. Secondary data may be internal to the firm, such as sales invoices and warranty cards, or may be external to the firm such as published data or commercially available data.

The government census is a valuable source of secondary data. Secondary data has the advantage of saving time and reducing data gathering costs. The disadvantages are that the data may not fit the problem perfectly and that the accuracy may be more difficult to verify for secondary data than for primary data.

Some secondary data is republished by organizations other than the original source. Because errors can occur and important explanations may be missing in republished data, one should obtain secondary data directly from its source. One also should consider who the source is and whether the results may be biased.

There are several criteria that one should use to evaluate secondary data:

- Whether the data is useful in the research study.
- How current the data is and whether it applies to time period of interest.
- Errors and accuracy - whether the data is dependable and can be verified.
- Presence of bias in the data.
- Specifications and methodologies used, including data collection method, response rate, quality and analysis of the data, sample size and sampling technique, and questionnaire design.
- Objective of the original data collection.
- Nature of the data, including definition of variables, units of measure, categories used, and relationships examined.

Primary Data

Often, secondary data must be supplemented by primary data originated specifically for the study at hand.

Some common types of primary data are:

- Demographic and socioeconomic characteristics.
- Psychological and lifestyle characteristics.
- Attitudes and opinions.
- Awareness and knowledge - for example, brand awareness.
- *Antentions*: For example, purchase intentions. While useful, intentions are not a reliable indication of actual future behaviour.

- *Motivation*: A person's motives are more stable than his/her behaviour, so motive is a better predictor of future behaviour than is past behaviour.
- Behaviour.

Primary data can be obtained by communication or by observation. Communication involves questioning respondents either verbally or in writing. This method is versatile, since one needs only to ask for the information; however, the response may not be accurate.

Communication usually is quicker and cheaper than observation. Observation involves the recording of actions and is performed by either a person or some mechanical or electronic device.

Observation is less versatile than communication since some attributes of a person may not be readily observable, such as attitudes, awareness, knowledge, intentions, and motivation.

Observation also might take longer since observers may have to wait for appropriate events to occur, though observation using scanner data might be quicker and more cost effective.

Observation typically is more accurate than communication. Personal interviews have an interviewer bias that mail-in questionnaires do not have. For example, in a personal interview the respondent's perception of the interviewer may affect the responses.

QUESTIONNAIRE DESIGN

The questionnaire is an important tool for gathering primary data. Poorly constructed questions can result in large errors and invalidate the research data, so significant effort should be put into the questionnaire design. The questionnaire should be tested thoroughly prior to conducting the survey.

MEASUREMENT SCALES

Attributes can be measured on nominal, ordinal, interval, and ratio scales:

- Nominal numbers are simply identifiers, with the only permissible mathematical use being for counting. *Example*: social security numbers.
- Ordinal scales are used for ranking. The interval between the numbers conveys no meaning. Median and mode calculations can be performed on ordinal numbers.
  Example: class ranking
- Interval scales maintain an equal interval between numbers. These scales can be used for ranking and for measuring the interval between two numbers. Since the zero point is arbitrary, ratios cannot be taken between numbers on an interval scale; however, mean, median, and mode are all valid. *Example*: temperature scale.

- Ratio scales are referenced to an absolute zero values, so ratios between numbers on the scale are meaningful. In addition to mean, median, and mode, geometric averages also are valid.
  Example: weight

VALIDITY AND RELIABILITY

The validity of a test is the extent to which differences in scores reflect differences in the measured characteristic. Predictive validity is a measure of the usefulness of a measuring instrument as a predictor. Proof of predictive validity is determined by the correlation between results and actual behaviour. Construct validity is the extent to which a measuring instrument measures what it intends to measure.

Reliability is the extent to which a measurement is repeatable with the same results. A measurement may be reliable and not valid. However, if a measurement is valid, then it also is reliable and if it is not reliable, then it cannot be valid. One way to show reliability is to show stability by repeating the test with the same results.

ATTITUDE MEASUREMENT

Many of the questions in a marketing research survey are designed to measure attitudes. Attitudes are a person's general evaluation of something.

Customer attitude is an important factor for the following reasons:

- Attitude helps to explain how ready one is to do something.
- Attitudes do not change much over time.
- Attitudes produce consistency in behaviour.
- Attitudes can be related to preferences.

Attitudes can be measured using the following procedures:

- *Self-reporting*: Subjects are asked directly about their attitudes. Self-reporting is the most common technique used to measure attitude.
- *Observation of behaviour*: Assuming that one's behaviour is a result of one's attitudes, attitudes can be inferred by observing behaviour. For example, one's attitude about an issue can be inferred by whether he/she signs a petition related to it.
- *Indirect techniques*: Use unstructured stimuli such as word association tests.
- *Performance of objective tasks*: Assumes that one's performance depends on attitude. For example, the subject can be asked to memorize the arguments of both sides of an issue. He/she is more likely to do a better job on the arguments that favour his/her stance.
- *Physiological reactions*: Subject's response to a stimuli is measured using electronic or mechanical means. While the intensity can be measured, it is difficult to know if the attitude is positive or negative.

- *Multiple measures*: A mixture of techniques can be used to validate the findings, especially worthwhile when self-reporting is used.

There are several types of attitude rating scales:

- *Equal-appearing interval scaling*: A set of statements are assembled. These statements are selected just as to their position on an interval scale of favourableness. Statements are chosen that has a small degree of dispersion. Respondents then are asked to indicate with which statements they agree.
- *Likert method of summated ratings*: A statement is made and the respondents indicate their degree of agreement or disagreement on a five point scale.
- *Semantic differential scale*: A scale is constructed using phrases describing attributes of the product to anchor each end. For example, the left end may state, "Hours are inconvenient" and the right end may state, "Hours are convenient". The respondent then marks one of the seven blanks between the statements to indicate his/her opinion about the attribute.
- *Stapel Scale*: Similar to the semantic differential scale except that:
  - Points on the scale are identified by numbers,
  - Only one statement is used and if the respondent disagrees a negative number should marked, and
  - There are 10 positions instead of seven.

  This scale does not require that bipolar adjectives be developed and it can be administered by telephone.
- *Q-sort technique*: The respondent if forced to construct a normal distribution by placing a specified number of cards in one of 11 stacks just as to how desirable he/she finds the characteristics written on the cards.

SAMPLING PLAN

The sampling frame is the pool from which the interviewees are chosen. The telephone book often is used as a sampling frame, but have some shortcomings. Telephone books exclude those households that do not have telephones and those households with unlisted numbers. Since a certain percentage of the numbers listed in a phone book are out of service, there are many people who have just moved who are not sampled. Such sampling biases can be overcome by using random digit dialing. Mall intercepts represent another sampling frame, though there are many people who do not shop at malls and those who shop more often will be over-represented unless their answers are weighted in inverse proportion to their frequency of mall shopping.

In designing the research study, one should consider the potential errors. Two sources of errors are random sampling error and non-sampling error.

Sampling errors are those due to the fact that there is a non-zero confidence interval of the results because of the sample size being less than the population being studied. Non-sampling errors are those caused by faulty coding, untruthful responses, respondent fatigue, etc.

There is a tradeoff between sample size and cost. The larger the sample size, the smaller the sampling error but the higher the cost. After a certain point the smaller sampling error cannot be justified by the additional cost.

While a larger sample size may reduce sampling error, it actually may increase the total error. There are two reasons for this effect. First, a larger sample size may reduce the ability to follow up on non-responses. Second, even if there is a sufficient number of interviewers for follow-ups, a larger number of interviewers may result in a less uniform interview process.

DATA COLLECTION

In addition to the intrinsic sampling error, the actual data collection process will introduce additional errors. These errors are called non-sampling errors. Some non-sampling errors may be intentional on the part of the interviewer, who may introduce a bias by leading the respondent to provide a certain response. The interviewer also may introduce unintentional errors, for example, due to not having a clear understanding of the interview process or due to fatigue.

Respondents also may introduce errors. A respondent may introduce intentional errors by lying or simply by not responding to a question. A respondent may introduce unintentional errors by not understanding the question, guessing, not paying close attention, and being fatigued or distracted.

Such non-sampling errors can be reduced through quality control techniques.

DATA ANALYSIS-PRELIMINARY STEPS

Before analysis can be performed, raw data must be transformed into the right format. First, it must be edited so that errors can be corrected or omitted. The data must then be coded; this procedure converts the edited raw data into numbers or symbols. A codebook is created to document how the data was coded. Finally, the data is tabulated to count the number of samples falling into various categories. Simple tabulations count the occurrences of each variable independently of the other variables.

Cross tabulations, also known as cross tabs, treats two or more variables simultaneously. However, since the variables are in a two-dimensional table, cross tabbing more than two variables is difficult to visualize since more than two dimensions would be required.

Cross tabulation can be performed for nominal and ordinal variables. Cross tabulation is the most commonly utilized data analysis method in marketing research. Many studies take the analysis no further than cross tabulation. This technique divides the sample into sub-groups to show how the dependent variable varies from one subgroup to another. A third variable can be introduced to uncover a relationship that initially was not evident.

CONJOINT ANALYSIS

The conjoint analysis is a powerful technique for determining consumer preferences for product attributes.

HYPOTHESIS TESTING

A basic fact about testing hypotheses is that a hypothesis may be rejected but that the hypothesis never can be unconditionally accepted until all possible evidence is evaluated. In the case of sampled data, the information set cannot be complete.

So if a test using such data does not reject a hypothesis, the conclusion is not necessarily that the hypothesis should be accepted. The null hypothesis in an experiment is the hypothesis that the independent variable has no effect on the dependent variable.

The null hypothesis is expressed as H0. This hypothesis is assumed to be true unless proven otherwise. The alternative to the null hypothesis is the hypothesis that the independent variable does have an effect on the dependent variable.

This hypothesis is known as the alternative, research, or experimental hypothesis and is expressed as H1. This alternative hypothesis states that the relationship observed between the variables cannot be explained by chance alone.

There are two types of errors in evaluating a hypotheses:

- *Type I error*: Occurs when one rejects the null hypothesis and accepts the alternative, when in fact the null hypothesis is true.
- *Type II error*: Occurs when one accepts the null hypothesis when in fact the null hypothesis is false.

Because their names are not very descriptive, these types of errors sometimes are confused. Some people jokingly define a Type III error to occur when one confuses Type I and Type II. To emphasise the difference, it is useful to consider a trial by jury in which the null hypothesis is that the defendant is innocent. If the jury convicts a truly innocent defendant, a Type I error has occurred. If, on the other hand, the jury declares a truly guilty defendant to be innocent, a Type II error has occurred.

Hypothesis testing involves the following steps:

- Formulate the null and alternative hypotheses.
- Choose the appropriate test.
- Choose a level of significance—determine the rejection region.
- Gather the data and calculate the test statistic.

- Determine the probability of the observed value of the test statistic under the null hypothesis given the sampling distribution that applies to the chosen test.
- Compare the value of the test statistic to the rejection threshold.
- Based on the comparison, reject or do not reject the null hypothesis.
- Make the marketing research conclusion.

In order to analyse whether research results are statistically significant or simply by chance, a test of statistical significance can be run.

TESTS OF STATISTICAL SIGNIFICANCE

The chi-square goodness-of-fit test is used to determine whether a set of proportions have specified numerical values. It often is used to analyse bivariate cross-tabulated data.

Some examples of situations that are well-suited for this test are:

- A manufacturer of packaged products test markets a new product and wants to know if sales of the new product will be in the same relative proportion of package sizes as sales of existing products.
- A company's sales revenue comes from Product A (50 per cent), Product B (30 per cent), and Product C (20 per cent). The firm wants to know whether recent fluctuations in these proportions are random or whether they represent a real shift in sales.

ANOVA

Another test of significance is the Analysis of Variance (ANOVA) test. The primary purpose of ANOVA is to test for differences between multiple means. Whereas the t-test can be used to compare two means, ANOVA is needed to compare three or more means. If multiple t-tests were applied, the probability of a TYPE I error (rejecting a true null hypothesis) increases as the number of comparisons increases. One-way ANOVA examines whether multiple means differ.

The test is called an F-test. ANOVA calculates the ratio of the variation between groups to the variation within groups (the F ratio). While ANOVA was designed for comparing several means, it also can be used to compare two means. Two-way ANOVA allows for a second independent variable and addresses interaction.

To run a one-way ANOVA, use the following steps:

- Identify the independent and dependent variables.
- Describe the variation by breaking it into three parts - the total variation, the portion that is within groups, and the portion that is between groups (or among groups for more than two groups). The total variation is the sum of the squares of the differences between each value and the grand mean of all the values in all the groups. The in-group variation is the sum of the squares of the differences in each

element's value and the group mean. The variation between group means is the total variation minus the in-group variation.
- Measure the difference between each group's mean and the grand mean.
- Perform a significance test on the differences.
- Interpret the results.

This F-test assumes that the group variances are approximately equal and that the observations are independent. It also assumes normally distributed data; however, since this is a test on means the Central Limit Theorem holds as long as the sample size is not too small. ANOVA is efficient for analysing data using relatively few observations and can be used with categorical variables. Note that regression can perform a similar analysis to that of ANOVA.

DISCRIMINANT ANALYSIS

Analysis of the difference in means between groups provides information about individual variables, it is not useful for determine their individual impacts when the variables are used in combination. Since some variables will not be independent from one another, one needs a test that can consider them simultaneously in order to take into account their interrelationship.

One such test is to construct a linear combination, essentially a weighted sum of the variables. To determine which variables discriminate between two or more naturally occurring groups, discriminant analysis is used. Discriminant analysis can determine which variables are the best predictors of group membership.

It determines which groups differ with respect to the mean of a variable, and then uses that variable to predict new cases of group membership. Essentially, the discriminant function problem is a one-way ANOVA problem in that one can determine whether multiple groups are significantly different from one another with respect to the mean of a particular variable.

A discriminant analysis consists of the following steps:
- Formulate the problem.
- Determine the discriminant function coefficients that result in the highest ratio of between-group variation to within-group variation.
- Test the significance of the discriminant function.
- Interpret the results.
- Determine the validity of the analysis.

Discriminant analysis analyses the dependency relationship, whereas factor analysis and cluster analysis address the interdependency among variables.

FACTOR ANALYSIS

Factor analysis is a very popular technique to analyse interdependence. Factor analysis studies the entire set of interrelationships without defining variables to be dependent or independent. Factor analysis combines variables to create a smaller set of factors. Mathematically, a factor is a linear combination of variables. A factor is not directly observable; it is inferred from the variables. The technique identifies underlying structure among the variables, reducing the number of variables to a more manageable set. Factor analysis groups variables just as to their correlation.

The factor loading can be defined as the correlations between the factors and their underlying variables. A factor loading matrix is a key output of the factor analysis. An example matrix is shown below.

	Factor 1	Factor 2	Factor 3
Variable 1			
Variable 2			
Variable 3			

Column's Sum of Squares: Each cell in the matrix represents correlation between the variable and the factor associated with that cell. The square of this correlation represents the proportion of the variation in the variable explained by the factor.

The sum of the squares of the factor loadings in each column is called an eigenvalue. An eigenvalue represents the amount of variance in the original variables that is associated with that factor. The communality is the amount of the variable variance explained by common factors.

A rule of thumb for deciding on the number of factors is that each included factor must explain at least as much variance as does an average variable.

In other words, only factors for which the eigenvalue is greater than one are used. Other criteria for determining the number of factors include the Scree plot criteria and the percentage of variance criteria.

To facilitate interpretation, the axis can be rotated. Rotation of the axis is equivalent to forming linear combinations of the factors. A commonly used rotation strategy is the varimax rotation. Varimax attempts to force the column entries to be either close to zero or one.

CLUSTER ANALYSIS

Market segmentation usually is based not on one factor but on multiple factors. Initially, each variable represents its own cluster. The challenge is to find a way to combine variables so that relatively homogenous clusters can be formed. Such clusters should be internally homogenous and externally heterogeneous. Cluster analysis is one way to accomplish this goal. Rather than being a statistical test, it is more of a collection of algorithms for grouping objects, or in the case of marketing research, grouping people. Cluster analysis is useful in the exploratory phase of research when there are no a-priori hypotheses. Cluster analysis steps:

- Formulate the problem, collecting data and choosing the variables to analyse.
- Choose a distance measure. The most common is the Euclidean distance. Other possibilities include the squared Euclidean distance, city-block distance, Chebychev distance, power distance, and per cent disagreement.
- Choose a clustering procedure.
- Determine the number of clusters. They should be well separated and ideally they should be distinct enough to give them descriptive names such as professionals, buffs, etc.
- Profile the clusters.
- Assess the validity of the clustering.

MARKETING RESEARCH REPORT

The format of the marketing research report varies with the needs of the organization. The report often contains the following:

- Authorization letter for the research,
- Table of Contents,
- List of illustrations,
- Executive summary,
- Research objectives,
- Methodology,
- Results,
- Limitations,
- Conclusions and recommendations,
- Appendices containing copies of the questionnaires, etc.

CONCLUDING THOUGHTS

Marketing research by itself does not arrive at marketing decisions, nor does it guarantee that the organization will be successful in marketing its products. However, when conducted in a systematic, analytical, and objective manner, marketing research can reduce the uncertainty in the decision-making process and increase the probability and magnitude of success.

2

Importance of Marketing Research

Research, as a general concept, is the process of gathering information to learn about something that is not fully known. Nearly everyone engages in some form of research. From the highly trained geologist investigating newly discovered earthquake faults, to the author of best selling spy novels gaining insight into new surveillance techniques, to the model train hobbyist spending hours hunting down the manufacturer of an old electric engine, each is driven by the quest for information. For marketers, research is not only used for the purpose of learning, it is also a critical component needed to make good decisions. Market research does this by giving marketers a picture of what is occurring (or likely to occur) and, when done well, offers alternative choices that can be made. For instance, good research may suggest multiple options for introducing new products or entering new markets. In most cases marketing decisions prove less risky (though they are never risk free) when the marketer can select from more than one option. Using an analogy of a house foundation, marketing research can be viewed as the foundation of marketing. Just as a well-built house requires a strong foundation to remain sturdy, marketing decisions need the support of research in order to be viewed favourably by customers and to stand up to competition and other external pressures. Consequently, all areas of marketing and all marketing decisions should be supported with some level of research. While research is key to marketing decision making, it does not always need to be elaborate to be effective. Sometimes small efforts, such as doing a quick search on the Internet, will provide the needed information. However, for most marketers there are times when more elaborate research work is needed and understanding the right way to conduct research, whether performing the work themselves or hiring someone else to handle it, can increase the effectiveness of these projects.

EXAMPLES OF RESEARCH IN MARKETING

As noted, marketing research is undertaken to support a wide variety of marketing decisions. The table below presents a small sampling of the research undertaken by marketing decision area.

Marketing Decision	Types of Research
Target Markets	Sales, market size; demand for product, customer characteristics, purchase behaviour, customer satisfaction, web site traffic
Product	Product development; package protection, packaging awareness; brand name selection; brand recognition, brand preference, product positioning
Distribution	Distributor interest; assessing shipping options; online shopping, retail store site selection
Promotion	Advertising recall; advertising copy testing, sales promotion response rates, sales force compensation, traffic studies (outdoor advertising), public relations media placement
Pricing	Price elasticity analysis, optimal price setting, discount options
External Factors	Competitive analysis, legal environment; social and cultural trends
Other	Company image, test marketing

DOING RESEARCH RIGHT

Marketing research is a process that investigates both organizations and people. Of course, organizations are made up of people so when it comes down to it, marketing research is a branch of the social sciences. Social science studies people and their relationships and includes such areas as economics, sociology and psychology.

To gain understanding into their fields, researchers in the social sciences use scientific methods that have been tested and refined over hundreds of years. Many of these methods require the institution of tight controls on research projects. For instance, many companies survey (*i.e.*, ask questions) a small percentage of their customers (called a sample) to see how satisfied they are with the company's efforts. For the information obtained from a small group of customers to be useful when evaluating how all customers feel, certain controls must be in place including controls on who should be included in the sample.

Thus, doing research right means the necessary controls are in place to insure it is done correctly and increase the chance the results are relevant. Relying on results of research conducted incorrectly to make decisions could prove problematic if not disastrous. Thousands of examples exist of firms using faulty research to make decisions, including many dot-com companies that failed between 1999 and 2002.

As one might expect, the trade-off for doing research right is the increase in cost and time needed to conduct the research. So a big decision for marketers, when it comes to doing research, is to determine the balance between the need for obtaining relevant information and the costs involved in carrying out the research.

RESEARCH VALIDITY AND RELIABILITY

As we discussed, not all research requires undertaking an elaborate study. But even marketers conducting small, informal research should know that any type of research performed poorly will not yield relevant results. In fact, all research, no matter how well controlled, carries the potential to be wrong. There are many reasons why research may not yield good results (a full discussion being beyond the scope of this tutorial), however, most errors can be traced to problems with how data is gathered. In particular, many research mistakes occur due to problems associated with research validity and research reliability.

RESEARCH VALIDITY

This problem with data gathering represents several concepts that to the non-researcher may be quite complex. But basically validity boils down to whether the research is really measuring what it claims to be measuring. For instance, if a marketer is purchasing a research report from a company claiming to measure how people prefer the marketer's products over competitors' products, the marketer should understand how the data was gathered to help determine if the research really captures the information the way the research company says it does.

While research validity is measured in several ways, those evaluating research results should keep asking this simple question: Is the research measuring what it is supposed to measure? If the marketer has doubts about the answer to this question then it is possible the results should also be questioned.

RESEARCH RELIABILITY

This problem relates to whether research results can be applied to a wider group than those who took part in a study. In other words, would similar results be obtained if another group containing different respondents or a different set of data points were used? For example, if 40 salespeople out of 2,000-person corporate sales force participate in a research study focusing on company policy, is the information obtained from these 40 people sufficient to conclude how the entire sales forces feels about company policies? What if the same study was done again with 40 different salespeople, would the responses be similar?

Reliability is chiefly concerned with making sure the method of data gathering leads to consistent results. For some types of research this can be measured by having different researchers follow the same methods to see if results can be duplicated. If results are similar then it is likely the method of data gathering is reliable. Assuring research can be replicated and can produce similar results is an important element of the scientific research method.

RISK IN MARKETING RESEARCH

The discussion above regarding doing research right shows that good marketing research, especially when it involves formal research projects, requires strict controls in order to produce relevant information. Being relevant means the probability is high that the research results reflect what is happening now or might happen in the future. But following the right procedures to produce a relevant study does not insure the results of research will be 100 per cent correct as there is always the potential that results are wrong.

Because of the risks associated with research, marketers are cautioned not to use the results of marketing research as the only input in making marketing decisions. Rather, smart marketing decisions require considering many factors, including management's own web site of what is best. But being cautious with how research is used should not diminish the need to conduct research. While making decisions without research input may work sometimes, long-term success is not likely to happen without regular efforts to collect information.

Additionally, risk in research extends to research produced by others. The research process often includes using information initially gathered by other sources, such as market research firms. However, in many instances the methods for collecting this information is not be fully disclosed, thus questions exist regarding research validity and reliability. Marketers using research collected by third-party sources should do so with a reasonable level of skepticism. In fact, it is wise for marketers to always make an effort to locate multiple information sources that address the same issue (*e.g.*, two or more sales forecasts reports). A good rule-of-thumb for all marketers is never to rely on one source for making definitive statements about a market.

NATURE OF MARKETING RESEARCH

The American Marketing Association, marketing research involves the "systematic gathering, recording, and analysing of data about problems relating to the marketing of goods and services." This definition provides a useful description of the nature of marketing research, but it fails to include preresearch analysis, which is an important aspect of the research process. Before data collection, careful planning is required to specify both the kind of information needed and the purpose of such information.

Without preresearch activities, there is a great danger that critical information may not be obtained and that what is obtained may turn out to be irrelevant or unsuitable. The gathering of information can never be a substitute for good managerial web site. A story told by the founder of Bata illustrates this point. Two shoe salesmen from two companies visited the same island and came away with vastly different interpretations of people not wearing shoes there.

One was returning home immediately because of a non-existment marketing opportunity. The other salesman, however, was very enthusiastic since all these potential customers were still without shoes. The moral of the story is that marketing research is only one part of the equation, and proper analysis and web siteal decisions are required. In terms of marketing research expenditures, the USA is a leader. Commercial firms' total worldwide expenditures for marketing, advertising, and opinion research totalled $15.5 billion in 2000. The top twenty-five firms accounted for 61 per cent of the total world expenditures.

MARKETING INFORMATION SOURCES

Once a researcher has identified the marketing problem and has completed a preresearch analysis, the relevant information must be collected. The two major sources of information are primary data and secondary data. Primary data may be defined as information that is collected firsthand, generated by original research tailor-made to answer specific, current research questions.

The major advantage of primary data is that the information is specific, relevant, and up-to-date. The desirability of primary data is, however, somewhat moderated by the high cost and amount of time associated with the collection of this type of data. Secondary data, in contrast, may be defined as information that has already been collected for other purposes and is thus readily available. Note that the advantages of primary data are the disadvantages of secondary data, and that the advantages of secondary data become the disadvantages of primary data.

As a rule, no research should be done without a search for secondary information first, and secondary data should be used whenever available and appropriate. To determine the suitability of the secondary data, a researcher should employ relevant criteria to evaluate the purpose, methodology, definitions of the concepts, and time period covered in the study yielding the secondary information. Transition economies, in particular, pose a special challenge in terms of data quality.

Extreme caution should be used when interpreting the foreign trade statistics in the Baltics, Russia, and the other countries of the former Soviet Union. With the economic transformation, coupled with an elimination of the large foreign trade organizations that relied on one currency with an administratively established exchange rate, the methodology of collecting and recording data has changed markedly. The evaluation process becomes much more complicated if secondary data from various countries must be compared in order to analyse the business potential of each country.

A problem for marketers is that secondary data on international marketing may not be comparable for several reasons. First, countries may employ different data collection methods. Second, there may be a problem with classification differences. Third, the unit of measurement employed could differ. Finally, definitional differences are another common problem because countries tend to use various definitions in collecting the same kind of information. For example, regarding the "urban" concept, Denmark defines it as a locality of 200 or more inhabitants, while it must be at least 20,000 for Nigeria. In the case of Bermuda and Singapore, the entire countries comprise an urban area.

PRIMARY RESEARCH

When secondary data are unavailable, irrelevant, or obsolete, the marketer must turn to primary research. One decision that must be made is whether to compile or buy the information. In other words, the question to be decided is whether outside agencies such as marketing research firms should be used to collect the information needed or whether the firm should use its own personnel for this purpose. A list of international marketing research firms may be found in the US Department of Commerce's *Trade List: Market Research Organizations Worldwide*, the American Marketing Association's *International Directory of Marketing Research Houses and Services*, and *Bradford's Directory of Marketing Research Agencies and Management Consultants in the USA and the World*. If outside personnel are to be used, the company should make a distinction among different types of information brokers who differ in terms of the extent to which value is added to the information delivered.

Some merely retrieve printed materials ordered by their clients who know what they want. Other brokers add value by locating information sources and may proceed to conduct interviews on behalf of their clients. If a marketer decides to conduct his or her own research without hiring outside consultants or researchers, there are many alternatives available to collect primary information. First, the marketer should subscribe to the newspapers in the competitor's home country.

These newspapers should include the local language papers and dailies with large circulations. Even a newspaper in a small town near the potential market area is useful, because that paper is likely to cover the news concerning a major company or employer in the area. Second, the marketer can learn about a foreign market by personally visiting it or by being a member of a trade mission. By attending trade fairs, the marketer can observe competitors' display booths and have the opportunity to talk with potential customers and distributors. A company should make an attempt to determine the effectiveness of the planned marketing mix. Some type of *experimental study* may be necessary to determine a cause-and-effect relationship. One type of field experimentation is test marketing. The technique may be used to test a planned national marketing programme for a new product in a limited geographic area.

A good test market should possess the following characteristics:

- Representativeness,
- Self-contained media, and
- Selfcontained trading area.

The concern about representativeness involves demographic comparability. The test market should be demographically similar to the country of which it is part and its population should portray the country's typical characteristics. This market should be large enough to provide meaningful data and yet not be so large as to make the costs of the study prohibitive.

The market should be self-contained from a media standpoint in order to avoid media spillage out of the market. If the market is not isolated in terms of media coverage, communication costs are wasted because an audience is being contacted outside of the intended market. Media should also be available at a reasonable cost. A city such as Tokyo is unsuitable for test marketing because of the exorbitant prices charged for TV time–time not at all readily available. Finally, the test market should be self-contained in terms of trading area. This is necessary in order to avoid trans-shipments into and out of the area.

If the city population increases during the daytime because outside people travel into the city for work or if a distributor delivers the product to others nearby cities, it is difficult to achieve accurate readings of sales, because the sales figure is actually overstated. Cities such as Tokyo and New York are definitely not self-contained. In North America, Winnipeg, the capital of the Canadian province of Manitoba, is considered a premier test market. Its fairly cosmopolitan and conservative population displays the same characteristics as a larger target audience or general market.

This city is favourably isolated because the nearest urban centres are Regina, Saskatchewan, and Minneapolis, Minnesota, both of which are approximately 300 miles away. Thus, the market is controllable because its residents are not exposed to conflicting or competing information from outside sources. In terms of media, Winnipeg has its own newspapers and TV stations; their easy access eliminates any problems related to media availability and waste.

Winnipeg has been used to test several product concepts before those products were made available in the US market. McDonald's first tested its chicken product in Winnipeg by combining it with french fries. Consumers, however, considered chicken to be a diet food and preferred the product without a bun or fries. Subsequently, McDonald's Chicken and Chips became Chicken McNuggets. If certain countries are demographically and psychologically similar, a firm can use a city in one country as a test market to research market conditions in another country.

As in the case of Hong Kong, empty nesters or people over age 40 whose children have entered the workforce, accounting for 36 per cent of all adults, will jump to 54 per cent by 2020. This demographic shift makes Hong Kong a useful test market to determine the future of the other affluent Asian markets. Hong Kong is leading the trend, and a product's success here may influence market development elsewhere.

SECONDARY RESEARCH

There are many different ways to collect secondary data, and there are many information sources for this purpose. Such sources may be grouped under either public or private sources.

PRIVATE SOURCES

A very basic method of finding business information is to begin with a public library or a university library. A library with a reasonable collection should contain standard reference guides, commercial and industrial directories, financial reference manuals, and other materials containing pertinent business information.

One useful source of information is the World Trade Centres Association which has more than 300 World Trade centres in eighty-nine countries. Established as a non-profit organization in 1970, the WTCA promotes international business relationships through a network of members worldwide. These centres offer referrals, contacts, and information for businesses. A local chamber of commerce in a metropolitan area pays a $165,000 licensing fee to join the WTCA. Another good source of information is a community's chamber of commerce. Being well informed on local business, this organization is capable of providing helpful advice.

In addition to a chamber of commerce at the national level, there are local chambers of commerce, which are often some of the best sources of information on trade and industry in specific localities. Larger organizations may publish classified buyers' guides, manufacturers' guides, or lists of international traders in their areas. Finally, foreign chambers of commerce are in a position to provide a great deal of relevant information about their countries because they act as public relations offices. Concerning country information, Dun's Marketing Services offers *Exporter's Encyclopaedia*, which provides comprehensive country-by-country information for over 200 markets. Several large accounting firms also publish their own country-by-country books.

PUBLIC SOURCES

Public sources of market information are numerous. Foreign governments, their embassies and consulates, and trade promotion agencies either have the information desired or are in a position to guide the marketer to the proper source of information. Germany, for example, has the Society for Information and Documentation, which promotes development of information science and exchanges scientific and technical data with other countries.

France's Center for Information and Documentation offers services similar to those provided by US information brokers. Furthermore, regional and international organizations, such as the World Bank, the OECD, and the IMF, routinely collect information on population and a nation's financial circumstances. The World Bank and its affiliates offer a number of publications.

As in the case of its Global Development Finance, it allows users to:

- Generate market analysis, forecasts, and comparisons,
- Examine current trends and assess their impact on investment opportunities,
- Develop investment strategies, and
- Analyse the investment risks associated with specific emerging markets.

The World Bank has launched the Country Analytic Work Web site to enable multilateral agencies to share information. Donor agencies share analysis, good practices and advice, and they develop and implement country strategies. Both the donors and their clients, through the web site, can use development resources more efficiently while avoiding duplication. The Organization for Economic Cooperation and Development is the international organization of the industrialized, market economy countries of Western Europe, North America, and Asia. At OECD headquarters in Paris, it regularly gathers statistical information on the foreign trade of its member countries and makes the statistics internationally comparable by converting the information into uniform units.

The OECD Secretariat compiles economic data and policy information, formulates forecasts, and provides analytical work to support the work of government representatives. The IMF has worldwide information-gathering resources. The IMF's research activities rely on the expertise of its more than 1100 economists who conduct a wide range of financial and monetary studies.

Based on these studies, the IMF publishes the *Occasional Papers* and *Economic and Financial Surveys* series, both of which are proven references. *Occasional Papers* are studies on economic and financial subjects of importance to the world economy. *World Economic and Financial Surveys* series, in contrast, are special-topic studies, and the core of the series is derived from *World Economic Outlook*. Twice a year, the IMF prepares *World Economic Outlook* which is a comprehensive assessment of each country's economic situation and prospects. Each May, *World Economic Outlook* examines what is happening and what is likely to happen in various countries; each October, it provides updated projections, showing the impact of key developments.

In addition, the IMF's *Staff Country Reports* cover a variety of topics on economic developments in individual member countries. Each in-depth report includes an overview, economic and financial data, analysis of trends, factors to consider in forecasting, comparative charts and graphs, and tabular presentations with interpretive comments. Because the IMF's projections affect the decisions of the IMF and its member countries, the IMF's research is based on the latest facts and figures.

The World Trade Organization has several resources for global trade statistics. Its web site provides selected statistics on trade in merchandise and services at world and regional levels, developments in major product categories, and historical developments in international trade at the aggregate level. Its trilingual CD-ROM contains statistical reports. For US firms, the most logical public source of information is the US government and its agencies.

A good starting point would be to contact the International Trade Division of the Department of Commerce. The International Trade Division maintains reference libraries in major cities where one can talk to trade experts and find statistical and trade reports for each country. At its main office in Washington, DC, there are experts assigned to cover a particular country. One US company interested in selling microwave toilets to Nigeria avoided a costly mistake after being advised that what Nigeria really needed was basic sewage systems.

Getting information from the US government has become easier. The federal government now offers a one-stop data site. One can learn about statistics, laws, and regulations. The CIA publishes the *World Factbook* that provides countries' basic statistics and cultural and political/legal information. The *World Factbook* can also be accessed online.

In conclusion, the US government collects large amounts of relevant data that it makes available at reasonable cost. From this large database, several data products and services are produced. Many of these services differ only in terms of how the information is retrieved and packaged for sale. A marketer should thus consult the International Trade Administration before ordering too many services, some of which may turn out to be redundant.

SAMPLING IN MARKETING RESEARCH

As with virtually all consumer market studies, it is neither feasible nor practical for a researcher to contact all the members of the population. The general rule is to contact a select group of consumers considered to be representative of the entire population. This practice is known as *sampling*. There are several kinds of sampling techniques, with probability and non-probability sampling methods being the two major categories. In probability sampling, it is possible to specify in advance the chance that each element in the population will have of being included in that sample, though not necessarily in equal probability for every element.

In non-probability sampling, it is not possible to determine such probability or to estimate the sampling error. The problem of poor sampling methods is not always under the control of the researcher. An ideal sampling method, for instance, may not be practical for many reasons when used in the various markets of the world.

In the USA, it is possible to use virtually all types of probability and non-probability sampling methods that closely reflect the population of a target market. The luxury of these options may not be available in other advanced countries. This problem is of a greater magnitude with sampling in developing economies. Probability sampling methods, though theoretically superior, may be difficult to employ, and the temptation to use non-probability methods becomes great. There are several reasons for this difficulty. A map of the country may not be available or out of date. Some cities in Saudi Arabia, for example, have no street names, and houses have no numbers. In Hong Kong, a large number of people live on boats.

The unavailability of block statistics thus precludes meaningful stratification. Lists of residents may be non-existent or inaccurate. Poor people may illegally build shacks and pay their neighbours to allow illegal hookups of electricity and water–thus, even utility companies' lists may not be as accurate as they might first appear. Poor road systems can create another problem because they preclude the use of the dispersed sample. Even when a proper location is identified, it is still difficult to identify the selected sample element.

For example, if the element is a homemaker of a particular housing unit, the researcher may be surprised upon arrival that that particular household has more than one home-maker. This can be a common situation in many parts of the world. The prevalence of extended families and joint tenancy makes it very easy for a housing unit to comprise several primary family units.

In some countries, a husband may be a polygamist, and all his wives may live together in the same house. In sum, while one should pay attention to sampling design, one should not be obsessed with it in light of sampling limitations in most parts of the world. In cross-national studies, sampling procedures become even more complicated.

A researcher may desire to use the same sampling method for all countries in order to maintain consistency. Theoretical desirability, however, often gives way to practicality and flexibility.

Sampling procedures may have to vary across countries in order to ensure reasonably the comparability of national groups. For durable products, a random sample may work well in the USA and the European Union, but a web siteal sample based on the more upscale segment of the population may be more meaningful in a less developed country, because relatively affluent consumers there are more likely to purchase and use such products. Thus, the relevance of the sampling method depends on whether it will yield a sample that is representative of a country's population and on whether comparable samples may be obtained from the intended groups of different countries. Furthermore, a researcher may have to distinguish samples obtained from rural and urban areas because dual economies exist in many countries, resulting in rural and urban inhabitants being distinctly different.

It is quite rare for a study to simultaneously investigate some forty or fifty countries. A researcher conducting international business research typically focuses on a few countries for comparison. Sivakumar and Nakata have proposed a methodology that aims to choose country combinations so as to strengthen hypothesis testing. Using a series of algorithms, they have rank-ordered the sets of countries by their power in hypothesis testing. Their tables eliminate web siteal or ad-hoc selection so that a sample can be better justified in terms of methodological rigour.

Still, in the end, practical considerations must also be given to access to fieldsites, availability of research collaboration, and non-culture variables to be studied. The experience of Honda demonstrates why it is critical to have an appropriate sample. Honda initially pushed to recycle a platform developed in Japan for its American sport-utility vehicle, while the American team insisted on a genuine American platform. The American subsidiary wanted an "apartment on wheels" SUV to target surfers, mountain bikers, and other youthful outdoor types who could live in a vehicle while on the road. It was critical for this SUV, Acura MDX, to have American features that included a third row of seats.

On the other hand, the top Japanese product development executives felt that people who needed a third row would buy a minivan instead. To overcome this resistance, the American team insisted that a top research-and-development Japanese executive visit Denver. There, he went to the homes of the families that drove Ford Expeditions, and he observed how mothers transported their own children and those of the neighbours to soccer games. He also saw firsthand how so many families used a vehicle's third row for their dogs. Had the research been done in Japan, the Japanese executive would have missed the dogfriendly behaviour of the American middle class.

MARKETING MANAGEMENT

Marketing Management is a business discipline which is focused on the practical application of marketing techniques and the management of a firm's marketing resources and activities. Rapidly emerging forces of globalization have compelled firms to market beyond the borders of their home country making International marketing highly significant and an integral part of a firm's marketing strategy. Marketing managers are often responsible for influencing the level, timing, and composition of customer demand accepted definition of the term. In part, this is because the role of a marketing manager can vary significantly based on a business' size, corporate culture, and industry context.

For example, in a large consumer products company, the marketing manager may performance as the overall general manager of his or her assigned product To create an effective, cost-efficient Marketing management strategy, firms must possess a detailed, objective understanding of their own business and the market in which they operate. In analyzing these issues, the discipline of marketing management often overlaps with the related discipline of strategic planning.

STRUCTURE

Traditionally, marketing analysis was structured into three areas: Customer analysis, Company analysis, and Competitor analysis. More recently, it has become fashionable in some marketing circles to divide these further into certain five "Cs": Customer analysis, Company analysis, Collaborator analysis, Competitor analysis, and analysis of the industry Context.

Department analysis is to develop a schematic diagram for market segmentation, breaking down the market into various constituent groups of customers, which are called customer segments or market segmentations.

Marketing managers work to develop detailed profiles of each segment, focusing on any number of variables that may differ among the segments: demographic, psychographic, geographic, behavioural, needs-benefit, and other factors may all be examined. Marketers also attempt to track these segments' perceptions of the various products in the market using tools such as perceptual mapping.

In company analysis, marketers focus on understanding the company's cost structure and cost position relative to competitors, as well as working to identify a firm's core competencies and other competitively distinct company resources.

Marketing managers may also work with the accounting department to analyse the profits the firm is generating from various product lines and customer accounts. The company may also conduct periodic brand audits to assess the strength of its brands and sources of brand equity.

The firm's collaborators may also be profiled, which may include various suppliers, distributors and other channel partners, joint venture partners, and others. An analysis of complementary products may also be performed if such products exist.

Marketing management employs various tools from economics and competitive strategy to analyse the industry context in which the firm operates. These include Porter's five forces, analysis of strategic groups of competitors, value chain analysis and others. Depending on the industry, the regulatory context may also be important to examine in detail.

In competitor analysis, marketers build detailed profiles of each competitor in the market, focusing especially on their relative competitive strengths and weaknesses using SWOT analysis.

Marketing managers will examine each competitor's cost structure, sources of profits, resources and competencies, competitive positioning and product differentiation, degree of vertical integration, historical responses to industry developments, and other factors.

Marketing management often finds it necessary to invest in research to collect the data required to perform accurate marketing analysis. As such, they often conduct market research to obtain this information.

Marketers employ a variety of techniques to conduct market research, but some of the more common include:

- Qualitative marketing research, such as focus groups.
- Quantitative marketing research, such as statistical surveys.
- Experimental techniques such as test markets.
- Observational techniques such as ethnographic observation.

Marketing managers may also design and oversee various environmental scanning and competitive intelligence processes to help identify trends and inform the company's marketing analysis.

Marketing Strategy

If the company has obtained an adequate understanding of the customer base and its own competitive position in the industry, marketing managers are able to make their own key strategic decisions and develop a marketing strategy designed to maximize the revenues and profits of the firm. The selected strategy may aim for any of a variety of specific objectives, including optimizing short-term unit margins, revenue growth, market share, long-term profitability, or other goals.

To achieve the desired objectives, marketers typically identify one or more target customer segments which they intend to pursue. Customer segments are often selected as targets because they score highly on two dimensions: 1) The segment is attractive to serve because it is large, growing, makes frequent purchases, is not price sensitive, or other factors; and 2) The company has the resources and capabilities to compete for the segment's business, can meet their needs better than the competition, and can do so profitably. In fact, a commonly cited definition of marketing is simply"meeting needs profitably."

The implication of selecting target segments is that the business will subsequently allocate more resources to acquire and retain customers in the target segment(s) than it will for other, non-targeted customers. In some cases, the firm may go so far as to turn away customers who are not in its target segment.The doorman at a swanky nightclub, for example, may deny entry to unfashionably dressed individuals because the business has made a strategic decision to target the"high fashion" segment of nightclub patrons.

In conjunction with targeting decisions, marketing managers will identify the desired positioning they want the company, product, or brand to occupy in the target customer's mind. This positioning is often an encapsulation of a key benefit the company's product or service offers that is differentiated and superior to the benefits offered by competitive products. For example, Volvo has traditionally positioned its products in the automobile market in North America in order to be perceived as the leader in"safety", whereas BMW has traditionally positioned its brand to be perceived as the leader in"performance."

Ideally, a firm's positioning can be maintained over a long period of time because the company possesses, or can develop, some form of sustainable competitive advantage. The positioning should also be sufficiently relevant to the target segment such that it will drive the purchasing behaviour of target customers.

Implementation Planning

After the firm's strategic objectives have been identified, the target market selected, and the desired positioning for the company, product or brand has been determined, marketing managers focus on how to best implement the chosen strategy. Traditionally, this has involved implementation planning across the "4Ps" of marketing: Product management, Pricing, Place and Promotion. Taken together, the company's implementation choices across the 4Ps are often described as the marketing mix, meaning the mix of elements the business will employ to "go to market" and execute the marketing strategy. The overall goal for the marketing mix is to consistently deliver a compelling value proposition that reinforces the firm's chosen positioning, builds customer loyalty and brand equity among target customers, and achieves the firm's marketing and financial objectives.

In many cases, marketing management will develop a marketing plan to specify how the company will execute the chosen strategy and achieve the business' objectives.

The content of marketing plans varies from firm to firm, but commonly includes:

- An executive summary.
- Situation analysis to summarize facts and insights gained from market research and marketing analysis.
- The company's mission statement or long-term strategic vision.
- A statement of the company's key objectives, often subdivided into marketing objectives and financial objectives.
- The marketing strategy the business has chosen, specifying the target segments to be pursued and the competitive positioning to be achieved.
- Implementation choices for each element of the marketing mix.

Project, Process, and Vendor Management

Once the key implementation initiatives have been identified, marketing managers work to oversee the execution of the marketing plan. Marketing executives may therefore manage any number of specific projects, such as sales force management initiatives, product development efforts, channel marketing prigrammes and the execution of public relations and advertising campaigns. Marketers use a variety of project management techniques to ensure projects achieve their objectives while keeping to established schedules and budgets.

More broadly, marketing managers work to design and improve the effectiveness of core marketing processes, such as new product development, brand management, marketing communications, and pricing. Marketers may employ the tools of business process reengineering to ensure these processes are properly designed, and use a variety of process management techniques to keep them operating smoothly.

Effective execution may require management of both internal resources and a variety of external vendors and service providers, such as the firm's advertising agency. Marketers may therefore coordinate with the company's Purchasing department on the procurement of these services.

Organizational Management and Leadership

Marketing management may spend a fair amount of time building or maintaining a marketing orientation for the business. Achieving a market orientation, also known as "customer focus" or the "marketing concept", requires building consensus at the senior management level and then driving customer focus down into the organization. Cultural barriers may exist in a given business unit or functional area that the marketing manager must address in order to achieve this goal. Additionally, marketing executives often performance as a "brand champion" and work to enforce corporate identity standards across the enterprise.

In larger organizations, especially those with multiple business units, top marketing managers may need to coordinate across several marketing departments and also resources from finance, research and development, engineering, operations, manufacturing, or other functional areas to implement the marketing plan. In order to effectively manage these resources, marketing executives may need to spend much of their time focused on political issues and inte-departmental negotiations.

The effectiveness of a marketing manager may therefore depend on his or her ability to make the internal "sale" of various marketing prigrammes equally as much as the external customer's reaction to such prigrammes.

Reporting, Measurement, Feedback and Control Systems

Marketing management employs a variety of metrics to measure progress against objectives. It is the responsibility of marketing managers–in the marketing department or elsewhere–to ensure that the execution of marketing prigrammes achieves the desired objectives and does so in a cost-efficient manner.

Marketing management therefore often makes use of various organizational control systems, such as sales forecasts, sales force and reseller incentive prigrammes, sales force management systems, and customer relationship management tools. Recently, some software vendors have begun using the term "marketing operations management" or "marketing resource management" to describe systems that facilitate an integrated approach for controlling marketing resources. In some cases, these efforts may be linked to various supply chain management systems, such as enterprise resource planning, material requirements planning, efficient consumer response, and inventory management systems.

Measuring the return on investment of and marketing effectiveness various marketing initiatives is a significant problem for marketing management. Various market research, accounting and financial tools are used to help estimate the ROI of marketing investments. Brand valuation, for example, attempts to identify the percentage of a company's market value that is generated by the company's brands, and thereby estimate the financial value of specific investments in brand equity. Another technique, integrated marketing communications, is a CRM database-driven approach that attempts to estimate the value of marketing mix executions based on the changes in customer behaviour these executions generate.

MARKETING ENVIRONMENT

Elements of the environment. The marketing *environment* involves factors that, for the most part, are beyond the control of the company. Thus, the company must *adapt* to these factors. It is important to observe how the environment changes so that a firm can adapt its strategies appropriately.

Consider these environmental forces:

- *Competition*: Competitors often "creep" in and threaten to take away markets from firms. For example, Japanese auto manufacturers became a serious threat to American car makers in the late 1970s and early 1980s. Similarly, the Lotus Corporation, maker of one of the first commercially successful spreadsheets, soon faced competition from other software firms. Note that while competition may be frustrating for the firm, it is good for consumers. Note that competition today is increasingly global in scope. It is important to recognize that competition can happen at different "levels." At the brand level, two firms compete in providing a very similar product or service. Coca Cola and Pepsi, for example, compete for the cola drink market, and United and American Airlines compete for the passenger air transportation market. Firms also face less direct—but frequently very serious—competition at the product level. For example, cola drinks compete against bottled water. Products or services can serve as substitutes for each other even though they are very different in form. Teleconferencing facilities, for example, are very different from airline passenger transportation, but both can "bring together" people for a "meeting." At the budget level, different products or services provide very different benefits, but buyers have to make choices as to what they will buy when they cannot afford—or are unwilling to spend on—both. For example, a family may decide between buying a new car or a high definition television set. The family may also have to choose between going on a foreign vacation or remodeling its kitchen. Firms, too, may have to make choices. The firm has the cash flow either to remodel its offices or install a more energy efficient climate control system; or the firm can choose either to invest in new product development or in a promotional campaign to increase awareness of its brand among consumers.

- *Economics*: Two economic forces strongly affect firms and their customers:
  - *Economic Cycles*: Some firms in particular are extremely vulnerable to changes in the economy. Consumers tend to put off buying a new car, going out to eat, or building new homes in bad times. In contrast, in good times, firms serving those needs may have difficulty keeping up with demand. One important point to realise is that different industries are affected to different degrees by changes in the economy. Although families can cut down on the quality of the food they buy—going with lower priced brands, for example—there are limits to the savings that can be made without greatly affecting the living standard of the family. On the other hand, it is often much easier to put off the purchase of a new car for a year or hold off on remodeling the family home. If need be, firms can keep the current computers—even though they are getting a bit slow—when sales are down. The economy goes through cycles. In the late 1990s, the U.S. economy was quite strong, and many luxury goods were sold. Currently, the economy fluctuates between increasing strength, stagnation, or slight decline. Many firms face consequences of economic downturns. Car makers, for example, have seen declining profit margins as they have had to cut prices and offer low interest rates on financing. Generally, in good economic times, there is a great deal of demand, but this introduces a fear of possible inflation. In the U.S., the Federal Reserve will then try to prevent the economy from "overheating." This is usually done by raising interest rates. This makes businesses less willing to invest, and as a result, people tend to make less money. During a recession,

unemployment tends to rise, causing consumers to spend less. This may result in a "bad circle," with more people losing their jobs due to lowered demands. Some businesses, however, may take this opportunity to invest in growth now that things can be bought more cheaply.

- *Inflation*: Over time, most economies experience some level of inflation. Therefore, it is useful to explicitly state whether a reference to money over time involves the actual dollar amount exchanged at any point or an "inflation adjusted" figure that "anchors" a given amount of money to the value of that money at some point in time. Suppose, for example, that cumulative inflation between 1960 and 2007 has been 1,000 per cent—that is, on the average, it costs ten times as much to buy the same thing in 2007 as it did 47 years earlier. If the cumulative inflation between 1960 and 1984 had been 500 per cent, we could talk about one 1984 dollar being worth fifty 1960 cents or two 2007 dollars. It is important to note that inflation is uneven. Some goods and services—such as health care and college tuition—are currently increasing in cost much higher than the average rate of inflation. Prices of computers, actually decline both in absolute numbers and in terms of the value for money paid once an adjustment has been made for the improvement in quality. That is, two years later, the computer has not only declined in price by 20 per cent, but it may also be 30 per cent better. In that case, then, there has actually been, over the period, a net deflation of 38.5 per cent for the category.

- *Political*: Businesses are very vulnerable to changes in the political situation. For example, because consumer groups lobbied Congress, more stringent rules were made on the terms of car leases. The tobacco industry is currently the target of much negative attention from government and public interest groups. Currently, the desire to avoid aiding the enemy may result in laws that make it more difficult for American firms to export goods to other countries. Many industries have a strong economic interest in policies that benefit the industry may have a negative impact on the nation as a whole but enhance profits for the industry. For example, regulations that limit the amount of sugar that can be imported into the United States is estimated to cost each American approximately $10.00 a year. The total increase in profits to the sugar industry is difficult to estimate because many of the large producers of refined sugar are privately held corporations, but it is likely that the net gain to the industry is as much as the roughly $3 billion lost by Americans a whole. However, the interests of the industry are much more concentrated. The industry can rally its stockholders, unions and employees, and suppliers together to lobby for their special interests. In turn, the industry can join forces with other agricultural interests which each support each other's prigrammes.

- *Legal:* Firms are very vulnerable to changing laws and changing interpretations by the courts. Firms in the U.S. are very vulnerable to lawsuits. McDonald's, for example, is currently being sued by people who claim that eating the chain's hamburgers caused them to get fat. Firms are significantly limited in what they can do by various laws—some laws, for example, require that disclosures be made to consumers on the effective interest rates they pay on products bought on installment. A particularly interesting group of laws relate to antitrust. These laws basically exist to promote fair competition among firms. As suggested, consider such laws when we cover pricing later in the term.
- *Technological:* Changes in technology may significantly influence the demand for a product. For example, the advent of the fax machine was bad news for Federal Express. The Internet is a major threat to travel agents. Many record stores have been wiped out of business by the trend towards downloading songs. Although technological change eliminates or at least greatly diminishes some markets, it creates opportunities for others. For example, although Federal Express has lost a considerable amount of business from documents that can now be faxed or sent by the Internet rather than having to be physically shipped, there has been a large increase in demand for packages to be delivered overnight or "second day air." Just-in-time manufacturing techniques, in addition to online sales, have dramatically increased the market for such shipments. Online sites such as eBay now makes it possible to sell specialty products that, in the old days, would have been difficult to distribute. Although it has been possible for more than a hundred years to sell merchandise by catalog, buyers of these specialty products often had no easy access to the catalogs.
- *Social*: Changes in customs or demographics greatly influence firms. Fewer babies today are being born, resulting in a decreased demand for baby foods. More women work outside the home today, so there is a greater demand for prepared foods. There are more unmarried singles today. This provides opportunities for some firms but creates problems for others. Today, there are more "blended" families that result as parents remarry after divorce. These families are often strapped for money but may require "duplicate" items for children at each parent's residence.

BASIC METHODS OF DATA COLLECTION

There are two principal methods for the collection of primary data:

- Observation, and
- The administration of survey questions.

In the case of observation, respondents are visually observed, regardless of whether they realise it or not. When the survey question method is used, respondents are asked certain questions relating to their characteristics or behaviour.

OBSERVATION

The principal advantage of the observation method is that, on a theoretical basis, it is supposed to be more objective than the use of survey questions. When using observation, a researcher does not have to depend on what respondents say or are willing to say.

Another reason why the observation method tends to yield more objective information lies in the fact that there is no influence exerted by an interviewer, regardless of whether such influence would be real or imagined by respondents. The lack of social interaction eliminates the possibility of influencing the respondent.

Individuals are usually reluctant to discuss personal habits or consumption, and observation avoids this problem. In the Middle East, Latin America, and Asia, interviewers are suspected of being tax investigators in disguise, making it difficult to obtain data about income and purchases. The degree of openness in a society may also vary. Because of the effectiveness of the observation technique, Edward T. Hall, an internationally known anthropologist, has replaced listening and asking with watching.

There are conflicting opinions about the kind of personnel that should be involved in direct observation. Some contend that local observers should be used because of their familiarity and understanding of the local culture, while others believe that familiarity breeds carelessness.

Local observers, by being familiar with local events, tend to take those occurrences for granted. Consequently, essential and rich detail may be left out of a report. For example, a local observer may fail to notice that students wear school uniforms if that is a common local practice. The failure to include this piece of information may be quite crucial for an American firm wanting to sell clothing to schoolchildren. If an American observer were used in the same way, it would be unlikely that such information would be missing, since school uniforms are the exception in the USA. Of course, the situation can also be reversed.

An American observer may see nothing unusual about students wearing blue jeans to school, but this kind of behaviour might be very conspicuous to a non-American observer. Whereas familiarity may result in some details being left out, lack of familiarity may lead an inexperienced observer to draw the wrong conclusion.

An American observer seeing two foreign males holding hands could draw a hasty conclusion that these men must be homosexual. But this conclusion could be based on an ignorance of the local culture. In many countries, there is nothing sexual or unusual about friends of the same sex holding hands. In such countries, what is unusual is for members of the opposite sex to hold hands in public. The only safe conclusion that can be made about observers is that there is no substitute for careful training. Observers must be explicitly instructed about what they are supposed to notice.

Training and practice are necessary if desired details are to be systematically noted and recorded. If bias cannot be completely eliminated through training, it may be necessary to use observers from various backgrounds to cover each other's blind spots. Clearly, no company can learn about the competition by interviewing competitors.

This is one situation where the observation technique can prove useful in gathering information. One common method used to gather data involves such traditional sources as media and business indexes.

A marketer can learn about competitors by reading newspaper or magazine stories about those companies. Problems with such sources are that stories appearing in the print media may be too general and that standard business sources are often outdated. Furthermore, print media may not provide information on competitors' plant operations, capacity, sales force, management structure, and distribution.

QUESTIONING

Survey questions can be used more frequently than observation because of speed and cost. With questioning, data can be collected quickly and at a minimum cost because the researcher does not have to waste time waiting for an event to happen to be observed.The survey question method is also quite versatile, because it can be used to explore virtually all types of marketing problems. Survey questions can be employed to acquire information on the past, present, and future.

They are even useful to learn about a consumer's internal workings–such as motives and attitudes–that are not immediately observable. There are three basic ways of administering questions: personal interview, telephone interview, and mail questionnaire.

The popularity of each questioning mode varies from country to country. In many developing countries, telephone and mail surveys are impractical for a variety of reasons.

Although personal, door-to-door, in-home interviews are the dominant mode for gathering research data in Great Britain and Switzerland, central location/ street interviews are the dominant technique in France.

While the telephone interview is quite popular in the USA, face-to-face interviews account for 77 per cent of all interviews conducted in Portugal. In the Nordic countries, where the education level is very high, mail interviews are common. When the personal interview is used, an interviewer must know and understand the local language.

This imperative can present a problem in a country such as India, where there are fourteen official languages. In addition, a great deal of personal and social interaction occurs in a personal interview, and the appearance of the interviewer must thus be taken into account. If an interviewer is dressed too smartly, farmers and villagers may be intimidated and may claim to use expensive products just to impress the interviewer. Personal interview style and technique may need to be adjusted from country to country.

A researcher will not be able to ask too many questions in Hong Kong. People there are constantly in a hurry, and will not tolerate lengthy interviews. Telephone interviews pose a special challenge for international researchers. State-run telephone monopolies are usually associated with poor service, and it is therefore difficult and at times impossible to conduct a telephone survey.

It is exceedingly difficult for residents in many countries to receive their own telephone lines–something Americans have always taken for granted. Consumers in other countries may have to pay several hundred dollars for the privilege of being put on a waiting list in the hope that new telephone lines and numbers become available. Often, a person will wait several years before eventually receiving a telephone.

Assuming that private telephones are available, there remain several problems associated with a telephone interview. First, some cities do not have telephone books. Second, foreign telephone owners are much more likely than their Western counterparts to be members of the educated and higher-income groups, making them untypical of the larger population. Finally, telephone conversational habits can be vastly different, and an interviewer may experience great difficulty in obtaining information over the telephone. Some people may be reluctant to give any information over the telephone to an unknown person. The mail questionnaire is a popular survey method due to its low cost and high degree of standardization.

Despite these advantages, its effectiveness is contingent on the country in which it is used. Unilever, for instance, will not use the mail questionnaire in Italy. One problem involves the scarcity of good mailing lists. No population is as mobile as the US population, but people in most countries generally do not bother to report their new address, not even for the purpose of forwarding mail. As a result, a government's list based on the census report and household registration is, as a rule, woefully out of date. Another problem is illiteracy. Without doubt, this is a significant problem in many less developed countries, but the USA is hardly immune to this problem.

Lack of familiarity with the mailed survey question method should be given careful consideration, because many people are not used to responding by mail. This may be due in part to the low volume of mail received outside of the USA. Finally, poor postal service, especially in rural areas, is a cause for complaint in most parts of the world. ESOMAR's web site provides tips on nuances to consider when conducting business research overseas. The site offers a guide to opinion polls. There are guidelines on tape and video recording, interviewing children, mystery shopping, and pharmaceutical marketing research.

DATA ANALYSIS AND PROCESS

Analysis of data is a process of inspecting, cleaning, transforming, and modeling data with the goal of highlighting useful information, suggesting conclusions, and supporting decision making. Data analysis has multiple facets and approaches, encompassing diverse techniques under a variety of names, in different business, science, and social science domains.

Data mining is a particular data analysis technique that focuses on modeling and knowledge discovery for predictive rather than purely descriptive purposes. Business intelligence covers data analysis that relies heavily on aggregation, focusing on business information. In statistical applications, some people divide data analysis into descriptive statistics, exploratory data analysis (EDA), and confirmatory data analysis (CDA). EDA focuses on discovering new features in the data and CDA on confirming or falsifying existing hypotheses. Predictive analytics focuses on application of statistical or structural models for predictive forecasting or classification, while text analytics applies statistical, linguistic, and structural techniques to extract and classify information from textual sources, a species of unstructured data. All are varieties of data analysis.

Data integration is a precursor to data analysis, and data analysis is closely linked to data visualization and data dissemination. The term *data analysis* is sometimes used as a synonym for data modeling.

TYPE OF DATA

Data can be of several types:

- Quantitative data data is a number:
  - Often this is a continuous decimal number to a specified number of significant digits.
  - Sometimes it is a whole counting number.
- Categorical data data one of several categories.
- Qualitative data data is a pass/fail or the presence or lack of a characteristic.

THE PROCESS OF DATA ANALYSIS

Data analysis is a process, within which several phases can be distinguished. Data cleaning is an important procedure during which the data are inspected, and erroneous data are—if necessary, preferable, and possible—corrected. Data cleaning can be done during the stage of data entry. If this is done, it is important that no subjective decisions are made. The guiding principle provided by Adèr (ref) is: during subsequent manipulations of the data, information should always be cumulatively retrievable.

In other words, it should always be possible to undo any data set alterations. Therefore, it is important not to throw information away at any stage in the data cleaning phase. All information should be saved (*i.e.*, when altering variables, both the original values and the new values should be kept, either in a duplicate data set or under a different variable name), and all alterations to the data set should carefully and clearly documented, for instance in a syntax or a log.

The most important distinction between the initial data analysis phase and the main analysis phase, is that during initial data analysis one refrains from any analysis that are aimed at answering the original research question. The initial data analysis phase is guided by the following four questions: The quality of the data should be checked as early as possible. Data quality can be assessed in several ways, using different types of analyses: frequency counts, descriptive statistics (mean, standard deviation, median), normality (skewness, kurtosis, frequency histograms, normal probability plots), associations (correlations, scatter plots). Other initial data quality checks are:

- Checks on data cleaning: have decisions influenced the distribution of the variables? The distribution of the variables before data cleaning is compared to the distribution of the variables after data cleaning to see whether data cleaning has had unwanted effects on the data.
- Analysis of missing observations: are there many missing values, and are the values missing at random? The missing observations in the data are analyzed to see whether more than 25 per cent of the values are missing, whether they are missing at random (MAR), and whether some form of imputation is needed.
- Analysis of extreme observations: outlying observations in the data are analyzed to see if they seem to disturb the distribution.
- Comparison and correction of differences in coding schemes: variables are compared with coding schemes of variables external to the data set, and possibly corrected if coding schemes are not comparable.

The choice of analyses to assess the data quality during the initial data analysis phase depends on the analyses that will be conducted in the main analysis phase.

QUALITY OF MEASUREMENTS

The quality of the measurement instruments should only be checked during the initial data analysis phase when this is not the focus or research question of the study. One should check whether structure of measurement instruments corresponds to structure reported in the literature.

There are two ways to assess measurement quality:

- Confirmatory factor analysis.
- Analysis of homogeneity (internal consistency), which gives an indication of the reliability of a measurement instrument. During this analysis, one inspects the variances of the items and the scales, the Cronbach's α of the scales, and the change in the Cronbach's alpha when an item would be deleted from a scale.

INITIAL TRANSFORMATIONS

After assessing the quality of the data and of the measurements, one might decide to impute missing data, or to perform initial transformations of one or more variables, although this can also be done during the main analysis phase. Possible transformations of variables are:

- Square root transformation (if the distribution differs moderately from normal).
- Log-transformation (if the distribution differs substantially from normal).
- Inverse transformation (if the distribution differs severely from normal).
- Make categorical (ordinal/dichotomous) (if the distribution differs severely from normal, and no transformations help).

One should check the success of the randomization procedure, for instance by checking whether background and substantive variables are equally distributed within and across groups. If the study did not need and/or use a randomization procedure, one should check the success of the non-random sampling, for instance by checking whether all subgroups of the population of interest are represented in sample.

Other possible data distortions that should be checked are:

- Dropout (this should be identified during the initial data analysis phase).
- Item non-response (whether this is random or not should be assessed during the initial data analysis phase).
- Treatment quality (using manipulation checks).

CHARACTERISTICS OF DATA SAMPLE

In any report or article, the structure of the sample must be accurately described. It is especially important to exactly determine the structure of the sample (and specifically the size of the subgroups) when subgroup analyses will be performed during the main analysis phase. The characteristics of the data sample can be assessed by looking at:

- Basic statistics of important variables,
- Scatter plots,
- Correlations,
- Cross-tabulations.

FINAL STAGE OF THE INITIAL DATA ANALYSIS

During the final stage, the findings of the initial data analysis are documented, and necessary, preferable, and possible corrective actions are taken.

Also, the original plan for the main data analyses can and should be specified in more detail and/or rewritten. In order to do this, several decisions about the main data analyses can and should be made:

- In the case of non-normals: should one transform variables; make variables categorical (ordinal/dichotomous); adapt the analysis method?
- In the case of missing data: should one neglect or impute the missing data; which imputation technique should be used?
- In the case of outliers: should one use robust analysis techniques?
- In case items do not fit the scale: should one adapt the measurement instrument by omitting items, or rather ensure comparability with other (uses of the) measurement instrument(s)?
- In the case of (too) small subgroups: should one drop the hypothesis about inter-group differences, or use small sample techniques, like exact tests or bootstrapping?
- In case the randomization procedure seems to be defective: can and should one calculate propensity scores and include them as covariates in the main analyses?

ANALYSES

Several analyses can be used during the initial data analysis phase:

- Univariate statistics,
- Bivariate associations (correlations),
- Graphical techniques (scatter plots).

It is important to take the measurement levels of the variables into account for the analyses, as special statistical techniques are available for each level:

- Nominal and ordinal variables:
    - o Frequency counts (numbers and percentages)
    - o Associations
- Circumambulations (crosstabulations),
- Hierarchical loglinear analysis (restricted to a maximum of 8 variables),
- Loglinear analysis (to identify relevant/important variables and possible confounders):

  - Exact tests or bootstrapping (in case subgroups are small).
  - Computation of new variables.
- Continuous variables:
  - Distribution.
- Statistics (M, SD, variance, skewness, kurtosis).
- Stem-and-leaf displays.
- Box plots.

MAIN DATA ANALYSIS

In the main analysis phase analyses aimed at answering the research question are performed as well as any other relevant analysis needed to write the first draft of the research report.

EXPLORATORY AND CONFIRMATORY APPROACHES

In the main analysis phase either an exploratory or confirmatory approach can be adopted. Usually the approach is decided before data is collected. In an exploratory analysis no clear hypothesis is stated before analysing the data, and the data is searched for models that describe the data well. In a confirmatory analysis clear hypotheses about the data are tested. Exploratory data analysis should be interpreted carefully. When testing multiple models at once there is a high chance on finding at least one of them to be significant, but this can be due to a type 1 error.

It is important to always adjust the significance level when testing multiple models with, for example, a bonferroni correction. Also, one should not follow up an exploratory analysis with a confirmatory analysis in the same dataset. An exploratory analysis is used to find ideas for a theory, but not to test that theory as well. When a model is found exploratory in a dataset, then following up that analysis with a comfirmatory analysis in the same dataset could simply mean that the results of the comfirmatory analysis are due to the same type 1 error that resulted in the exploratory model in the first place. The comfirmatory analysis therefore will not be more informative than the original exploratory analysis.

STABILITY OF RESULTS

It is important to obtain some indication about how generalizable the results are. While this is hard to check, one can look at the stability of the results. Are the results reliable and reproducible? There are two main ways of doing this:

- Cross-validation: By splitting the data in multiple parts we can check if analyzes (like a fitted model) based on one part of the data generalize to another part of the data as well.
- Sensitivity analysis: A procedure to study the behaviour of a system or model when global parameters are (systematically) varied. One way to do this is with bootstrapping.

STATISTICAL METHODS

A lot of statistical methods have been used for statistical analyses. A very brief list of four of the more popular methods is:

- General linear model: A widely used model on which various statistical methods are based (*e.g.* t test, ANOVA, ANCOVA, MANOVA). Usable for assessing the effect of several predictors on one or more continuous dependent variables.
- Generalized linear model: An extension of the general linear model for discrete dependent variables.
- Structural equation modelling: Usable for assessing latent structures from measured manifest variables.
- Item response theory: Models for (mostly) assessing one latent variable from several binary measured variables (*e.g.* an exam).

FREE SOFTWARE FOR DATA ANALYSIS

- ROOT- C++ data analysis framework developed at CERN.
- PAW- FORTRAN/C data analysis framework developed at CERN.
- JHepWork- Java (multi-platform) data analysis framework developed at ANL.
- KNIME- the Konstanz Information Miner, a user friendly and comprehensive data analytics framework.
- Data Applied- an online data mining and data visualization solution.
- R- a programming language and software environment for statistical computing and graphics.
- DevInfo- a database system endorsed by the United Nations Development Group for monitoring and analysing human development.
- Zeptoscope Basic- Interactive Java-based plotter developed at Nanomix.

NUCLEAR AND PARTICLE PHYSICS

In nuclear and particle physics the data usually originate from the experimental apparatus via a data acquisition system. It is then processed, in a step usually called *data reduction*, to apply calibrations and to extract physically significant information. Data reduction is most often, especially in large particle physics experiments, an automatic, batch-mode operation carried out by software written ad-hoc. The resulting data *n-tuples* are then scrutinized by the physicists, using specialized software tools like ROOT or PAW, comparing the results of the experiment with theory.

The theoretical models are often difficult to compare directly with the results of the experiments, so they are used instead as input for Monte Carlo simulation software like Geant4, predict the response of the detector to a given theoretical event, producing simulated events which are then compared to experimental data.

TECHNIQUES OF DATA COLLECTION

SOCIAL SURVEY

The basic procedure in survey is that people are asked a number of questions on that aspect of behaviour which the sociologist is interested in. A number of people carefully selected so that their representation of their population being studied are asked to answer exactly the same question so that the replies to different categories of respondents may be examined for differences. One type of survey relies on contacting the respondents by letter and asking them to complete the questionnaire themselves before returning it. These are called Mail questionnaires. Sometimes questionnaires are not completed by individuals separately but by people in a group under the direct supervision of the research worker. A variation of the procedure can be that a trained interviewer asks the questions and records the responses on a schedule from each respondent.

These alternate procedures have different advantages and disadvantages. Mail questionnaires are relatively cheap and can be used to contact respondents who are scattered over a wide area. But at the same time the proportion of people who return questionnaires sent through post is usually rather small. The questions asked in main questionnaires have also to be very carefully worded in order to avoid ambiguity since the respondents cannot ask to have questions clarified for them. Using groups to complete questionnaires means that the return rate is good and that information is assembled quickly and fairly. Administrating the interview schedules to the respondents individually is probably the most reliable method. Several trained interviewers may be employed to contact specific individuals. The questionnaires and schedules can consist of both close-ended and open-ended questions. Also a special attention needs to be paid to ensure that the questionnaires are filled in logical order.

Where aptitude questions are included great care must be exercised to ensure the proper words are used. In case of schedules emphasis and interactions may also be standardized between different individuals and from respondents to respondents. Finally proper sampling techniques must be used to ensure that the sample under study represents the universe of study. In order to enhance the reliability of data collected through questionnaires and schedules, these questionnaires and schedules must be pretested through pilot studies.

INTERVIEWING

Social surveys may depend either on questionnaires that are self-administered or on schedules completed by trained research workers personally interviewing then is not a method of data collection distinct from social surveying but rather a technique which may vary from the brief formal contact as when the interviewer is working for the firms public opinion consultants or a market research organization and simply asks a housewife a few highly specific questions on limited range of topics to a long interview in which the research worker allows the respondents to develop points at leisure and take up others as he chooses.

The brief formal interview in which the working of the questions and the order in which they are asked is fixed is called structured interview while the freer discursive interview is called unstructured interview. The object of using structured interview is to standardize the interview as much as possible and thus to reduce the effect that the interviewer's personal approach or biases may have upon the result and even when structured interviews are used, proper training can do a lot to ensure further the reliability and validity of research. The personality of the interviewer and the social characteristics that the respondents attribute to him can be having influence on the result.

The effort of interviewer's bias can be estimated by comparing one interviewer's result with other. The problem of interviewer's bias in an unstructured interview is much greater. Here the interviewer is left to his common devices as far as the way he approaches a respondent is concerned. There is no fixed list of questions to work through. Instead the interviewer may work from a guide that will remind him of the topics he wishes to cover.

The training of the interviewer is crucial here not simply training in the social skills of keeping the conversation going on a topic that the respondent may not be very interested in but also in acquiring sensitivity to those things his respondents tells him which are specially relevant to the theoretical topics he is pursuing. This means that unstructured interviews can be carried out by people trained in sociological theory. They are then able to size upon stray comments made by the respondents which can be developed and lead on to important theoretical insight.

OBSERVATION: PARTICIPANT AND NON- PARTICIPANT

The rationale behind the use of observation in sociological research is that the sociologist should become party to a set of social actions sufficiently able to be able to assess directly the social relationship involved. The degree of involvement may vary considerable from being merely a watcher on the sidelines to be deeply involved in and being a part of what is going on. The former type of observation techniques are called non-participant while the latter is called participant observation. Sometimes one way observations screen have been used to watch groups in actions that they are unaware that they are being watched and the observer cannot affect their actions by his presence. The sociologist is visibly present and is a part of the situation either as a sociologist or in another guise. Where the sociologist is merely an observer it is usually assumed that he knows enough about what the actors are doing to be able to understand their behaviour. Any sociological observer has then to some extent be a participant observer he must at least share sufficient cultural background with the actors to be able to construe their behaviour meaningfully but the degree of participation and of sharing of meaning may vary considerably. Examples of such studies are Nel Anderson's study of Hobo-Indians and William White study of Street Corner Society.

SAMPLING

For practical and cost reasons, it is often impossible to collect information about the entire population of people or things in which social researchers are interested. In these cases, a sample of the total is selected for study. Most statistical studies are based on samples and not on complete enumerations of all the relevant data.

The main criteria when sampling are to ensure that a sample provides a faithful representation of the totality from which it is selected, and to know as precisely as possible the probability that a sample is reliable in this way. Randomization meets these criteria, because it protects against bias in the selection process and also provides a basis on which to apply statistical distribution theory that allows an estimate to be made of the probability that conclusions drawn from the sample are correct. A statistical sample is a miniature picture or cross-section of the entire group or aggregate from which the sample is taken. The entire group from which a sample is chosen is known as the population, universe or supply.

RESEARCH MEASUREMENT IN MARKETING

The best research design and the best sample are useless without proper measurements. A measuring method or instrument that works quite satisfactorily in one culture may fail to achieve the intended purpose in another country. Special care must therefore be taken if the reliability and validity of the measurement are to be ensured. Questions and scales must be assessed in order to make certain that they perform the function properly. A measuring instrument exhibits reliability when it yields the same result repeatedly, assuming no change in the object being measured.

As an example, if a person steps on a weighing scale five times and gets five different results, then something is certainly wrong with the scale, since that person's weight does not change appreciably within a short span of time. The same reliability problem applies to international marketing research.

An English-language questionnaire, when used within foreign markets, increases the chances that misinterpretation, misunderstanding, and administration variation will occur. Respondents' inconsistent answers are likely to be an indicator of the possible unreliability of the instrument. Validity is an indication of whether a measuring instrument is able to measure what it purports to measure.

A thermometer has been universally accepted as being a valid instrument for measuring temperature, but its validity must be seriously questioned if it is used to measure something else, such as the length of a room or the amount of rainfall. Reliability is a prerequisite for the existence of validity. If an instrument is not reliable, there are no circumstances under which it may be valid. Reliability, although a necessary condition for validity, is not a sufficient condition. Just because an instrument is reliable, the instrument is not automatically valid. Linguistic and conceptual non-equivalencies in questionnaire instruments that are used in crossnational surveys could conceivably operate to produce differences in the reliability of measurements, thus affecting the validity of conclusions drawn about market similarities or differences. The occurrence of reliability differentials in cross-national samples varies just as to the type of variable.

CONCEPTUAL EQUIVALENCE

Conceptual equivalence is concerned with whether a particular concept of interest is interpreted and understood in the same manner by people in various cultures. Such concepts as hunger and family welfare are universally understood and pose little problem. Other concepts, however, are culturally specific. The concept of dating between the sexes, which is taken for granted by Americans, is incomprehensible to citizens of countries where the arranged marriage is the norm and where a man can see a member of the opposite sex only in the presence of her family or a chaperon.

Culture specific concepts such as these can have implications for marketers. For example, Pizza Hut initially found that it could not conduct marketing research in Thailand because Thai consumers at the time did not know what a pizza was.

Demographics, in spite of being apparent and easily understood, should not be readily embraced in terms of conceptual equivalence without an examination of the varying frames of reference. A demographic variable such as sex is universal, and a question of this nature can be used in a cross-cultural study. Age, on the other hand, is not always considered in the same way–the Chinese include the time during pregnancy in their age.

Educational level, likewise, does not have the same meaning everywhere. The meaning of primary school, grade school, secondary school, high school, college, and university varies greatly. A primary school can range from four years to eight years, depending on the country. In some countries, a college may be nothing more than a vocational school. A college education in one country may not at all be equivalent to that in another. It is thus wise in many instances to ask about the number of years of schooling attended by the respondent. Let us consider the measurement of poverty.

The measurement process usually comprises three steps:

- Choosing an indicator of individual economic welfare,
- Setting a poverty line, and
- Identifying an aggregate poverty measure.

The three steps mentioned are anything but easy because the process has a number of contentious issues. There are several conceptual difficulties associated with each step. In the case of the household welfare indicator, the disputes include such issues as: should the indicator be consumption or income, what should each one include, and whether and how should it consider cost-of-living differences? Regarding the poverty line, at what overall level should it be set, and should the level vary in real terms by subgroup or date? Finally, with regard to the aggregate poverty measure, how should it treat inequality among the poor?

One has to wonder whether economists are well equipped to answer these questions or whether behavioural scientists can do a better job by focusing on individuals' perceptions of their well-being. The measurement issues and debates play an important role in the debate over globalization's impact on poverty and inequality.

While some point out that the proportion of people living in extreme poverty in the developing world fell sharply in 1990s, others argue that globalization has created greater poverty. Some contend that income equality has been rising in the world, whereas others argue the opposite. Such conflicting claims stem not only from differences in data and methods used but also from the important conceptual distinctions.

The opposing positions of proglobalizers and antiglobalizers represent a question of interpretation. One kind of conceptual equivalence a researcher should pay close attention to is functional equivalence. A particular object may perform varying functions or may satisfy different needs in different countries. A bicycle is a recreation device in some countries and a basic transportation device in others. Antifreeze is used to prevent freezing of engine coolant in cold countries but to prevent overheating in countries with warm climates. A hot milk-based drink is perceived as having restful, relaxing, and sleep-inducing properties in the United Kingdom; Thai consumers, in contrast, view the same drink as stimulating, energy giving, and invigorating.

Thais consume hot milk as either a substitute for or a supplement to breakfast. Therefore, a valid comparison requires the use behaviour to have been developed in response to similar problems in different cultures. Use differences must be built into the measuring instrument if meaningless results are to be avoided. Definitional or classification equivalence is another type of conceptual equivalence that requires careful treatment. This factor involves the way in which an object is defined or categorized–either perceptually by consumers or officially by law or government agencies.

In addition, even demographic characteristics are subject to the problem of definitional or classification equivalence. Age is one such example.

Persons in the same age group in different countries are not necessarily at the same stage of life or family life. When a boy becomes a man or a legal adult depends on the definition used by a particular country.

The age of legal adulthood may vary anywhere from the very early teens to 21 years. In India, a "boy" of only 13 or 14 years of age can legally marry a girl who is a few years younger. As a result, chronologically identical age groups within two or more countries do not necessarily lead to comparable equivalent groups. It is thus not possible to standardize age groupings and have the same definitional or classification equivalence on an international basis.

INSTRUMENT EQUIVALENCE

In devising and using a measure, a researcher should distinguish between two kinds of measuring instruments: emic and etic. Emic instruments are tests constructed to study a phenomenon within one culture only.

Etic instruments, on the other hand, are those that are "culture universal" or "culture independent." As such, when properly translated, etic measuring instruments may be used in other cultures. International marketing research often necessitates some measurement adaptation to overcome the problems of reliability and validity.

The rest of this section on measurement is devoted to the problems and adjustments of measurement in terms of conceptual equivalence, instrument equivalence, linguistic equivalence, response style, measurement timing, and external validity. A measuring instrument should be evaluated in terms of its international suitability.

Let us consider the CETSCALE instrument which is used to measure consumer ethnocentrism. Consumers who are ethnocentric do not like to purchase foreign products because such purchases are unpatriotic and harm the domestic economy and employment.

The instrument was originally validated with samples of American consumers only. Subsequently, the instrument was applied to samples from France, Japan, Germany, and the USA.

The CETSCALE was found to be a reliable measure across the four countries. It also has some degree of validity as evidenced by the consistent pattern of correlations across each country's sample.

An investigation of product-country images, lifestyles, and ethnocentric behaviours of Turkish consumers detected the robustness of the CETSCALE, thus lending further support to the earlier studies which were conducted in Western countries. Another study investigated whether the CETSCALE could be used as a measure of consumer ethnocentricism on an international basis.

In order to assess the instrument's reliability and validity in as many countries and different conditions as possible, the study focused on Spanish consumers' ethnocentric tendencies. The findings indicated that the scale measured a unidimensional construct and that the degree of measurement error was quite acceptable. In consumer research, the most popular rating scales are the Likert scale and the semantic differential scale.

When a Likert scale is employed, a respondent is asked to respond by indicating agreement and the relative intensity of such an agreement to each item or question. The degree of agreement usually ranges from "strongly agree" to "strongly disagree." The semantic differential scale measures the meaning of an object to a respondent who is asked to rate that concept on a series of bipolar rating scales.

A researcher must keep in mind that the Likert and semantic differential scales, though proven to be satisfactory in measuring behaviour and opinion in the USA, may not be understood or may not elicit the same manner of response in other markets. One study found significant main effects due to country and type of scale used as well as the interaction effects. The Likert and semantic differential scales appear to have emic properties and should be treated as culture-specific instruments.

The nature of the measurement scale can affect responses. Asking whether a particular object is a 10 on a scale of 1 to 10 may be meaningful to American respondents but may not be understood by respondents in most other countries where this rating scheme is uncommon.

It is imperative that scales be tailor-made and tested carefully in each culture in terms of relevance and appropriateness. One issue that may pose a problem is whether a scale should be in balance. A balanced scale is one that has the same number of choices for the positive side as well as for the negative side of the scale.

Should scales have a positive or negative skew? It is possible that people in certain cultures may tend to rate positively. As such, should a researcher offer a larger number of alternatives among the positive categories to achieve discrimination? Another issue related to rating scales is the number of choices provided with each question. A 7-point scale, for example, may not yield more information than a 5-point scale in the USA, but the former may prove useful elsewhere.

In general, a higher-point scale is needed when a group is relatively homogeneous, since more information is required to distinguish among members of the group. The 3-category scales were more equivalent than the 5-category scales. This finding raises several interesting questions. "Do scales with fewer categories pose fewer equivalence problems? Is it more difficult to systematically bias scales with fewer categories because choices are constrained?

If so, it would create a trade-off between designing items to capture variance more accurately and designing items less susceptible to response bias." Content validity should be routinely examined. Content validity is critical when a measuring instrument developed for one population is going to be used with another population. A test has content validity when it consists of items or questions judged to be representative of the specified universe of content. A test to measure the spelling ability of fifth-grade students should comprise words which students at that level of education are supposed to have learned. If a test were to contain a relatively large number of sports terms, for example, it would not have content validity because it would be unfair to those not interested in sports.

One researcher has constructed a scale to measure *Guanxi*, a behaviour that is pervasive in China. Naturally, the items used must reflect the typical activities in Chinese society. Standardized tests, such as IQ, SAT, and GMAT tests, are somewhat controversial due to content validity or the lack of it. In the USA, such tests are criticized by the poor and various ethnic minorities for being biased because the questions purportedly reflect the experience of white, middle-class Americans.

As such, the questions are not representative of the universe of content of interest. The problem is greatly amplified when US colleges require foreign students to take these standardized tests to determine admission eligibility. Uniformity is usually desirable, but that should be achieved at the expense of content validity. A researcher must keep in mind that some questions are culturally specific, making them difficult for foreigners, no matter how acculturated or smart they may be, to understand.

Some of the questions in US are meaningful to Americans but incomprehensible to Britons. A foreign language can complicate matters even more. It would be unreasonable to say that non-English-speaking children are unintelligent just because they cannot answer questions written in English. A researcher must remember that the content validity of an instrument depends on the purpose of the study as well as on the groups of people under investigation.

The universe of content can vary from group to group and from culture to culture. Standardized tests, therefore, may not necessarily work. Identical questions do not guarantee comparable data from different countries, and some variations in questions may be necessary.

LINGUISTIC EQUIVALENCE

Linguistic differences can easily invalidate the results of a study. There is no question that poor translation works against sound research methodology. Particularly disadvantageous are imprecise literal translations made without regard to the intended purpose or meaning of the study. Linguistic equivalence must be ensured when cross-cultural studies are conducted in different languages.

The goal of linguistic equivalence requires the researcher to pay close attention to potential translation problems. Translators should pay attention to idiomatic vocabulary, grammatical and syntactical differences in languages, and the experiential differences between cultures as expressed in language. Vocabulary equivalence requires a translation that is equivalent to the original language in which the instrument was developed.

Idiomatic equivalence becomes a problem when idioms or colloquialisms unique to one language cannot be translated properly into another. Grammatical and syntactical equivalence poses a problem when long passages must be translated. With regard to experiential equivalence, care should be taken that accurate inferences in a given statement are drawn by respondents from various cultures. As in the case of one study exploring strategic alliances in the emerging Latin American countries, the survey instrument was developed in English and was translated into Portuguese and Spanish by native speakers who were business professors.

Back translation was later performed on each local language instrument until conceptual and functional equivalence was achieved. There are several translation techniques that can be used: back translation, parallel-blind translation, committee approach, random probe, and decentering. With *back translation*, the research question is translated by one translator and then translated back into the source language by another translator. Any discrepancy between the first and last research questions indicates translation problems. In a *parallel-blind translation*, the question is translated by several individuals independently, and their translated statements are then compared. The *committee approach* differs from the *parallel-blind* technique in the sense that the former permits committee members to discuss the research questions with one another during the translation.

A *random probe* involves placing probes at random locations in both the source and translated question during pretesting in order to ensure that the respondents understand questions in the same way.

In *decentering*, both the source version and target version are viewed as open to modification. If translation problems are recognized for the source document, then it should be modified to be more easily translatable. Consequently, the source question becomes more lucid and precise. For example, the statement "I am an aerobic instructor" may be changed to "I am a dance-exercise teacher."

Regardless of the method of translation, there will always be concepts that cannot be translated into certain languages or that cannot be asked in a meaningful way in certain cultures. 7Up's "uncola" slogan is an example of such a concept. Some language purists may even contend that linguistic comparability is an unattainable goal. In any case, none of the translation methods can guarantee linguistic equivalence, but the recognition of potential translation difficulties should at least minimize problems. When Gillette globally launched Venus, a tripleblade razor for women, the product hit twenty-nine countries simultaneously.

A global campaign must pay attention to local languages and requirements; so a web site was designed to serve as a global template for fifteen regional sites. Since a package might contain as many as three languages, the company set up a translation war room in London filled with designers, translators, and lawyers.

Because the promotional phrases of "soft, protective cushions" and "reveal the goddess in you" carried significance nuances, the translators were required to express back the core idea in their native language. In the case of the word "goddess," Gillette chose the lower case so as to avoid a cultural or religious controversy.

RESPONSE STYLE

Response styles are "tendencies to respond systematically to questionnaire items on some basis other than what items were specifically designed to measure." Some common response styles are: acquiescence, extreme responding, use of the middle response category on the rating scales, and socially desirable responding.

Such response styles, by contaminating respondents' answers to substantive questions, threaten the validity of empirical findings of both domestic and international marketing research. One large, representative sample of consumers from eleven European Union countries showed systematic effects of response styles on the scale scores as a function of two scale characteristics.

The correlations between the scales could be biased upward or downward depending on correlation between response style components. Furthermore, a secondary analysis of a comprehensive collection of measurement scales found many scales to fail to control adequately for response styles. People from different cultures have different response styles when dealing with the same questions. Asian people, for example, are generally very polite and may avoid making negative statements about a product.

In such a case, a researcher may have to employ an even-number scale in order to receive an objective response. The even number scale, however, may create another problem in the sense that it may elicit an opinion that does not truly exist. A researcher may then want to consider whether to use an odd-number scale so that respondents have an option of making a neutral response.

Another issue concerning response style variation is the willingness–or lack of it–on the part of a respondent to take an extreme position, especially when such a position is not a popular one. It may thus be appropriate to adjust for respondents' extreme positions and/or response style by using "normalized" scores rather than raw scores. More often than not, one must be sensitive to the logic of a language. English-speaking people, for example, use the words *yes* and *no* in a manner that differs from the way non-English-speaking people do. Thus, "yes" is not always "yes," and sometimes "no" may mean "yes" instead.

The English and Western languages require the answer to be "yes" when the answer is affirmative. It is "no" when the answer is negative. For other languages, however, "yes" or "no" refers to whether a person's answer affirms or negates the question asked. Consider the question, "Don't you like it?" An American who does not like the item in question would say "no," but a non-Westerner would probably say "yes," indicating agreement with the question.

For the non-Westerner, the statement "Yes, I don't like it" is perfectly logical. Therefore, it is a good idea to phrase questions in simple, positive terms. Questions with negatives should be avoided. It should be noted that an interviewer is part of the measuring instrument. As such, the characteristics of the interviewer may interact with a respondent's response style. As shown in one study, response quality was affected by interaction effects of respondent and interviewer gender and ethnicity. Overall, Anglos and female interviewers were able to generate more responses. Also in support of the general deference theory, both Hispanic and Anglo respondents deferred to an interviewer from a different background when asked about the interviewer's culture but not when queried about non-cultural questions.

MEASUREMENT TIMING

A cross-national study can be done simultaneously, sequentially, or independently. A researcher may initially think it advantageous for a study to be conducted simultaneously in the countries of interest. But simultaneous studies in different markets may present problems of data comparability, especially due to seasonal factors. Consider a study of soft drink consumption, which is generally highest in the summer. Winter in Canada occurs when it is summer in Argentina. Simultaneous studies in such a case would yield invalid results. History is a specific external event that may affect the outcome or respondent behaviour within a study. Acting as an extraneous variable, history complicates cross-national studies. For example, an important election held in one country and not in another may considerably affect the results of a study. Likewise, sales in the USA during the Christmas season are much higher than sales during the rest of the year, whereas sales in China and Hong Kong tend to be higher than normal during the period of the Chinese New Year.

Another complicating factor can be a product's life-cycle stage. The same product may be in different stages of its life cycle in different countries. Because of the phenomenon of an international product's life cycle, less developed countries may lag behind more advanced nations in adopting the product. The sales of the product in two or more countries for the same period may not be comparable, casting doubt on the wisdom of conducting simultaneous studies. Because of this problem, it may be better in some cases to conduct "simultaneous" studies when the countries are in the same product-life-cycle stage. In addition, it may be prudent to conduct sequential studies for a particular stage in the product's life cycle when the product is not introduced at the same time in the countries of interest.

EXTERNAL VALIDITY

There are two major types of validity: internal and external. So far this stage has only discussed internal validity. A study is said to have internal validity when it accurately measures the characteristic or behaviour of interest. However, a researcher is prudent to ask whether the findings concerning a particular sample in a particular study will hold true for subjects who did not take part in the study.

External validity is concerned with the generalization of research results to other populations. Ordinarily, there is a limit on how far research findings can be generalized. Consequently, the findings may not be applicable to other groups or populations, other products, other cities, other countries, or other cultures. Consider the health concerns about the use of saccharin. Many studies have provided evidence for a link between saccharin and cancer. The scientific evidence has shown that saccharin is a carcinogen and that it may act as a cancer catalyst in the sense that it assists the carcinogen to work. Internal validity has never been much of an issue because studies have repeatedly proven that saccharin indeed causes cancer, at least in laboratory rats.

Critics of this evidence have concentrated on the issue of external validity. Producing a disease in rats is not a valid basis for predicting the effect of saccharin on humans. The US Food and Drug Administration, however, has dismissed this criticism by pointing out that the analysis is not accompanied by any proof that the mechanism causing cancer in rats would be different in humans.

As far as the FDA is concerned, the studies in question are both internally and externally valid. Ironically, after several decades, new evidence seems to indicate that saccharin is safe for consumption after all. The FDA, surprisingly, has reacted conservatively when test results submitted have used foreign subjects.

Although the FDA has accepted results using rats as surrogates for human beings, it had long shown great reluctance in accepting foreigners as being similar to Americans in terms of the impact of drug treatment. New FDA rules now permit a drug company to submit the results of clinical studies done abroad to support claims of safety and efficacy. Such studies are permitted as long as they have been conducted by competent foreign researchers, can be validated, and are applicable to the US population.

External validity is generally not a problem when the matter of concern is physiological in nature. The same cannot be said about psychological matters. Thus, people may have similar demographics but diverse attitudes and behaviour. The behaviour of one consumer group or the general behaviour of people in one country should not simply be extended to another group or people. It may not be reasonable to assume that a study of a marketing problem in one country or the results obtained within one culture will also be applicable to a marketing problem or people in other cultures. Because of differences between cultures, the problem of external validity is amplified when marketers engage in international marketing research. Since research in the area of satisfaction has focused primarily on American subjects, the degree of generalization of the results must be evaluated. Towards this end, one study tests the basic disconfirmation of expectations model in a very different culture. Based on the matched samples of American and Taiwanese respondents, the results confirm the generalizability of the model in this particular Asian culture. Along the same lines, 100 American and 100 Chinese Singaporean customers were used to study whether the Fishbein behavioural intention model could be used to explain their retail bargaining behaviour. While the Chinese have a higher level of bargaining intention as well as a more competitive bargaining style, the two groups' bargaining attitudes and subjective norms do not differ.

Another study evaluates the applicability of the Narver and Slater market orientation scale in the context of service firms in Central Europe's transition economies. The survey measures the levels of market orientation in 205 business-to-business services companies and 141 consumer services companies in Hungary, Poland, and Slovenia. The results are consistent with the prediction found in predominantly Western marketing literature, thus establishing the scale's reliability and validity.

Service firms with the higher levels of market orientation are:

- More often found in turbulent, rapidly changing markets,
- More likely to pursue longer term market-building goals,
- More likely to pursue differentiated positioning through superior levels of service, and
- Better performers on both financial and market-based criteria.

3

Trends in Marketing Research

In recent years the evolution of marketing research has been dramatic with marketers getting access to a wide variety of tools and techniques to improve their hunt for information. Below we discuss a few important trends shaping the marketing research field.

GAINING AN INFORMATION ADVANTAGE

In its role as the foundation of marketing, marketing research is arguably marketing's most important task. Today marketers not only view research as a key ingredient in making marketing decisions they also consider information to be a critical factor in gaining advantage over competitors.

Because organizations recognize the power information has in helping create and maintain products that offer value, there is an insatiable appetite to gain even more insight into customers and markets.

Marketers in nearly all industries are expected to direct more resources to gathering and analyzing information especially in highly competitive markets.

Many of the trends discussed below are directly related to marketers' quest to acquire large amounts of customer, competitive and market information.

INTERNET TECHNOLOGIES

To address the need for more information, marketing companies are developing new methods for collecting data. This has led to the introduction of several new technologies to assist in the information gathering process. Many of these developments are Internet-based technologies that include:

- *Enhanced Tracking*: The Internet offers an unparalleled ability to track and monitor customers. Each time a visitor accesses a web site they provide marketers with extensive information including how they arrived at the web site (*e.g.*, via a search engine) and what they did when on the web site (*e.g.*, what products were investigated). In many ways the vast data available through Internet tracking has yet to be used by the majority of marketers. However, as tracking software becomes more sophisticated the use of tracking data will be a routinely used research tool.

- *Improved Communication*: Not only is the Internet enabling marketers to monitor customers' web site activity, it also offers significant improvement in customer-to-company communication which is vital for marketing research. For instance, the ability to encourage customers to offer feedback on the company's products and service is easy using web site popup notices and e-mail reminders. The use of the Internet for conducting online focus group research is expanding.
- *Research Tools*: A large number of Internet services have added options for conducting research. These include the ubiquitous search engines, tools for conducting online surveys, and access to large databases containing previous research studies (*i.e.*, secondary research).

OTHER TECHNOLOGIES

In addition to the Internet, marketing research has benefited from other technological improvements including.

- *Virtual Reality and Simulations*: Marketers can use computer developed virtual worlds to simulate real world customer activity such as store shopping. While this type of research is mostly performed in a controlled laboratory setting, there are emerging virtual worlds on the Internet where marketers can test concepts and communicate with customers.
- *Global Positioning Systems*: GPS enables marketers to track inventory and even track mobile sales and service personnel. Soon GPS will be a common feature of customers' communication devices, such as cell phones, offering marketers the potential to locate and track customers.
- *Data Analysis Software*: Research includes gathering information and it also involves analyzing what is collected. A number of software and statistical programmes have been refined to give marketers greater insight into what the data really means.

AFFORDABLE RESEARCH

For many years formal research projects were considered something that only the largest marketers could afford due to the expense of carrying out relevant research.

However, the technologies discussed above make it affordable for companies of all sizes to engage in research that were financially prohibitive just few years ago.

For instance, surveying customers is quick and easy using one of the many online survey services which charge low fees to create, distribute and analyse results.

MERGING OF DATA SOURCES

The wide range of technologies used to gather data has led to the creation of data centres where information is stored. Today many of these data centres are sharing information with other centres in a manner that offers the marketer a fuller picture of their customers. Many companies have multiple contact points where customers can interact with the company (*e.g.*, in-person, on the web, via phone call). In the past the information gathered at these points was often stored separately so if a customer contacted the company through one contact point they may not be recognized if they also contacted the company through a different point.

Companies now see the value in knowing what customers do across all contact points and work to integrate customer information. Additionally, some marketers are going outside their own data collection and seek information on their customers from other sources, such as information provided by credit card companies. This information is then merged with the company-owned information to get a fuller picture of customer activity.

PRIVACY CONCERNS

The continual demand for customer information, along with advances in technology and the merging of information sources, has lead marketing organizations to gather information in ways that raise concerns among privacy advocates. Many customers are unaware of the amount and nature of the data marketers collect. As new information gathering techniques and technologies emerge customer response to issues of privacy may determine whether these methods are feasible or forbidden.

RESPONDENT COOPERATION AT ISSUE

The growing concern with privacy is leading many customers to limit their participation in a company's research activities. This includes customers choosing not to respond to company requests to take part in research studies that may come via telephone or e-mail solicitation. Customers are also becoming more aware of how their Internet activities are tracked and are responding by using techniques to restrict marketers tracking efforts. For example, marketers can place small data files called cookies on customers' computer and then use this to track user activity. Many customers are learning to disable the cookies and, in doing so, limit the marketer's ability to track customer activity.

RESEARCH AS A PROMOTIONAL TOOL

While most people do not equate marketing research with promotion, the fact is many companies are discovering research can also function as a major promotional tool. The practice of distributing company-produced research reports to potential customers and the news media has been used for a number of years in scientific and technology industries. In recent years the practice has expanded into many other fields, particularly among firms involved in consulting, health care and financial industries. Such reports often provide readers with information related to product features and benefits, comparisons with competitor's offerings and target market perceptions. These reports are produced using high quality graphs and charts backed up by carefully created narratives that proudly emphasize the company's strengths.

TARGETING MARKETS

The basic concepts needed as a foundation for building a strong marketing programme. In particular, it has emphasized the importance of understanding customers since they are the reason an organization is in business. With customer knowledge in hand, it is now time to turn our attention to the process of addressing customers' needs through actions undertaken by the marketer.

WHAT IS A MARKET?

The simplest way to define a market is to think of it as consisting of all the people or organizations that may have an interest in purchasing a company's products or services. In other words, a market comprises all customers who have needs that may be fulfilled by an organization's offerings. Yet just having a need is not enough to define a market. Many people may say they have a need for a California mansion that overlooks the Pacific Ocean but most would not be considered potential customers of a real estate agent who is attempting to sell such a property. So other factors come into play when defining a market.

The first factor is that markets consist of customers who are qualified to make a purchase. Qualified customers are defined as those who:

Seek a solution to a need, and

Are eligible to make a purchase, and

Possess the financial ability to make the purchase, and

Have the authority to make the decision.

Note that a customer must meet ALL factors listed above, though for some markets the customer may have a surrogate who will handle some of these qualifications for a targeted customer.

For instance, a market may consist of pre-teen customers who have a need for certain clothing items but the actual purchase may rest with the pre-teens' parents. So the parents could possibly assume one or more surrogate roles (*e.g.*, financial ability, authority) that will result in the pre-teen being a qualified customer.

A second factor for defining a market rests with the company's ability to service the market. To an organization a market can only exist if the solutions sought by customers are ones that the company can satisfy with their offerings. If a company identifies a group of customers who are qualified to make purchases they only become a market for the company once the company is in a position to execute marketing activities designed to service those customers.

Thus, for the purposes of this tutorial, a market is defined as a group of customers who are qualified to make purchases of products or services that a marketer is able to offer. However, even if an organization can offer products and services to a market, not all markets will fit an organization's goals and objectives. With this in mind, we now turn our attention to examining the process marketers follow to choose which markets are best to target with their marketing effort.

SELECTING TARGET MARKETS THROUGH MARKET SEGMENTATION

The market selected by a company as the target for their marketing efforts (*i.e.*, target market) is critical since all subsequent marketing decisions will be directed towards satisfying the needs of these customers. But what approach should be taken to select markets the company will target?

One approach is to target at a very broad level by identifying the market as consisting of qualified customers who have a basic need that must be satisfied. For example, one could consider the beverage market as consisting of all customers that want to purchase liquid refreshment products to solve a thirst need. While this may be the largest possible market a company could hope for (it would seem to contain just about everyone in the world!) in reality there are no commercial products that would appeal to everyone in the world since individual nutritional needs, tastes, purchase situations, economic conditions, and many other issues lead to differences in what people seek to satisfy their thirst needs.

Because people are different and seek different ways to satisfy their needs, nearly all organizations, whether for-profits or not-for-profits, industrial or consumer, domestic or international, must use a Market Segmentation approach to target marketing. This approach divides broad markets, consisting of customers possessing different characteristics, into smaller market segments in which customers are grouped by characteristic shared by others in the segment.

To successfully target markets using a segmentation approach, organizations should engage in the following three-step process.

Identify segments within the overall market. Choose the segment(s) that fits best with the organization's objectives and goals. Develop a marketing strategy that appeals to the selected target market(s)

IDENTIFY MARKET SEGMENTS

The first step in targeting markets is to separate customers who make up large, general markets into smaller groupings based on selected characteristics or variables (also referred to as bases of segmentation) shared by those in the group.

General markets are most often associated with basic product groups, such as automobile, beverage, footwear, home entertainment, etc. The purpose of segmentation is to look deeper within the general market in order to locate customers with more specific needs within the product group (*e.g.*, seek hybrid automobiles) and who also share similar characteristics (*e.g.*, college educated, support environmental issues, etc.). When grouped together these customers may form a smaller segment of the general market. By focusing market research on these smaller segments the marketer can learn a great deal about these customers and with this information can begin to craft highly targeted marketing campaigns.

For this tutorial, we take the approach that the variables used to segment markets can be classified into a three-stage hierarchy with higher stages building on information obtained from lower stages in order to reach greater precision in identifying shared characteristics. Yet, the more precise a marketer wishes to be with their segmentation efforts the more this process requires sufficient funding and strong research capabilities. For instance, a marketer entering a new market may not have the ability to segment beyond the first two stages since the precision available in Stage 3 segmentation may demand an established relationship with customers in the market.

The three-stage segmentation process presented below works for both consumer and business markets (*e.g.*, manufacturers, reseller, etc.), though, as one might expect, the variables used to segment these markets may be different. Each segmentation stage includes an explanation along with suggestions for variables the marketer should consider. This is not meant to be an exhaustive list, as other variables are potentially available, but for marketers who are new to segmentation these will offer a good starting point for segmenting markets.

Segmentation Variables

Segmentation Variables Consumer Markets	Segmentation Variables Business Markets
Demographics age group (e.g., teens, retirees, young adults), gender, education level, ethnicity, income, occupation, social class, marital status Geographics location (e.g., national, regional, urban/suburban/rural, international), climate	Demographics type (e.g., manufacturer, retailer, wholesaler), industry, size (e.g., sales volume; number of retail outlets), age (e.g., new; young growth, established growth, mature) Geographics location (e.g., national, regional, urban/suburban/rural, international), climate Business Arrangement ownership (e.g,. private versus public, independent versus chain), financial condition (e.g., credit rating, income growth, stock price, cash flow)

Stage 1 segmentation consists of variables that can be easily identified through demographics (*i.e.*, statistics that describe a population), geographics (*i.e.*, location issues) and financial information. For both consumer and business segmentation this information focuses mostly on easy to obtain data from such sources as government data (*e.g.*, census information), examining secondary data sources (*e.g.*, news media), trade associations and financial reporting services. While Stage 1 segmentation does not offer the segmentation benefits available with higher-level stages, the marketer benefits from accomplishing the segmentation task in a short time frame and at lower cost.

Segmentation Variable

Some firms, especially companies with limited funds or those who feel they need to move quickly to get their product to market, will stop the search for segmentation variables at the Stage 1 level. However, moving beyond Stage 1 segmentation offers a rich amount of customer information that will allow marketers to more effectively and efficiently target customers' needs.

To segment using Stage 2 variables marketers must use market research techniques that help gain insight into customers' current purchase situation and the environment in which the customer operates.

Information at this stage includes learning what options customers have chosen to satisfy their needs, what circumstances within customers' environment could affect how purchases are made, and understanding local conditions that could impact purchase decisions.

Segmentation Variables Consumer Markets	**Segmentation Variables Business Markets**
Current Purchasing Situation: brands used, purchase frequency, current suppliers	Current Purchasing Situation: brands used, purchase frequency, current suppliers
Purchase Ready : possess necessary equipment, property, knowledge and skill sets	Purchase Ready: possess necessary equipment, property, knowledge and skill sets
Local Environment: cultural, political, legal	Local Environment: cultural, political, legal
	Customers Served by the Business identify the business' market
	Business' Perceived Image identify how targeted businesses are perceived by their customers

Marketers might locate some of this information through the same sources used in Stage 1 (*e.g.*, may find out brands most frequently purchased) but most of these variables require the marketer to engage in at least casual contact with customers in the market. This can be done through primary research methods, such as surveying the market, having sales personnel contact customers, purchasing research reports from commercial research firms or hiring consultants to undertake research projects. The cost and time needed to acquire this information may be significantly greater than that of Stage 1 segmentation.

Segmentation Variables

Marketers choosing to segment at the Stage 3 level face an enormous challenge in gathering useful segmentation information but, for those who do commit to segmenting at this level, the rewards may include gaining competitive advantage over rivals whose segmentation efforts have not dug this deep.

However to reach the reward the marketer must invest significant time and money to amass the detailed market intelligence needed to achieve Stage 3 segmentation. Additionally much of what is needed at Stage 3 is information that is often well protected and not easily shared by customers. In fact, many customers are unwilling to share certain personal information (*e.g.*, psychological) with marketers with whom they are not familiar.

Segmentation Variables Consumer Markets	Segmentation Variables Business Markets
Benefits Sought price, overall value, specific feature, ease-of-use, service, etc. Product Usage how used, situation when used, etc. Purchase Conditions time of day/month/year when purchased, credit terms, trade-in option, etc. Characteristics of Individual Buyer purchase experience, how purchase is made, influencers on purchase decision, importance of purchase Psychographics personality, attitudes, and lifestyle combined with demographics	Benefits Sought price, overall value, specific feature, services, profit margins, promotional assistance; etc. Product Usage how used (e.g., raw material, component product, major selling item at retail level), situation when used, etc. Purchase Conditions length of sales cycle, set product specifications, bid pricing, credit terms, trade-in option, product handling, etc. Characteristics of Buying Center purchase experience, number of members, make-up of key influencers, willingness to assume risk;

Consequently, segmenting on Stage 3 variables is often not an option for marketers new to a market unless they purchase this access via other means (*e.g.*, hire a consultant who knows the market to undertake customer research). To get access to this information, marketers who already serve the market with other products may be able to use primary research such as focus groups, in-depth interviews, observation research and other high level market research techniques.

CHOOSING MARKET SEGMENTS

The second step in selecting target markets requires the marketer to critically evaluate the segments identified in Step 1 in order to select those which are most attractive.

For small firms this step may not be very involving since they may lack the resources needed to do it effectively. So they are often left with using their own intuition or judgement to determine which segments are the most promising. For companies with the time and money to commit to this step, the results may identify the segments that are primary candidates for current marketing efforts and also present segments that are future targets for the company's offerings. In determining whether a segment is worthy of being a target market, the marketer needs to address the following questions:

- Is the segment large enough to support the marketer's objectives? This is an especially critical question if the marketer is entering a market served by many competitors.
- Is the segment showing signs of growth? One of the worst situations for a marketer is to enter a market whose growth is flat or declining, especially if competitors already exist.
- Does the company have the necessary skills, knowledge and expertise to service the segment? The company should understand and be able to communicate with the customers in the segment, otherwise they may face a significant learning curve in understanding how to effectively market to a segment.
- Does the segment meet the mission of the company? The segment should not extend too far beyond the direction the company has chosen to take.

Once one or more segments have been identified the marketer must choose the most attractive option(s) for their marketing efforts. At this point the choice becomes the firm's target market(s).

DEVELOP MARKETING STRATEGY TO APPEAL TO TARGET MARKET(S)

The results of analyzing market segments leads the marketer to consider one of the following target marketing strategies.

- *Undifferentiated or Mass Marketing*: Under this strategy the marketer attempts to appeal to one large market with a single marketing strategy. While this approach offers advantages in terms of lowering development and production costs, since only one product is marketed, there are few markets in which all customers seek the same benefits. While this approach was very popular in the early days of marketing (*e.g.*, Ford Model-T), few companies now view this as a feasible strategy.

- *Differentiated or Segmentation Marketing:* Marketers choosing this strategy try to appeal to multiple smaller markets with a unique marketing strategy for each market. The underlying concept is that bigger markets can be divided into many sub-markets and an organization chooses different marketing strategies to reach each sub-market it targets. Most large consumer products firms follow this strategy as they offer multiple products (*e.g.*, running shoes, basketball shoes) within a larger product category (*e.g.*, footwear).
- *Concentrated or Niche Marketing:* This strategy combines mass and segmentation marketing by using a single marketing strategy to appeal to one or more very small markets. It is primarily used by smaller marketers who have identified small sub-segments of a larger segment that are not served well by larger firms that follow a segmentation marketing approach. In these situations a smaller company can do quite well marketing a single product to a narrowly defined target market.
- *Customized or Micro-Marketing:* This newest target marketing strategy attempts to appeal to targeted customers with individualized marketing programmes. For micro-marketing segmentation to be effective the marketer must, to some degree, allow customers to "build-their-own" products. This approach requires extensive technical capability for marketers to reach individual customers and allow customers to interact with the marketer. The Internet has been the catalyst for this target marketing strategy. As more companies learn to utilize the Internet micro-marketing is expected to flourish.

PRODUCT POSITIONING

No matter which target marketing strategy is selected, the overall marketing strategy should involve the process of positioning the firm's offerings in ways that will appeal to targeted customers. Positioning is concerned with the perception customers hold regarding a product or company. In particular, it relates to marketing decisions an organization undertakes to get customers to think about a product or company in a certain way compared to its competitors.

The goal of positioning is to convince customers to believe the marketer's offerings are different in some way from its competitors on an important benefit sought by the market. For instance, if a customer has discovered she has a need for an affordable laptop computer, a company such as Dell may come to mind since their marketing efforts position their products as offering good value at a reasonable cost.

To position successfully the marketer must have thorough knowledge of the key benefits sought by the market. Obviously the more effort the marketer expends on segmentation (*i.e.*, reached Stage 3) the more likely they will know the benefits sought by the market. Once known, the marketer must: 1) tailor marketing efforts to ensure their offerings satisfy the most sought after benefits, and 2) communicate to the market in a way that differentiates the marketer's offerings from competitors. For firms that seek to appeal to multiple target markets (*i.e.*, segmentation marketing), positioning strategies may differ for each market. For example, a marketer may sell the same product to two different target markets, but in one market the emphasis is on styling while in another market the emphasis is on ease-of-use benefits. The important point is that the overall market strategy must be evaluated for each target market since what works well in one market may not work as well in another market.

QUANTITATIVE RESEARCH

Believing that the research question was even more fundamental than the paradigm one felt allegiance to, several years ago we began to discuss the qualitative-quantitative debate from that perspective. The dichotomy and the debate disappeared, and the ideas presented here began to develop. This book describes our stance at a point in time, not the conclusions of our ideas, which continue to emerge, to grow, and to build from our work as researchers and as teachers.

While clearly a work in progress, which continues to evolve, the framework of an interactive continuum presented here has been enlightening to colleagues and students who operate within the current world of often-misunderstood and frequently debated paradigm shifts. At the conclusion of this chapter, the reader should be able to:

- Describe the history of qualitative and quantitative research methods and the debate about their relative values.
- Describe the typical purpose and outline of qualitative research.
- Describe the typical purpose and outline of quantitative research.
- Discuss the advantages and disadvantages of a dichotomy versus a continuum conceptualization of research design.

Qualitative and quantitative researches have philosophical roots in the naturalistic and the positivistic philosophies, respectively. Virtually all qualitative researchers, regardless of their theoretical differences, reflect some sort of individual phenomenological perspective. Most quantitative research approaches, regardless of their theoretical differences, tend to emphasize that there is a common reality on which people can agree.

From a phenomenological perspective, Douglas and Geertz believe that multiple realities exist and multiple interpretations are available from different individuals that are all equally valid. Reality is a social construct.

If one functions from this perspective, how one conducts a study and what conclusions a researcher draws from a study are considerably different from those of a researcher coming from a quantitative or positivist position, which assumes a common objective reality across individuals. There are different degrees of belief in these sets of assumptions about reality among qualitative and quantitative researchers. For instance, Blumer (1980), a phenomenological researcher who emphasizes subjectivity, does not deny that there is a reality one must attend to.

The debate between qualitative and quantitative researchers is based upon the differences in assumptions about what reality is and whether or not it is measurable. The debate further rests on differences of opinion about how we can best understand what we "know," whether through objective or subjective methods.

William Firestone (1987), in an article in the "Educational Researcher", differentiates qualitative from quantitative research based on four dimensions: assumptions, purpose, approach, and research role. Regarding assumptions, Firestone asks: is objective reality sought through facts or is reality socially constructed? Related to purpose, he asks: is it looking for causes or for understanding? To determine approach, he asks whether the research is experimental/ correlational or a form of ethnography. Lastly, related to the researcher's role, he asks whether the researcher is detached or immersed in the setting.

Shaker (1990), in a discussion of programme evaluation models, presents them as a metaphorical journey—moving from quantitative perspectives in the past to more recent naturalistic and qualitative assumptions. While positing a chronological continuum, Shaker would not seem to oppose our notion of question-driven research and evaluation. While he describes the "new identity" for evaluation as being "based on naturalistic approaches," he places this in the context of a "pragmatic commitment to finding methods that yield results in practice as we find it, rather than as we wish it to be".

The qualitative, naturalistic approach is used when observing and interpreting reality with the aim of developing a theory that will explain what was experienced. The quantitative approach is used when one begins with a theory (or hypothesis) and tests for confirmation or disconfirmation of that hypothesis.

It is important here to set the stage for abandoning the dichotomy. To do so, we examine a few of the key events in the chronicle of scientific evolution that established the debate in the first place. As long as one view of how we can explain the workings of the world reigns supreme, there is no debate.

The debate rests on a dichotomy characterized by a lessening of the dominance of one paradigm over another, leveling the playing field so that the debate could occur. In fact, the debate may be but one more phase in the ebb and flow of an everchanging philosophy of knowledge. For example, in The Enlightened Eye, Eisner (1991) cautions against the dichotomy and asserts that qualitative and quantitative research can be combined. He warns against qualitative researchers merely adopting a "soft form of positivism".

The genesis of the current qualitative-quantitative debate in educational research occurred as far back as 1844, when Auguste Comte claimed that the methods of natural science could be justified in studying social science. Science, in this view, is the collection and study of facts that can be observed through sensory input. These are the traditional data investigated by natural scientists—the physicists, the chemists, the biologists.

This view holds that true science is accumulated through the study of phenomena that can be physically sensed, observed, and counted. The "unknowables," as Herbert Spencer described them in his 1910 essay, those things that cannot be sensed but might rely on reason or thought, are banished from scientific investigation. Both Comte and Spencer were positivists.

Interestingly, this "positivism" was a move away from a more speculative, more "unknowable" view. It was a move away from relying on theological and metaphysical explanations of the world. It was a move towards what could be "positively" (confirmed through sensory data) determined. The philosophy maintained a grip on social science from the late 1800s through the early 1900s.

In the early 1900s, John Dewey, among others, questioned the absolutism of this position, viewing science as not separate and distinct from problem solving. His pragmatism considered science less rigidly than did the positivists. In his Sources of a Science of Education (1929), written some time after his initial speculations, he pointed out that practice should be the ground of our enquiry. Because of the value placed on experience for learning and the emphasis on practice, he appreciated the deeper complexity of what educational and social scientists study.

During the same period, a group of scholars who made up what became known as the famous Vienna Circle met and developed a new philosophy of science, logical positivism. Supporting Comte's positivism, they combined it with the symbolic logic of mathematics. Hypotheses derived using the rigour of mathematics (the symbolic) could be combined with fact gathering (the positivism) to test their confirmability (which was eventually modified to disconfirmability).

Although counter to an impetus by Dewey to diffuse the positivistic assumptions made by researchers, this hypothetico-deductive system was dominant in the middle years of the 20th century in psychology and sociology. Education, which borrowed traditions of enquiry from these disciplines, was affected as well. The respect for precision in measurement, mathematically systematic tests of hypotheses, and a quest for value-free science solidified this paradigm.

During the 1940s and 1950s, the quantitative paradigm dominated the social science and the educational research scene. Behaviourists and organizational theorists utilized empirical fact gathering and hypothesis testing almost exclusively in studying educational and social phenomena. In the mid- 1960s, while the quantitative perspective continued to prevail, a shift began as skepticism towards the domination of logical positivism and the evident chasm between human social systems and mathematical logic grew. New epistemologies began to emerge that acknowledged, for example, the value-laden nature of human social interactions. That human beings construct reality for themselves and that knowledge itself is transmitted in social ways were beginning to be assumed. Questions arose about the tenability of applying natural science methodology to these complex human dynamics.

In 1962, in The Structure of Scientific Revolutions, the most significant work on this issue, Thomas Kuhn explored the shifts in science's dominant paradigms. His doctorate in theoretical physics led him to look back into the history of science as he sought to know more about its foundations. He describes how, by randomly exploring the literature, he was exposed to Jean Piaget and, in the late 1950s, to a historical analysis of social science and psychology. Kuhn's study of methodology drove him to leave physics and become a historian of science.

He conceptualizes the notion of paradigms, "universally recognized scientific achievements that for a time provide model problems and solutions to a community of practitioners," and proposes that competing paradigms emerge chronologically when the dominant one no longer serves the explanatory needs of the scientific community.

For the most part, using the context of physics from the perspectives of Sir Isaac Newton and Albert Einstein, Kuhn explains these periods of competition, or scientific revolutions, in the natural sciences. He acknowledges that competing paradigms can possibly coexist on equal footing following such a revolution, or "paradigm shift," although, he cautions, it may be only rarely possible. He proposes that the predominant paradigm affects researchers not only methodologically but also in how they see the world. Kuhn's conceptualization of "paradigm" has been reinterpreted by others since his work, and many definitions are incorporated in the literature of the 1990s.

The quantitative paradigm continued to reign over social science and, according to Culbertson (1988), prevailed in education until the mid-1980s. At that time the logical positivists were losing supremacy. (The strong traditional bias towards quantitative science might even be based on Americans' preference for facts we can observe and count, a sense that that's what science "is.")

Concurrent with Kuhn's early notions of paradigms in the 1960s, society was undergoing radical changes. While some began to question the efficacy of the positivists' tools in explaining human organizational and social phenomena, education was moving into a more complex social context. Culbertson points to such 1960s and 1970s issues as racial integration, poverty, equal opportunity, schools as tools in global economic competition, the Soviet Union's threat to our math and science pre-eminence, and the need to account for the success and failure of the nation's children and posits that, in this context of increased complexity, some began to search for policy tools that the quantitative paradigm did not seem sufficiently able to explain.

That education served economic, political, and policy ends enhanced the opportunity for scholars interested in the culture of schools to begin to use anthropological strategies in their enquiry. These same interests fed the scholars' attempts to approach their research from the perspective of the critical theorists, as well as that of the feminists. Although always an important issue, the policy makers' interest in the world of classroom practice grew, and they increasingly expressed concerns that research and practice were unconnected and that this disconnection was in part due to the use of tightly controlled laboratory-like quantitative assumptions. A move among some social scientists in the direction of deriving theory from practice, rather than the other way around, characterized this change as well.

Graduate programmes preparing educational and social science researchers as well as professional journals have increasingly directed their attention towards qualitative research. Allotting time and space to what had been considered the "alternative" paradigm led to wide discussions in the journals and at professional meetings. The editors of the American Educational Research Journal, for example, announced in 1987 that particular emphasis on qualitative methodology would be forthcoming as they evaluated manuscripts.

This was a major legitimation of the paradigm for educational researchers. A plethora of books, articles, and presentations on the trustworthiness of the qualitative paradigm materialized. Some extolled the virtues of qualitative research as the only avenue to "truth," while others claimed that only by holding onto the quantitative traditions can we have confidence in our knowledge base.

In many forums the debate was manifest. Which is more scientific: the deductive methods of the logical positivists (quantitative researchers) or the inductive methods of the naturalists (qualitative researchers)? Can the results of qualitative research be generalized as are the results of quantitative research? Can science be value laden (qualitative) or only legitimate if value free (quantitative)? What epistemological assumptions are violated by adopting one paradigm or the other?

While to some the debate has ended, to others, especially those we encounter in researcher-preparation programmes, the debate has either not yet materialized to the full extent of its fury or continues unabated. Our strong sense is twofold. First, we continue to prepare students for an "either-or" world, a dichotomous world that no longer exists. We still prepare students who leave our colleges and universities with a monolithic perspective. Either they become well-trained statisticians, or they become cultural anthropologists, methodologically weak in asking research questions and in justifying either one or the other set of strategies. Second, researchers in education and in the social sciences have not yet constructed a way to ensure their success in utilizing both paradigms. The interactive continuum model in this book serves as a kind of framework directed towards both those needs.

The dichotomy of qualitative and quantitative research is one we deny but one we exploit here for heuristic purposes. The dichotomy, while not an ontological construct, does allow us to separate the idea. We slice it thin to examine it and make the case in this chapter that it does not exist in the scientific research realm. All research in education stands on basic underlying assumptions. This is true for quantitative methods as well as qualitative methods. To the extent that these assumptions withstand the scrutiny of scientific enquiry, the methods can be supported, taught to novice researchers, and used professionally and ethically without reservation. Since the mid-1980s when quality in all educational professions came under public review, it has become particularly crucial to delineate the foundational bases of educational research. Within the realm of this book, such bases will be examined.

QUALITATIVE VERSUS QUANTITATIVE

All behavioural research is made up of a combination of qualitative and quantitative constructs. In this book, the notion of the qualitative-quantitative research continuum, as opposed to a dichotomy, is explored on scientific grounds. We believe that conceptualizing the dichotomy (using separate and distinct categories of qualitative and quantitative research) is not consistent with a coherent philosophy of science and, further, that the notion of a continuum is the only construct that fits what we know in a scientific sense. A secondary theme is equally important; that is, what are known as qualitative methods are frequently beginning points, foundational strategies, which often are followed by quantitative methodologies.

Qualitative research methods are those generally subsumed under the heading ethnography.

Other headings and names include case studies, field studies, grounded theory, document studies, naturalistic enquiry, observational studies, interview studies, and descriptive studies. Qualitative research designs in the social sciences stem from traditions in anthropology and sociology, where the philosophy emphasizes the phenomenological basis of a study, the elaborate description of the "meaning" of phenomena for the people or culture under examination.

This is referred to as the verstehen approach. Often in a qualitative design only one subject, one case, or one unit is the focus of investigation over an extended period of time. According to Glaser and Strauss (1967), qualitative data are often coded a posteriori from interpretations of those data.

Quantitative research, on the other hand, falls under the category of empirical studies, according to some, or statistical studies, according to others. These designs include the more traditional ways in which psychology and behavioural science have carried out investigations. Quantitative modes have been the dominant methods of research in social science.

Quantitative designs include experimental studies, quasi-experimental studies, pretest-postest designs, and others, where control of variables, randomization, and valid and reliable measures are required and where generalizability from the sample to the population is the aim. Data in quantitative studies are coded according to a priori operational and standardized definitions.

It is necessary to adopt some standard by which one can measure whether the qualitative, the quantitative, or a continuum that includes both methodologies is the most effective mode in reaching truth. We assume the standard of science as a way of knowing.

Mouly (1970) asserts that, although there are two ways other than science to "know" something (*i.e.*, "experience" and "reasoning"), only through science can we generalize and provide for theory building. Some would have us believe that we can know something based on "authority" This basis has similarly been discredited because of the frequent inability to verify the facts, as well as the conflicting points of view among authorities.

Other philosophers go even further and suggest one can "know truth" also through "serendipity," "intuition," "compromise," and "consensus." Conjecture surrounding how we can know about truth, repeatable and verifiable truth, runs the gamut from "faith" to simple sensory perception. The assumption here is that science, as reflected in the scientific method, is the only defensible way of locating and verifying truth. Therefore, the criteria for comparison of the constructs underlying the dichotomy (qualitative vs. quantitative) and the interactive continuum (qualitative to quantitative to qualitative, etc.) are their scientific bases

The search for knowledge (or "truth") is the purpose of research. This search and, concomitantly, this research is most effective when built on the scientific method. In the ongoing debate between the positivists and the naturalists we tend to support the idea that the modern-day scientific method is both inductive and deductive, objective and subjective.

Design validity is more likely to be built into studies when the researcher is open to both paradigms rather than precluding one or the other. When faced with the question, "Which is better?" we would refuse to answer; indeed, we would be unable to answer, given the choices presented. There is no such answer. The better paradigm (qualitative or quantitative) is the one that serves to answer the specific research question.

We began our thinking on these issues over a decade ago. Our thoughts began to solidify in an interactive continuum model in 1985. Others have written about integrating qualitative and quantitative methods. Cook and Reichardt (1979) predates our original work and, like us, they suggest that the researcher's method can be separated from the researcher's worldview. Their book differs from ours in that their ideas are presented in an introductory essay to a collection of essays by research methodologists.

Their purpose was to bring together the combined works of many who were then struggling with the issues. Michael Patton (1980) presents a diagram of what he calls "mixed paradigms" in his book, Qualitative Evaluation Methods. His conceptualization, like ours, acknowledges that, between the qualitative and quantitative paradigms, there is a continuum of methods. His book, however, addresses qualitative methods only. It is not an exhaustive examination of assumptions, methods of research, and ways to critique research studies as we intend ours to be.

Creswell (1994), too, has authored a volume, Research Design: Qualitative and Quantitative Approaches, and he intends it to assist the researcher in making decisions about design. His book seems most closely focused on writing a dissertation proposal, and it is organized in that sequence. It does not include critiquing research as ours does, and he does not present an overall model of his thinking. The book is replete with examples from both qualitative and quantitative studies.

Our book contributes to the current discourse on research methods and assumptions underlying social science research by Depicting an overall model of qualitative-quantitative interactive continuum Suggesting ways to assess quality of published research Providing a strong emphasis on validity. In the last decade, a debate has continually raged as though one or the other paradigm should eventually win. Discounting the debate is not the issue of importance.

The key issue, we believe, should be improving the quality of research through an integrated way of viewing qualitative and quantitative research methods. Both paradigms coexist in the world of enquiry, and together they form an interactive continuum.

COMPONENT OF QUALITY MANAGEMENT

The main components of Quality Management:

- Quality Control,
- Quality Assurance,
- Quality Improvement,
- Software Quality Factors.

QUALITY CONTROL

Quality control is a process employed to ensure a certain level of quality in a product or service. It may include whatever actions a business deems necessary to provide for the control and verification of certain characteristics of a product or service. The basic goal of quality control is to ensure that the products, services, or processes provided meet specific requirements and are dependable, satisfactory, and fiscally sound.

Essentially, quality control involves the examination of a product, service, or process for certain minimum levels of quality. The goal of a quality control team is to identify products or services that do not meet a company's specified standards of quality.

If a problem is identified, the job of a quality control team or professional may involve stopping production temporarily. Depending on the particular service or product, as well as the type of problem identified, production or implementation may not cease entirely. Usually, it is not the job of a quality control team or professional to correct quality issues. Typically, other individuals are involved in the process of discovering the cause of quality issues and fixing them.

Once such problems are overcome, the product, service, or process continues production or implementation as usual. Quality control can cover not just products, services, and processes, but also people. Employees are an important part of any company.

If a company has employees that don't have adequate skills or training, have trouble understanding directions, or are misinformed, quality may be severely diminished. When quality control is considered in terms of human beings, it concerns correctable issues. However, it should not be confused with human resource issues.

Often, quality control is confused with quality assurance. Though the two are very similar, there are some basic differences. Quality control is concerned with the product, while quality assurance is process "oriented".

Even with such a clear-cut difference defined, identifying the differences between the two can be hard. Basically, quality control involves evaluating a product, activity, process, or service. By contrast, quality assurance is designed to make sure processes are sufficient to meet objectives. Simply put, quality assurance ensures a product or service is manufactured, implemented, created, or produced in the right way; while quality control evaluates whether or not the end result is satisfactory.

Example: Quality Control refers to quality related activities associated with the creation of project deliverables. Quality control is used to verify that deliverables are of acceptable quality and that they are complete and correct. Examples of quality control activities include deliverable peer reviews and the testing process.

Quality Assurance refers to the process used to create the deliverables, and can be performed by a manager, client, or even a third-party reviewer. Examples of quality assurance include process checklists and project audits. If your project gets audited, for instance, an auditor might not be able to tell if the content of a specific deliverable is acceptable (quality control). However, the auditor should be able to tell if the deliverable seems acceptable based on the process used to create it (quality assurance).

That's why project auditors can perform a quality assurance review on your project, even if they do not know the specifics of what you are delivering. They don't know your project, but they know what good processes look like.

Here's an example to drive home the point. Let's say a project manager asked the sponsor to approve the Business Requirements Report. If you were the sponsor, how would you validate that the business requirements seemed complete and correct?

One solution would be for you to actually review the document and the business requirements. If you did that, you would be performing a quality control activity, since your actions would be based on validating the deliverable itself.

However, let's say the document was thirty pages long and that you (as the sponsor) did not have the expertise, the time, or the inclination to do a specific content review. In that case, you wouldn't ask to review the document itself. Instead, you would ask the project manager to describe the process used to create the document. Let us say you received the following reply:

Project manager - "I gathered eight of your major users in a facilitated session. After the meeting, I documented the requirements and asked the group for their feedback, modifications, etc. I then took these updated requirements to representatives from the Legal, Finance, Manufacturing and Purchasing groups and they added requirements that were needed to support company standards. We then had a meeting with the four managers in your area that are most impacted by this system. These managers added a few more requirements. I then asked your four managers to sign off on the requirements and you can see their signatures on the last page." If you were the sponsor, would you now feel comfortable to sign the requirements? If it were me, I would feel pretty comfortable. That's the difference.

Quality control activities are focused on the deliverable itself. Quality assurance activities are focused on the process used to create the deliverable. They are both powerful techniques and both must be performed to ensure that the deliverables meet your customers quality requirements.

Quality Assurance

Quality assurance, or QA for short, is the activity of providing evidence needed to establish quality in work, and that activities that require good quality are being performed effectively. All those planned or systematic actions necessary to provide enough confidence that a product or service will satisfy the given requirements for quality.

Quality Assurance Activities

Quality assurance covers all activities from design, development, production, installation, servicing and documentation. This introduced the rules:

"fit for purpose" and "do it right the first time". It includes the regulation of the quality of raw materials, assemblies, products and components; services related to production; and management, production, and inspection processes. One of the most widely used paradigms for QA management is the PDCA (Plan-Do-Check-Act) approach, also known as the Shewhart cycle.

- *Failure testing:* Quality assurance covers all activities from design, development, production, installation, servicing and documentation. This introduced the rules: "fit for purpose" and "do it right the first time". It includes the regulation of the quality of raw materials, assemblies, products and components; services related to production; and management, production, and inspection processes.
- *Statistical control:* Many organizations use statistical process control to bring the organization to Six Sigma levels of quality, in other words, so that the likelihood of an unexpected failure is confined to six standard deviations on the normal distribution. This probability is less than four one-millionths. Items controlled often include clerical tasks such as order-entry as well as conventional manufacturing tasks.

Traditional statistical process controls in manufacturing operations usually proceed by randomly sampling and testing a fraction of the output. Variances of critical tolerances are continuously tracked, and manufacturing processes are corrected before bad parts can be produced.

- *ISO 17025:* ISO 17025 is an international standard that specifies the general requirements for the competence to carry out tests and or calibrations. There are 15 management requirements and 10 technical requirements. These requirements outline what a laboratory must do to become accredited.

Management system refers to the organization's structure for managing its processes or activities that transform inputs of resources into a product or service which meets the organization's objectives, such as satisfying the customer's quality requirements, complying with regulations, or meeting environmental objectives.

For software development organization, CMMI (Capability Maturity Model Integration) standards are widely used to measure the Quality Assurance.

These CMMI standards can be divided in to 5 steps, which a software development company can achieve by performing different quality improvement activities within the organization.

Company Quality

During the 1980s, the concept of "company quality" with the focus on management and people came to the fore. It was realised that, if all departments approached quality with an open mind, success was possible if the management led the quality improvement process. The company-wide quality approach places an emphasis on four aspects:

- Elements such as controls, job management, adequate processes, performance and integrity criteria and identification of records.
- Competence such as knowledge, skills, experience, qualifications.
- Soft elements, such as personnel integrity, confidence, organizational culture, motivation, team spirit and quality relationships.
- Infrastructure (as it enhances or limits functionality).

  The quality of the outputs is at risk if any of these aspects is deficient in any way.

The approach to quality management given here is therefore not limited to the manufacturing theatre only but can be applied to any business activity:

- Design work,
- Administrative services,
- Consulting,
- Banking,
- Insurance,
- Computer software,
- Retailing,
- Transportation.

It comprises a quality improvement process, which is generic in the sense it can be applied to any of these activities and it establishes a behaviour pattern, which supports the achievement of quality.

This in turn is supported by quality management practices which can include a number of business systems and which are usually specific to the activities of the business unit concerned. In manufacturing and construction activities, these business practices can be equated to the models for quality assurance defined by the International Standards contained in the ISO 9000 series and the specified Specifications for quality systems.

Still, in the system of Company Quality, the work being carried out was shop floor inspection which did not control the major quality problems. This led to quality assurance or total quality control, which has come into being recently.

Concepts and Definitions of Software Quality Assurance (SQA)

Software Quality Assurance (SQA) is defined as a planned and systematic approach to the evaluation of the quality of and adherence to software product standards, processes, and procedures. SQA includes the process of assuring that standards and procedures are established and are followed throughout the software acquisition life cycle. Compliance with agreed-upon standards and procedures is evaluated through process monitoring, product evaluation, and audits. Software development and control processes should include quality assurance approval points, where an SQA evaluation of the product may be done in relation to the applicable standards.

Standards and Procedures

Establishing standards and procedures for software development is critical, since these provide the framework from which the software evolves. Standards are the established criteria to which the software products are compared. Procedures are the established criteria to which the development and control processes are compared.

Standards and procedures establish the prescribed methods for developing software; the SQA role is to ensure their existence and adequacy. Proper documentation of standards and procedures is necessary since the SQA activities of process monitoring, product evaluation and auditing rely upon unequivocal definitions to measure project compliance. Types of standards include:

Documentation Standards specify form and content for planning, control, and product documentation and provide consistency throughout a project. The NASA Data Item Descriptions (DIDs) are documentation standards.

Design Standards specify the form and content of the design product. They provide rules and methods for translating the software requirements into the software design and for representing it in the design documentation.

Code Standards specify the language in which the code is to be written and define any restrictions on use of language features. They define legal language structures, style conventions, rules for data structures and interfaces, and internal code documentation. Procedures are explicit steps to be followed in carrying out a process.

All processes should have documented procedures. Examples of processes for which procedures are needed are configuration management, non-conformance reporting and corrective action, testing, and formal inspections.

If developed according to the NASA DID, the Management Plan describes the software development control processes, such as configuration management, for which there have to be procedures, and contains a list of the product standards. Standards are to be documented according to the Standards and Guidelines DID in the Product Specification. The planning activities required to assure that both products and processes comply with designated standards and procedures are described in the QA portion of the Management Plan.

Software Quality Assurance Activities

Product evaluation and process monitoring are the SQA activities that assure the software development and control processes described in the project's Management Plan are correctly carried out and that the project's procedures and standards are followed.

Products are monitored for conformance to standards and processes are monitored for conformance to procedures. Audits are a key technique used to perform product evaluation and process monitoring. Review of the Management Plan should ensure that appropriate SQA approval points are built into these processes.

Product evaluation is an SQA activity that assures standards are being followed. Ideally, the first products monitored by SQA should be the project's standards and procedures.

SQA assures that clear and achievable standards exist and then evaluates compliance of the software product to the established standards. Product evaluation assures that the software product reflects the requirements of the applicable standard(s) as identified in the Management Plan. Process monitoring is an SQA activity that ensures that appropriate steps to carry out the process are being followed. SQA monitors processes by comparing the actual steps carried out with those in the documented procedures. The Management Plan specifies the methods to be used by the SQA process monitoring activity.

A fundamental SQA technique is the audit, which looks at a process and/or a product in depth, comparing them to established procedures and standards. Audits are used to review management, technical, and assurance processes to provide an indication of the quality and status of the software product.

The purpose of an SQA audit is to assure that proper control procedures are being followed, that required documentation is maintained, and that the developer's status reports accurately reflect the status of the activity. The SQA product is an audit report to management consisting of findings and recommendations to bring the development into conformance with standards and/or procedures.

TOTAL QUALITY MANAGEMENT

In the global marketplace increased levels of competition have resulted in quality becoming of increasing importance to organizations and consequently total quality management (TQM) has become a key management issue. A considerable number of companies are applying TQM and the topic is the subject of many books and papers. As the end of the twentieth century approaches, TQM appears to be a well-accepted system of management. Yet two decades ago the term was not used. What has been the process of development of TQM theory and practice and when and why did the term come into being? This paper attempts to answer these questions. Before discussing the origins of TQM it is necessary to examine definitions of the term.

This is not an easy task as almost every writer on the subject has their own definition, by and large devising it to suit their own beliefs, prejudices and business and academic experiences. To some degree this is also true in the organizations which have introduced a TQM approach to managing the business.

The result is a proliferation of unique definitions which confounds comparisons and adds to the difficulties of understanding and analysis. Even with the publication of an international definition of TQM in ISO 8402(1994) there is ample evidence that writers and researchers do not stick to this definition and create their own unique offering.

Moreover, as Hackman and Wageman (1995) state, a large number of interventions not related with TQM are being encompassed under the TQM banner; this further complicates the issue of definition and understanding.

Despite the divergence of views on what constitutes TQM there are a number of common elements running through the various definitions (*e.g.* top management support, customer and supplier relationships and employee involvement). Several writers have tried to define the different dimensions that shape TQM.

Table contains an analysis by the authors of the common dimensions. The development of TQM begins with a brief historical review of the different stages that preceded the birth of TQM.

A comparative analysis of the Japanese approach to quality management and an examination of Feigenbaum's (1961) concept of total quality control is made, these constitute two of the major inputs into the development of TQM. The visions of the quality management gurus are also examined.

A HISTORICAL PERSPECTIVE

Powell (1995) makes the points that: "TQM's origins can be traced to 1949, when the Union of Japanese Scientists and Engineers formed a committee of scholars, engineers, and government officials devoted to improving Japanese productivity, and enhancing their post-war quality of life" and "American firms began to take serious notice of TQM around 1980".

It can be argued that many of the TQM dimensions were being applied by organisations before the TQM movement appeared; consequently, it is not easy to establish the exact date of birth of the term TQM. Stuelpnagel (1993) considers that in Ford and Crowter's book *My Life and Work*, published in 1926, the origins of TQM can be found.

Nevertheless, it is clear that the term and the philosophy as a whole appeared around the mid 1980s. Bemowski (1992) states that the term TQM was initially coined in 1985 by the Naval Air Systems Command to describe its Japanese-style management approach to quality improvement. Perhaps, the main reason for the origin of the term TQM could be a substitution in the previously used term of total quality control (TQC), the word "control" by "management" with the reasoning that quality is not just a matter of control, it has to be managed.

This is reinforced by Deming's (1982) view that sampling inspection should be suppressed and also by Crosby (1979) who makes the point that control is not necessary when a zero defects level is achieved. The term "control" is sometimes understood as meaning control over the workforces activities, and this is clearly not the aim of TQM. In the USA the development of quality management resulted from the penetration of its markets by Japanese products which started in the 1970s, together with the impact of the writings of Crosby, Deming, Feigenbaum and Juran.

Consequently, companies and academics studied the works of these authors and others, such as Ishikawa, and, integrating their approaches with quality management, gave rise to the concept of TQM. This movement was exported to other countries, the UK being one of the first.

Dale, who started his research in quality management back in 1981, believes that the term TQM arose in the UK from the activities of the Department of Trade and Industry National Quality Campaign which was launched in 1983 and the pioneering work of organisations such as IBM.

He relates a discussion with John MacDonald (one of the stalwarts of the UK quality management and the first managing director of Crosby Associates UK Ltd) who mentioned that around mid 1986 he was using the term TQM in his cross-Atlantic communication with Philip Crosby, who responded with the retort "what is TQM"? It is also worth mentioning that in the early to mid-1980s the use of qualityrelated terms and acronyms was nothing like as pronounced as it is today.

Table has been created from an analysis of the ABI-INFORM database, which includes brief summaries of business articles published since 1986. The number of references with the terms TQM, quality management (QM) and total quality (TQ) included in them has been searched.

The number of papers including the term TQM in 1986, 1987 and 1988 is small, which confirms the view already expressed that the term only started to be used in the literature since the mid-1980s.

It can be seen that at the beginning of the 1990s, the use of the term was already widespread, reaching a peak in 1993. Since then, the number of papers using the term has been in decline, although maintaining some importance in relation to volume of material.

It is the authors' opinion that this decrease in the number of papers is because TQM is widely known and accepted and is not attracting the attention from writers as it once did. However, some of the most recent incorporations into TQM, such as benchmarking and self assessment, have been the subject of further treatment in the management literature.

If the origins of the TQM dimensions are traced and analysed, the following key points emerge:

- Those related with workforce management and the need for top management leadership have their origins in the USA, arising from the Hawthorne studies.
- With respect to process flow management, SPC has its roots in the USA with Shewhart (1931) and the UK with Dudding (BS 600 (1935)). On the other hand, mistake proofing systems are a Japanese idea, as is the importance of cleanliness and organisation of tools and housekeeping using the fives and CANDO (cleanliness, arrangement, neatness, discipline and orderliness) principles.

- The concern about consumers needs has been of inherent interest to marketing theorists since it first appeared, the maindevelopment work on this subject has beenconducted in the USA. The increase in competition and demanding consumers have been the main reasons for companies treating this need to listen to "customers' voices" in a serious manner.
- Most of the recommendations about design processes have arisen from observation of Japanese procedures and best practices. Taguchi methods were developed by Genichi Taguchi, a statistician and electrical engineer who was involved in rebuilding the Japanese telephone system. Quality function deployment (QFD) methods were also developed in Japan, but, as with the case of many other Japanese management tools and techniques, they have been popularized world-wide by North American writers such as Hauser and Clausing (1988).
- The grounds of the supplier relationship dimension can be found mostly in JIT theories, which were first developed in Toyota.
- The role of the quality department has been widely analysed by American writers such as Feigenbaum (1991) and Juran *et al.* (1974).
- Benchmarking was first developed in Xerox, an American company and popularised by the work of Camp (1989).

A brief résumé of the historical events that have influenced the development of TQM theory and practice, indicating a gradual emergence of TQM. The use of statistical methods and the fundamentals of the system of workforce management began to be developed early in the century and Japan developed its TQM approach gradually from the end of the Second World War.

At the end of the 1970s and the beginning of the 1980s, Japanese pressure and the success of some American writers created a general concern about the focus on quality management in the USA, and from this country to the rest of the world.

The publication of the Malcolm Baldrige National Quality Award and other similar awards in other countries was the official recognition of the importance of TQM.

QUALITY ASSURANCE

Quality assurance, or QA for short, is the systematic monitoring and evaluation of the various aspects of a project, service or facility to maximize the probability that minimum standards of quality are being attained by the production process. QA cannot absolutely guarantee the production of *quality* products.

Two principles included in QA are: "Fit for purpose"- the product should be suitable for the intended purpose; and "Right first time"- mistakes should be eliminated. QA includes regulation of the quality of raw materials, assemblies, products and components, services related to production, and management, production and inspection processes. *Quality* is determined by the product users, clients or customers, not by society in general. It is not the same as 'expensive' or 'high quality'. Low priced products can be considered as having high quality if the product users determine them as such.

EARLY EFFORTS TO CONTROL THE QUALITY OF PRODUCTION

During the Middle Ages, guilds adopted responsibility for quality control of their members, setting and maintaining certain standards for guild membership. Royal governments purchasing material were interested in quality control as customers. For this reason, King John of England appointed William Wrotham to report about the construction and repair of ships. Centuries later, Samuel Pepys, Secretary to the British Admiralty, appointed multiple such overseers.

Prior to the extensive division of labour and mechanization resulting from the Industrial Revolution, it was possible for workers to control the quality of their own products.

The Industrial Revolution led to a system in which large groups of people performing a similar type of work were grouped together under the supervision of a foreman who was appointed to control the quality of work manufactured.

WARTIME PRODUCTION

At the time of the First World War, manufacturing processes typically became more complex with larger numbers of workers being supervised. This period saw the widespread introduction of mass production and piecework, which created problems as workmen could now earn more money by the production of extra products, which in turn occasionally led to poor quality workmanship being passed on to the assembly lines.

To counter bad workmanship, full time inspectors were introduced into the to identify, quarantine and ideally correct product quality failures. Quality control by inspection in the 1920s and 1930s led to the growth of quality inspection functions, separately organised from production and large enough to be headed by superintendents.

The systematic approach to quality started in industrial manufacture during the 1930s, mostly in the USA, when some attention was given to the cost of scrap and rework.

With the impact of mass production required during the Second World War made it necessary to introduce an improved form of quality control known as Statistical Quality Control, or SQC. Some of the initial work for SQC is credited to Walter A. Shewhart of Bell Labs, starting with his famous one-page memorandum of 1924.

SQC includes the concept that every production piece cannot be fully inspected into acceptable and non-acceptable batches. By extending the inspection phase and making inspection organizations more efficient, it provides inspectors with control tools such as sampling and control charts, even where 100 per cent inspection is not practicable.

Standard statistical techniques allow the producer to sample and test a certain proportion of the products for quality to achieve the desired level of confidence in the quality of the entire batch or production run.

POSTWAR

In the period following World War II, many countries' manufacturing capabilities that had been destroyed during the war were rebuilt. General Douglas MacArthur oversaw the re-building of Japan. During this time, General MacArthur involved two key individuals in the development of modern quality concepts: W. Edwards Deming and Joseph Juran. Both individuals promoted the collaborative concepts of quality to Japanese business and technical groups, and these groups utilized these concepts in the redevelopment of the Japanese economy.

Although there were many individuals trying to lead United States industries towards a more comprehensive approach to quality, the U.S. continued to apply the Quality Control (QC) concepts of inspection and sampling to remove defective product from production lines, essentially ignoring advances in QA for decades.

ACCURACY OF QUALITY ASSURANCE

One of the primary devices of QA is metrics, or measurability. One QA process involves product evaluation and testing to determine if they meet specifications, such as performance measures. As a result, quality assurance can involve delays in production until all rework or remediation steps have been undertaken.

The costs related to products that do not meet minimum quality standards can be unacceptably high.

STEPS FOR A TYPICAL QUALITY ASSURANCE PROCESS

There are many forms of QA processes, of varying scope and depth. The application of a particular process is often customized to the production process.

A typical process may include:

- Test of previous articles.
- Plan to improve.
- Design to include improvements and requirements.
- Manufacture with improvements.
- Review new item and improvements.
- Test of the new item.

QUALITY ASSURANCE VERSUS QUALITY CONTROL

Quality control emphasizes testing of products to uncover products which do not meet specifications (*i.e.*, do not meet the minimum level of quality). Quality assurance attempts to improve and stabilize production, and associated processes, to avoid, or at least to minimize, issues that led to the products which do not meet the metrics in the first place..

To maximize QA effectiveness, several methodologies may be used. QA does not eliminate the need for QC, as metrics testing is still required. QC activities are treated as one aspect of the overall QA process.

FAILURE TESTING

Valuable processes to perform on a whole consumer product is failure testing or stress testing. In mechanical terms this is the operation of a product until it fails, often under stresses such as increasing vibration, temperature, and humidity. This exposes many unanticipated weaknesses in a product, and the data are used to drive engineering and manufacturing process improvements. Often quite simple changes can dramatically improve product service, such as changing to mold-resistant paint or adding lock-washer placement to the training for new assembly personnel.

STATISTICAL CONTROL

Many organizations use statistical process control to bring the organization to Six Sigma levels of quality, in other words, so that the likelihood of an unexpected failure is confined to six standard deviations on the normal distribution. This probability is less than four one-millionths. Items controlled often include clerical tasks such as order-entry as well as conventional manufacturing tasks.

Traditional statistical process controls in manufacturing operations usually proceed by randomly sampling and testing a fraction of the output. Variances in critical tolerances are continuously tracked and where necessary corrected before bad parts are produced.

TOTAL QUALITY MANAGEMENT

The quality of products is dependent upon that of the participating constituents, some of which are sustainable and effectively controlled while others are not. The process(es) which are managed with QA pertain to Total Quality Management.

If the specification does not reflect the true quality requirements, the product's quality cannot be guaranteed. For instance, the parameters for a pressure vessel should cover not only the material and dimensions but operating, environmental, safety, reliability and maintainability requirements.

CHARACTERISTIC QUALITIES OF PRODUCT

Thus far we have considered the subject of quality in its various relationships and have traced the basic influence of measurement in order to prepare the way for a better understanding of quality itself. We are no w in a position to ask "What is it that constitutes quality?"

The first answer is that each attribute or characteristic shape, dimension, strength, finish, colour, and so forth which defines one kind of article is a quality of that article. The more definite and specific we make the descriptions of the dominating qualities, the more accurately do we understand just what the product is intended to be, and, incidentally, wherein it is to differ from other articles of the same general class of goods. To state a quality at all accurately, it must be compared with some arbitrarily selected standard. For example, we might say a rod is to have length, but we have not described the rod as regards dimension until we state the relationship between its length and that of something else. We can secure a more exact definition of the dimensional quality of the rod if we say that its length is to be the same as that of a sample rod which has been selected as standard. But, as a matter of fact, in this case the comparison would be made with the well-accepted standard of dimension and the length stated in standard units of feet, inches, or both, depending on convenience.

This well-known and seemingly elementary example is simple only because we have a thoroughly established and well-known method of comparison or measurement for dimensional quality; but what about some of the other qualities? With respect to colour, for instance, there is, as yet, no accepted method of analysis and comparison with a standard. To say an article is to be painted red is nearly as loose a definition of colour quality as to describe dimensional quality by saying that a rod had length because there can be an enormous number of tints and shades of red. In the absence of a colour scale for numerical comparison, we are reduced to saying that the colour will be like a given standard sample. We must also take precautions to see that the colour of the sample itself does not change in the course of time, and thereby carry the product away from the standard as originally set.

The question of whether such qualities as colour can be reduced to a basis of definite measurement with the same ease of treatment as dimension must be deferred, at this time. Meanwhile, dimension will be used chiefly to illustrate the discussion as it proceeds. It should be borne in mind, however, that the general principle applies to the treatment of all qualities, that no quality can be described without comparing it to some standard which process is measurement and that the application of the idea of measurement must not be confined to dimension alone.

This is one excellent reason why every industrial executive who is interested in the subject under discussion should be familiar, in a general way at least, with the principles underlying the precision of measurement and the theory of errors to secure an important attitude of mind and a necessary sense of discrimination, of proportion and perspective.

QUALITY VARIES CONTINUALLY

One of the first things that this knowledge will reveal is that there is no such thing as an absolutely accurate measurement. No matter how carefully the unknown is compared with an accepted standard, errors are bound to creep in; and very shortly a certain critical point is reached beyond which these errors can be reduced only through the use of extreme precautions, if at all.

This thought leads at once to one of the most important conceptions of what constitutes quality, an idea that must be kept in mind throughout the subsequent study of the control of quality, namely, that quality is a variable. Quantity relates to the product en masse, and in this sense is abstract and impersonal. Quality, however, is different for each separate article produced. Hence the quality of the factory product varies from piece to piece. This fact must be clearly appreciated before an attempt is made to fix upon the standards of quality desired, or to take up the consideration of the organization and arrangement of manufacturing equipment and methods most suitable for securing these desired standards with greatest economy. In practice, the degree of quality varies continually from the standard desired. Further, the degree of quality varies with respect to time, in the sense that the attempt to make many things alike results inevitably in quality gradually slipping away from this desired standard as the work proceeds. This tendency of quality in all its forms to vary and change is always present as a potential force, and acts except in so far as it is held in check by external means provided for control purposes.

4

Application of Marketing Research Methodology

Market research focuses on assessing the preferences and choices of consumers and potential consumers. The Market Research Application (MRA) of SAS/STAT software is an intuitive point-and-click interface that provides statistical and graphical techniques for market research data analysis. The Market Research Application provides easy access to five important types of data analysis commonly used in market research. These are,

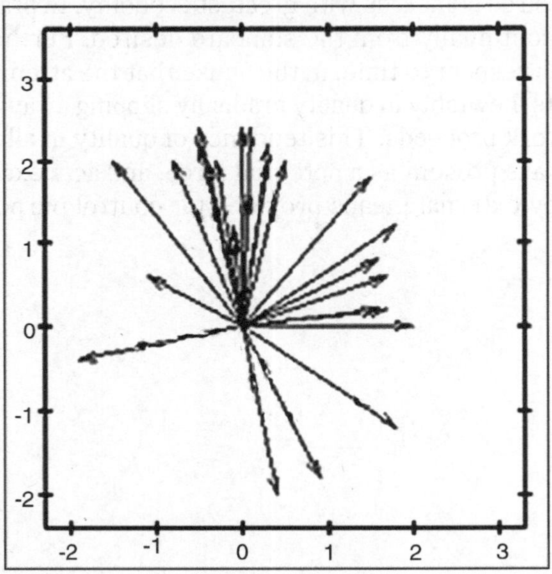

STATISTICS

CONJOINT ANALYSIS

Conjoint analysis is used to evaluate consumer preference. If products are composed of attributes, conjoint analysis determines which combination of attribute levels are most preferred by consumers. Consumers indicate their preferences by ranking a number of different combinations of attribute levels. Conjoint analysis assumes that consumers make purchases by simmultaneously considering several attributes of a product. The ability to analyse several attributes at once distinguishes conjoint analysis from traditional market research methods where each attribute is studied separately. Conjoint analysis helps you discover how consumers make trade-offs between the various possible attribute combinations available. Usually, conjoint analysis consists of a main-effects analysis of variance with ordinally scaled dependent variables. Consumer preferences are the dependent variables, and product attributes are the independent variables.

The following are some of the questions that can be answered with a conjoint analysis:

- How important is each product attribute to consumers?
- Which existing products do consumers prefer?
- What combination of product attributes do consumers prefer most?
- How well will my product do in the current market?

Correspondence Analysis

Market research frequently involves categorical data. Correspondence analysis characterizes the associations between the levels of two or more categorical variables by performing a weighted principal component analysis of a contingency table.

The result of a correspondence analysis is a two-dimensional graphical representation of the association between rows and columns of the table. The plot contains a point for each row and each column of the table. Rows with similar patterns of counts produce points that are close together, and columns with similar patterns of counts produce points that are close together. Simple correspondence analysis analyzes a contingency table made up of one or more column variables and one or more row variables. In multiple correspondence analysis, only column variables are used and a Burt table is produced.

The following are some of the questions that can be answered with a correspondence analysis.

- Who are my customers?
- Who else should be my customers?
- What new products should I create?
- Who should I target with my new products?

Discrete Choice Modeling

Discrete choice analysis is used to evaluate consumer choice. In conjoint analysis, consumer preferences for a product are evaluated by having a number of consumers rank different combinations of attribute levels. In discrete choice analysis, each consumer chooses one combination of attribute levels from a particular set of attribute level combinations. A set of attribute level combinations is called a *choice set*. Each consumer may be asked to choose one combination from each of several different choice sets.

The attributes of the product that define the choices are called *choice attributes* to distinguish them from other attributes that may be of interest but do not contribute to the definition of the choices. For example, you may want to include demographic variables related to the consumers in the analysis. The following are some of the questions that can be answered with a discrete choice analysis.

- Which combination of attribute levels is most likely to be chosen by consumers?
- Which combination of attribute levels is least likely to be chosen by consumers?
- What is the probability of my product being chosen by a consumer?

Multidimensional Scaling

Multidimensional scaling (MDS) analysis takes consumer judgements of similarity (or difference) of pairs of products and produces a map of the perceived relationship among the products. Each consumer evaluates the similarity (or difference) of each pair of products. MDS determines the relative similarity perceived by consumers among all the products. The results enable you to identify products that consumers see as similar. The following are some of the questions that can be answered with a multidimensional scaling analysis.

- Which products do consumers see as similar to my product?
- Which products do consumers see as different from my product?

Multidimensional Preference Analysis

In a conjoint analysis, consumers indicate their preferences for products that are composed of attributes. Sometimes in market research, the available data consist of consumer preferences for products for which attributes are not defined. Multidimensional preference analysis (MDPREF) is used to analyse such data. MDPREF analysis is a principal component analysis of a data matrix with columns that correspond to consumers and with rows that correspond to products. The analysis results in a plot that reveals patterns of consumer preference for the products. The following are some of the questions that can be answered with a multidimensional preference analysis.

- Who are my customers?
- Who else should be my customers?
- What new products should I create?

You invoke the application by issuing the command market on any command line. To view an example of conjoint analysis using the Market Research Application.

LIMITATION OF MARKETING RESEARCH

ROLE AND LIMITATIONS

In essence, management is about decision making. Decision is invariably surrounded by uncertainties and, therefore, risks. Marketing research is charged with helping to reduce such uncertainties, "...but will never remove it. At best, marketing research will increase the probability that the decisions which management has to take will help attain the organisation's marketing objectives.

THE ROLE AND LIMITATIONS OF MARKETING RESEARCH

"Marketing research does not make decisions and it does not guarantee success". Marketing managers may seek advice from marketing research specialists, and indeed it is important that research reports should specify alternative courses of action and the probability of success, where possible, of these alternatives. However, it is marketing managers who make the final marketing decision and not the researcher.

The second observation, that marketing research does not guarantee success, is simply a recognition of the environment within which marketing takes place. In the fields of science and engineering researchers are often working with deterministic models of the world where,

$$y = f(x).$$

That is, x is a necessary and sufficient condition for y to occur. For instance, an increase in pressure is usually necessary and sufficient to bring about a rise in air temperature. In the social sciences, and this includes marketing and marketing research, the phenomenon under investigation rarely, if ever, lends itself to deterministic modelling.

Consider the marketing problem of determining how much to spend on promotion in order to achieve a given market share.

The link between promotional expenditure and sales is not so direct as that between pressure and temperature. There are a great many more intervening variables, including: the media used, the effectiveness of the promotional message, the length and frequency of the campaign, not to mention the many dimensions of the product, price and distribution. Marketing researchers work with probabilistic models of the form:

$$y = f(x1)..(fx2)...f(xn)...$$

This reflects the fact that in order for a target market share to be reached some promotion (amount unknown) is necessary but will not be sufficient, on its own, to achieve the target. Y is a function of a number of variables and the interactions between them.

The model is further complicated by the fact that these interactions are themselves often not understood. It is for these reasons that marketing researchers cannot guarantee that decisions based on their information will always prove 'successful'. Rather the best that a competent researcher and a well designed study will be able to offer is a reduction in the amount of uncertainty surrounding the decision.

EXPLANATION

Marketing research is the systematic and objective search for, and analysis of, information relevant to the identification and solution of any problem in the field of marketing.

The key words in this definition are; systematic, objective and analysis. Marketing research seeks to set about its task in a systematic and objective fashion. This means that a detailed and carefully designed research plan is developed in which each stage of the research is specified. Such a research plan is only considered adequate if it specifies: the research problem in concise and precise terms, the information necessary to address the problem, the methods to be employed in gathering the information and the analytical techniques to be used to interpret it.

Maintaining objectivity in marketing research is essential if marketing management is to have sufficient confidence in its results to be prepared to take risky decisions based upon those results. To this end, as far as possible, marketing researchers employ the scientific method. The characteristics of the scientific method are that it translates personal prejudices, notions and opinions into explicit propositions (or hypotheses). These are tested empirically. At the same time alternative explanations of the event or phenomena of interest are given equal consideration.

Not many years ago an agricultural engineering company developed an improved rice milling machine. The machine was introduced into Thailand where existing rice milling machines were of a design which resulted in a high percentage of brokens (broken kernels).

The new rice mill produced a negligible percentage of brokens. Intuitively a successful product would be predicted, launched with hardly any need for marketing research when the new mill had such obvious advantages over existing products. The agricultural engineering company went through the expensive and time-consuming process of importing the machine into Thailand. They set up extensive distribution and servicing facilities only to be surprised when the mill failed to gain acceptance. In Thailand, smallholders take their rice to a miller.

Since they do not have sufficient cash to pay for milling their rice they get paid in 'brokens'. The miller then sells the 'brokens' for animal feed. The more effective milling machine simply did not fit into the Thai rice processing system. The company's assessment of the market was hardly objective. They saw the 'brokens' as a problem which their product solved. The prospective customer did not see it as a problem at all.

The third of the key terms in the definition given a little earlier was analytical.

The marketing researcher's task goes beyond the collecting of data. He/she must also interpret the data in terms of what the it means to the organisation which commissioned the research.

Knowing that 60 per cent of those interviewed thought that product A was superior to product B is, in itself, of little value. The organisation needs to know the alternative ways it can respond to this data.

Data is equivalent to the raw materials of manufacturing; it has to be converted into information before it becomes useful in decision making. The process of convening data into information is achieved through analysis.

Although the need for precision and thoroughness in marketing research has been stressed here, it is to be remembered that, in practice, there is a perpetual conflict between the demands of expediency and the search for truth. The reality is that management is frequently under pressure to make timely decisions.

Therefore management often seeks answers through marketing research in the shortest time possible and, moreover, at minimum cost. On such occasions its methods tend to be less theoretically rigorous and its analysis more superficial.

The Market Research Brief

Marketing research can be concerned with any of a variety of aspects of the market: the product, sales, buyer behaviour, promotion, distribution, pricing, packaging, etc. Since the researcher cannot investigate everything about a market, he/she must be selective. The question remains as to how the researcher decides where to focus the study, and to what depth each issue should be investigated.

The answer should lie in a document called the research brief. The research design is a set of guidelines given to the researcher by the person(s) who have commissioned the research and/or the individual(s) who are to make use of the results in their decision making. The brief must inform the researcher which aspects of the market are particularly important.

In particular, the Research Brief Should Include

- The purpose of the research.
- The objectives stated in a clear, concise, attainable, measurable and quantifiable way.
- A time horizon.
- A resource allocation, including the budget and facilities.
- A reporting period.

Each of these components of the brief is explained in a little more detail in the section that follows.

PURPOSE OF THE RESEARCH

It is not at all unusual for marketing managers to neglect to tell the researcher the precise purpose of the research. They often do not appreciate the need to do so. Instead, they simply state what they think they need to know. This is not quite the same thing.

To appreciate the difference consider the case of the marketing research agency which was contacted by the International Coffee Organization (ICO) and asked to carry out a survey of young people in the age group 15-24. They wanted information on the coffee drinking habits of these young people: how much coffee they drank, at what times of day, with meals or between meals, instant or ground coffee, which other beverages they preferred and so on. In response, the research organization developed a set of wide-ranging proposals which included taking a large random sample of young people.

In fact much of the information was interesting rather than important. Important information is that information which directly assists in making decisions and the ICO had not told the research company the purpose of the research. The initial reason for the study had been a suspicion, on the part of the ICO, that an increasing percentage of young people were consuming beverages other than coffee, particularly soft drinks, and simply never developed the coffee drinking habit.

Had this been explained to the research company then it is likely that their proposals would have been radically different. To begin with, the sample would have been composed of 15-24 year old non-coffee drinkers rather than a random sample of all 15-24 year olds. Second, the focus would have been non-coffee drinking habits rather than coffee drinking habits.

Unless the purpose of the research is stated in unambiguous terms it is difficult for the marketing researcher to translate the decision-maker's problem into a research problem and study design.

CLEAR AND CONCISE OBJECTIVES

Suppose that the marketing manager states that he needs to know the potential market for a new product his/her organization has been developing. At first glance this might appear to meet all of the requirements of being clear, concise, attainable, measurable and quantifiable. In practice it would possibly meet only one of these criteria, *i.e.* it is concise!

Here is another case to be considered. A small engineering firm had purchased a prototype tree-lifter from a private research company. This machine was suitable for lifting semi-mature trees, complete with root-ball intact and transplanting such trees in another location. It was thought to have potential in certain types of tree nurseries and plantations.

The problem with the objective is that the marketing manager needs to know the potential market for the new tree-lifter is that it is not attainable.

One could find out how many tree-lifters were currently being sold but this is not the same as the objective set by the marketing manager. The market potential for any new brand is a function of at least 4 things, as shown in Figure.

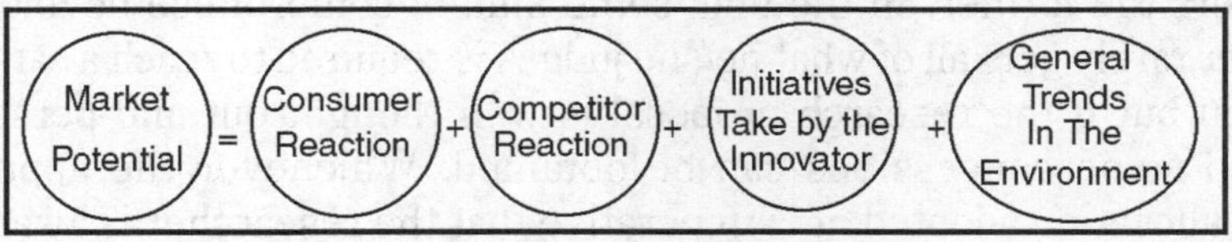

Fig. The Components of Market Potential.

It was possible to test customer reaction to the concept of the new tree-lifter by showing pictures, line drawings and by supplying product specifications to prospective buyers. However, since the company had not decided their pricing policy an important element could not be tested. In large measure, it was also possible to gauge the likely reaction from competitors. The researchers began by looking at the basis of competition to determine whether it was on price, product quality or unique product features. The researchers were able to look at precedents. They examined the pattern of response on past occasions when one or other of those companies already in the market had launched a new product. An audit of the environment was undertaken too, but the missing component was the company's' own plans for exploiting the market. Since the company had no involvement in the agricultural engineering sector, prior to acquiring the rights to the tree-lifter, they had no agreements with distributors, no idea of which, if any, of the distributors would be prepared to stock their product; they had no salesmen trained in selling into this industry and so on. The product's potential depended very much on such initiatives.

The solution would have been to undertake a study which would have described the market in detail in terms of customers, competitors and the environment. The company could then have put a marketing plan together and conducted a follow-up study to test their propositions out on the marketplace.

SETTING OF TIME HORIZON

Inevitably there are deadlines which the marketing research activity must fit and these must be stated clearly at the outset of the research. As was said earlier, because of time pressures, management is often seeking quick answers from marketing research. If the researcher is aware of the time constraints then this will become an overriding factor when he/she plans the research design. He or she is likely to put forward a design which is less elegant, and gives rise to less precise information but delivers the results on schedule.

Budget and Facilities

There are essentially two approaches to establishing the resource allocation to a particular marketing research exercise. Management can start with the problem and work out how much it will cost to solve it. Alternatively, they can decide how much the management can afford to spend, at the time, and seek the best answer they can for the time, money and manpower allocated.

In practice the decision-makers prefer the latter approach and the researchers the former. In the end, some kind of compromise develops. The researcher rarely gets all of what he/she judges is required to reach a satisfactory conclusion but if the research proposal is well thought out and persuasively presented some concessions can be obtained. Whichever the approach to resource allocation adopted, it is imperative that the researcher is aware of the financial and other constraints within which he/she must complete the work.

REPORTING PERIOD

The researcher must also know from the outset of the study the points in time when interim reports are required, if any, and the deadline for the final report. The form of interim reports should also be specified at the outset, whether verbal or written, and whether presentations are to be made to a group (nature and size of the group) or an individual. In addition there are several characteristics of a good research brief and these are that it:

- Means the same thing to all concerned,
- Does not ask for irrelevant information,
- Defines the relevant populations to be measured,
- Identifies the correct variables to be measured,
- Specifies the degree of accuracy really needed within the main results,
- Specifies an order of priorities when the sample has to be broken down for the purposes of analyzing data for subgroups, and
- Does not pre-judge the selection of research techniques and procedures.

Research Proposal

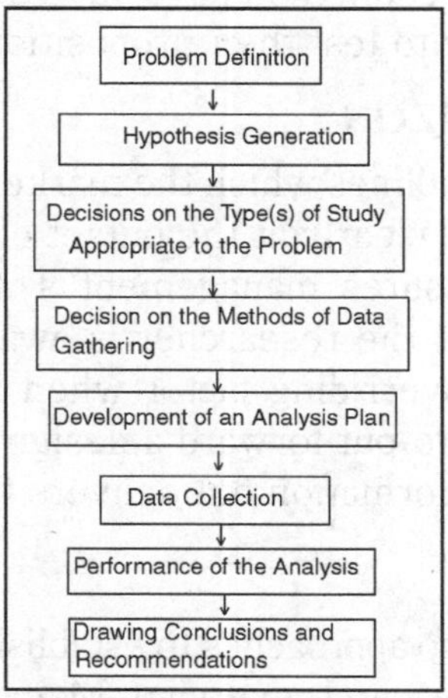

Fig.. The Research Design.

Having received the research brief, the researcher responds with a research proposal. This is a document which develops after having given careful consideration to the contents of the research brief. The research proposal sets out the research design and the procedures to be followed. The eight steps are set out in figure. These are only briefly discussed here since the remainder of this textbook consists of a detailed explanation of each step.

PROBLEM

The point has already been made that the decision-maker should clearly communicate the purpose of the research to the marketing researcher but it is often the case that the objectives are not fully explained to the individual carrying out the study.

Decision-makers seldom work out their objectives fully or, if they have, they are not willing to fully disclose them. In theory, responsibility for ensuring that the research proceeds along clearly defined lines rests with the decision-maker. In many instances the researcher has to take the initiative.

In situations, in which the researcher senses that the decision-maker is either unwilling or unable to fully articulate the objectives then he/she will have to pursue an indirect line of questioning.

One approach is to take the problem statement supplied by the decision-maker and to break this down into key components and/or terms and to explore these with the decision-maker. For example, the decision-maker could be asked what he has in mind when he uses the term market potential.

This is a legitimate question since the researcher is charged with the responsibility to develop a research design which will provide the right kind of information.

Another approach is to focus the discussions with the person commissioning the research on the decisions which would be made given alternative findings which the study might come up with. This process frequently proves of great value to the decision-maker in that it helps him think through the objectives and perhaps select the most important of the objectives.

Whilst seeking to clarify the objectives of the research it is usually worthwhile having discussions with other levels of management who have some understanding of the marketing problem and/or the surrounding issues. Other helpful procedures include brainstorming, reviews of research on related problems and researching secondary sources of information as well as studying competitive products. Kerlinger2 suggests that a well-defined marketing research problem tends to have three common characteristics as shown in figure.

HYPOTHESIS GENERATION

Whilst it is true that the purpose of research is to address some question, nonetheless one does not test research questions directly. For example, there may be interest in answering the question: “Does a person’s level of education have any bearing upon whether or not he/she adopts new products?" Or, "Does a person's age bear any relation to brand loyalty behaviour?". Research questions are too broad to be directly testable. Instead, the question is reduced to one or more hypotheses implied by these questions.

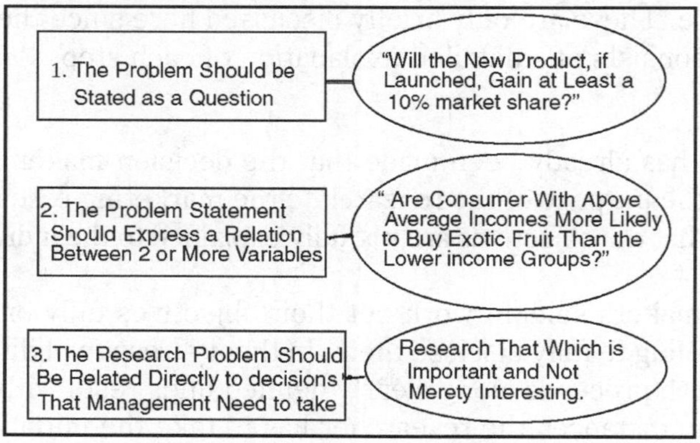

Fig. Characteristics of a Sound a Hypothesis is a Conjectural Statement Regarding the Relation Between two or more Variables.

There are two key characteristics which all hypotheses must have: they must be statements of the relationship between variables and they must carry clear implications for testing the stated relations. These characteristics imply that it is relationships, rather than variables, which are tested; the hypotheses specify how the variables are related and that these are measurable or potentially measurable. Statements lacking any or all of these characteristics are not research hypotheses.

Hypothesis

"There is no relationship between a farmer's educational level and his degree of innovativeness with respect to new farming technologies." Again there is a clear statement of the relationship being investigated but there are question marks over the measurability with respect to at least one of the variables *i.e.* "...a farmer's degree of innovativeness." We may also encounter difficulties in agreeing an appropriate measure of the other variable, *i.e.* "level of education". If these problems can be resolved then we may indeed have a hypothesis.

Hypotheses are central to progress in research. They will direct the researcher's efforts by forcing him/her to concentrate on gathering the facts which will enable the hypotheses to be tested. The point has been made that it is all too easy when conducting research to collect "interesting data" as opposed to "important data". Data and questions which enable researchers to test explicit hypotheses are important. The rest are merely interesting. There is a second advantage of stating hypotheses, namely that implicit notions or explanations for events become explicit and this often leads to modifications of these explanations, even before data is collected.

On occasion a given hypotheses may be too broad to be tested. However, other testable hypotheses may be deduced from it. A problem really cannot be solved unless it is reduced to hypothesis form, because a problem is a question, usually of a broad nature, and is not directly testable.

DECISION OF STUDY

Marketing research can be carried out on one of three levels: exploratory, descriptive or causal.

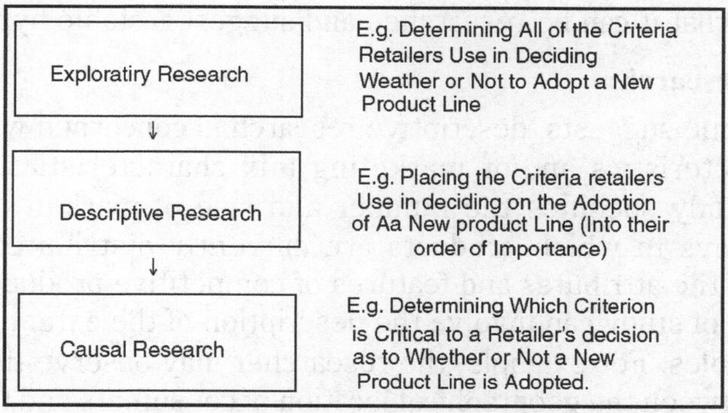

Fig. Three Types of Marketing Research Study.

Exploratory Research

The chief purpose of exploratory research is to reach a better understanding of the research problem. This includes helping to identify the variables which should be measured within the study. When there is little understanding of the topic it is impossible to formulate hypotheses without some exploratory studies. For example, crop residues such a straw are high in lignin (a wood-like substance) and low in nutrients. This makes them a poor animal feed since the lignin acts against digestibility and the low nutrient content means poor food value. However, if treated in a strong alkali, plus a little heat, the lignin breaks down and the nutrient content increases.

A company was established to exploit this technology and did so successfully for 4 seasons. After this period sales began to slow down. Three other manufacturers had entered the market by this time. The company, Animal Feed Systems, did not know whether the whole industry had slowed down or if only their product was suffering. Nor did they know if the problem was temporary in that perhaps the market comprised of "early adopters" had been saturated but it was only a matter of time before other farmers began to buy their systems when they saw how well they worked. It was also possible that if a problem did exist it could lie in any one of a number of areas: animal populations might be declining, distributors may not be promoting the product aggressively, customers may be experiencing difficulties in getting the chemicals, and so on and on.

This is a good example of a situation where insufficient knowledge prevented the development of clear objectives, since the problem could not be articulated with any precision and therefore research of an exploratory nature was required.

Such research can take the form of literature searches, informal personal interviews with distributors and users/non-users of the product and/or focus group interviews with farmers and/or distributors.

Exploratory research is intended to help researchers formulate a problem in such a way that it can be researched and suggest testable hypotheses.

Descriptive Research

As the name suggests, descriptive research is concerned with describing market characteristics and/or marketing mix characteristics. Typically, a descriptive study specifies the number and size of market segments, the alternative ways in which products are currently distributed, listing and comparison of the attributes and features of competitive products, etc.

This type of study can involve the description of the extent of association between variables. For example, the researcher may observe that there is an association between the geographical location of consumers and their tendency to consume red meat.

Note that the researcher is able to describe the relationship rather than explain it. Nonetheless if the relationship between the two is fairly stable this descriptive information may be sufficient for the purposes of prediction. The researcher may, for example, be able to predict how fast the per capita consumption of red meat is likely to rise over a given time period.

The principal difference between exploratory and descriptive research is that, in the case of the latter, specific research questions have been formulated before the research is undertaken. When descriptive research is conducted the researcher must already know a great deal about the research problem, perhaps because of a prior exploratory study, and is in a position to clearly define what he/she wants to measure and how to do it.

Causal Research

Causal research deals with the "why" questions. That is, there are occasions when the researcher will want to know why a change in one variable brings about a change in another.

If he/she can understand the causes of the effects observed then our ability to predict and control such events is increased.

In summary then there are three distinct types of marketing research study: exploratory, descriptive and causal. The purpose of each is summarized in figure. In some cases, a research programme will be of one kind or another, but in other instances these three typologies will represent phases within a single marketing research investigation.

EVALUATING HYPOTHESES

Karl Popper's hypothetico-deductive method (also known as the method of "conjectures and refutations") demands falsifiable hypotheses, framed in such a manner that the scientific community can prove them false (usually by observation). According to this view, a hypothesis cannot be "confirmed", because there is always the possibility that a future experiment will show that it is false.

Hence, failing to falsify a hypothesis does not prove that hypothesis: it remains provisional. However, a hypothesis that has been rigorously tested and not falsified can form a reasonable basis for action, *i.e.*, we can act as if it is true, until such time as it is falsified. Just because we've never observed rain falling upward, doesn't mean that we never will—however improbable, our theory of gravity may be falsified some day.

Popper's view is not the only view on evaluating hypotheses. For example, some forms of empiricism hold that under a well-crafted, well-controlled experiment, a lack of falsification *does* count as verification, since such an experiment ranges over the full scope of possibilities in the problem domain.

Should we ever discover some place where gravity did not function, and rain fell upward, this would not falsify our current theory of gravity (which, on this view, has been verified by innumerable well-formed experiments in the past)—it would rather suggest an expansion of our theory to encompass some new force or previously undiscovered interaction of forces. In other words, our initial theory as it stands is verified but incomplete. This situation illustrates the importance of having well-crafted, well-controlled experiments that range over the full scope of possibilities for applying the theory.

In recent years philosophers of science have tried to integrate the various approaches to evaluating hypothesis, and the scientific method in general, to form a more complete system that integrates the individual concerns of each approach. Notably, Imre Lakatos and Paul Feyerabend have produced novel attempts at such a synthesis. Both men also happen to be former students of Popper.

Most students believe that they are going to be experimenting anytime they are given a laboratory assignment in science. However, more often than not, students are doing something other than experiments. This is not necessarily bad. A good deal of science is observational and descriptive.

For example, the study of bio-diversity usually involves looking at wide variety of specimens and maybe sketching and recording their unique characteristics. However, there are other times when we science teachers are trying to teach students how scientists work and how we can verify things which others may say or believe is so without any proof.

To learn about what is not known or to verify a notion, the so-called "scientific method" might be carried out and an actual experiment may be conducted. It does not matter that your experiment has been done a thousand times before or that your teacher already knows the results. What matters is that you don't know the results and that you can independently find a verifiable answer. In real experiments, real hypotheses should be written before the actual experiment.

In early usage, scholars often referred to a clever idea or to a convenient mathematical approach that simplified cumbersome calculations as a *hypothesis*; when used this way, the word did not necessarily have any specific meaning. Cardinal Bellarmine gave a famous example of the older sense of the word in the warning issued to Galileo in the early 17th century: that he must not treat the motion of the Earth as a reality, but merely as a hypothesis.

In common usage in the 21st century, a *hypothesis* refers to a provisional idea whose merit requires evaluation.

For proper evaluation, the framer of a hypothesis needs to define specifics in operational terms. A hypothesis requires more work by the researcher in order to either confirm or disprove it. In due course, a confirmed hypothesis may become part of a theory or occasionally may grow to become a theory itself.

Normally, scientific hypotheses have the form of a mathematical model. Sometimes, but not always, one can also formulate them as existential statements, stating that some particular instance of the phenomenon under examination has some characteristic and causal explanations, which have the general form of universal statements, stating that every instance of the phenomenon has a particular characteristic.

Any useful hypothesis will enable predictions by reasoning (including deductive reasoning).

It might predict the outcome of an experiment in a laboratory setting or the observation of a phenomenon in nature.

The prediction may also invoke statistics and only talk about probabilities. Karl Popper, following others, has argued that a hypothesis must be falsifiable, and that one cannot regard a proposition or theory as scientific if it does not admit the possibility of being shown false.

Other philosophers of science have rejected the criterion of falsifiability or supplemented it with other criteria, such as verifiability (*e.g.*, verificationism) or coherence (*e.g.*, confirmation holism). The scientific method involves experimentation on the basis of hypotheses in order to answer questions and explore observations.

In framing a hypothesis, the investigator must not currently know the outcome of a test or that it remains reasonably under continuing investigation. Only in such cases does the experiment, test or study potentially increase the probability of showing the truth of a hypothesis. If the researcher already knows the outcome, it counts as a "consequence" — and the researcher should have already considered this while formulating the hypothesis.

If one cannot assess the predictions by observation or by experience, the hypothesis classes as not yet useful, and must wait for others who might come afterwards to make possible the needed observations. For example, a new technology or theory might make the necessary experiments feasible.

In the United States of America, teachers of science in primary schools have often simplified the meaning of the term "hypothesis" by describing a hypothesis as "an educated guess". The failure to emphasize the explanatory or predictive quality of scientific hypotheses omits the concept's most important and characteristic feature: the purpose of hypotheses. People generate hypotheses as early attempts to explain patterns observed in nature or to predict the outcomes of experiments. For example, in science, one could correctly call the following statement a hypothesis: identical twins can have different personalities because the environment influences personality.

In contrast, although one might have informed one's self about the qualifications of various political candidates, making an educated guess about the outcome of an election would qualify as a scientific hypothesis only if the guess includes an underpinning generic explanation.

WHAT IS A REAL HYPOTHESIS?

A hypothesis is a tentative statement that proposes a possible explanation to some phenomenon or event. A useful hypothesis is a testable statement which may include a prediction. A hypotheses should not be confused with a theory. Theories are general explanations based on a large amount of data.

For example, the theory of evolution applies to all living things and is based on wide range of observations. However, there are many things about evolution that are not fully understood such as gaps in the fossil record. Many hypotheses have been proposed and tested.

WHEN ARE HYPOTHESES USED?

The key word is testable. That is, you will perform a test of how two variables might be related. This is when you are doing a real experiment. You are testing variables. Usually, a hypothesis is based on some previous observation such as noticing that in November many trees undergo colour changes in their leaves and the average daily temperatures are dropping. Are these two events connected? How?

Any laboratory procedure you follow without a hypothesis is really not an experiment. It is just an exercise or demonstration of what is already known.

How Are Hypotheses Written?

- Chocolate may cause pimples.
- Salt in soil may affect plant growth.
- Plant growth may be affected by the colour of the light.

- Bacterial growth may be affected by temperature.
- Ultra violet light may cause skin cancer.
- Temperature may cause leaves to change colour.

All of these are examples of hypotheses because they use the tentative word "may.". However, their form is not particularly useful. Using the word may does not suggest how you would go about proving it. If these statements had not been written carefully, they may not have even been hypotheses at all.

For example, if we say "Trees will change colour when it gets cold." we are making a prediction. Or if we write, "Ultraviolet light causes skin cancer." could be a conclusion. One way to prevent making such easy mistakes is to formalize the form of the hypothesis. Formalized Hypotheses example: If skin cancer is related to ultraviolet light, then *people with a high exposure to uv light will have a higher frequency of skin cancer*.

If leaf colour change is related to temperature, then *exposing plants to low temperatures will result in changes in leaf colour.*

Notice that these statements contain the words, if and then. They are necessary in a formalized hypothesis. But not all if-then statements are hypotheses.

For example, "If I play the lottery, then I will get rich." This is a simple prediction. In a formalized hypothesis, a tentative relationship is stated.

For example, if the frequency of winning is related to frequency of buying lottery tickets.

"Then" is followed by a prediction of what will happen if you increase or decrease the frequency of buying lottery tickets. If you always ask yourself that if one thing is related to another, then you should be able to test it.

Formalized hypotheses contain two variables. One is "independent" and the other is "dependent." The independent variable is the one you, the "scientist" control and the dependent variable is the one that you observe and/or measure the results. In the statements above the dependent variable is blue and the independent variable is red.

The ultimate value of a formalized hypothesis is it forces us to think about what results we should look for in an experiment.

SCIENTIFIC HYPOTHESIS

People refer to a trial solution to a problem as a hypothesis — often called an "educated guess" — because it provides a suggested solution based on the evidence. Experimenters may test and reject several hypotheses before solving the problem.

According to Schick and Vaughn, researchers weighing up alternative hypotheses may take into consideration:

- Testability (compare falsifiability as discussed above).
- Simplicity (as in the application of "Occam's razor", discouraging the postulation of excessive numbers of entities).

- Scope - the apparent application of the hypothesis to multiple cases of phenomena.
- Fruitfulness - the prospect that a hypothesis may explain further phenomena in the future.
- Conservatism - the degree of "fit" with existing recognized knowledge-systems.

If that outcome suggests conducting an experiment, it is typically because of rather precise statements (*i.e.*, hypotheses) that reflect relationships believed to exist between two variables among a population of interest to company management.

The hypothesis serves as a guide for the other components and, therefore, represents the first decision by the researcher about these four components. It specifies the relationship of interest between two variables, which are the independent variables and dependent variables among a certain population.

While the relationship pertains to the population, conclusions about the relationship and population are based on a subset or sample of that population known as subjects.

A hypothesis is an unproven proposition. The proposition is usually a statement about reality that is empirically testable. It should be in direct response to the question(s) formulated in regard to the problem definition stage of the marketing research process.

Hypotheses in marketing research commonly regard a specific type of question that focuses on the causal relationship thought to exist between two or more variables.

An example of these relationships is those which may exist between an effect on marketplace behaviour (such as attitude, intent to purchase, or actual sales of a product) that is caused by an aspect of the marketing mix (such as a product's composition, its price, advertising programme, and/or distribution).

When the problem definition stage focuses on causal relationships, an experiment with its ability to test specific hypotheses is commonly the most appropriate choice of research method. This choice is because the research control associated with an experiment allows the greatest certainty when making conclusions that reject or support a hypothesis about marketing dynamics.

For example, the problem definition stage may yield questions about the effect on marketing effectiveness that is caused by different product designs, prices, distribution outlets, or promotion approaches.

There are literally thousands of potential marketing strategy and corresponding marketing research questions that can be addressed through experiments via hypotheses. A research question to be answered may, for example, focus on the impact of package Colour on marketing effectiveness.

Since the researcher can control the Colour of the package, the hypothesis in a respective experiment would focus on: "Does package Colour cause an effect on product sales." Thus, an experiment for Procter and Gamble could test the hypothesis that: "When given a choice, more consumers will purchase Crest toothpaste in a green container than a white container."

INDEPENDENT VARIABLES

An independent variable is a factor which the researcher controls. It is called independent because the researcher can choose what it should be and can manipulate it to study the effect it causes. The independent variable is specified in the hypothesis. For example, since hypotheses in marketing research commonly relate to aspects of the marketing mix, the independent variable is frequently a controllable variable of the marketing mix, involving the product, price, promotion, and/or distribution.

In the above hypothesis about Crest toothpaste, the Colour of the toothpaste container is the independent variable which can be manipulated or controlled by the researcher to be white, green, red, or any other Colour of interest to company management.

MULTIPLE VALUES

The independent variable is commonly comprised of more than one value. An independent variable value is the specific manipulation being studied in regard to the independent variable. In the Crest toothpaste example, the container Colour is the independent variable and the specific Colours tested (white and green) are the independent variable values. Other independent variable values (*i.e.*, other Colours) could be added to this Crest toothpaste experiment.

A strength of experiments is that different values of an independent variable can be tested at the same time. As a consequent, the effects of each tested value can be determined. To do so, different participants in an experiment (*i.e.*, subjects) are exposed to different values of the independent variable known as experimental treatments.

An experimental treatment is the independent variable value to which subjects in an experiment are exposed. Experiments with more than one independent variable value are said to have the respective number of experimental treatments. At times, the term experimental condition is used in place of experimental treatment. Therefore, for practical purposes, experimental condition is synonymous with experimental treatment and, in reality, these two terms are used interchangeably.

An independent variable can have many values. Management may question which of three values or four values is most effective. If the independent variable is package Colour, four values could be green, red, yellow, and blue. The number of values that an independent variable has in an experiment is theoretically unlimited. But the difficulty in conducting an experiment increases as the number of values for an independent variable increases. This difficulty is due to an increased number of participants (subjects) required to conduct the experiment, increased expenses and problems to collect the data, and increased efforts for analyzing and interpreting the results. Consequently, for practical purposes, experiments typically are conducted with a maximum of two to four values for an independent variable.

This figure shows that purchase values of the product under study are tabulated separately for the red packages, green packages, and yellow packages. It also shows that in an experimental design such as this one, the data analysis permits comparison of purchase data for each of the different independent variable values.

QUANTITATIVE AND QUALITATIVE VALUES

An independent variable can have a single value or multiple values that are qualitative as with labels, or quantitative as with numerical amounts. Qualitative values and quantitative values are both involved in experiments conducted in marketing research.

A marketing research experiment involving qualitative values for an independent variable could be advertisement appeal (humorous and serious), retail store (specialty store and mass discounter), or package Colour.

In the Crest toothpaste example, the white and green container Colours represent two qualitative values of the independent variable, and together they represent a categorical variable — an independent variable with a limited number of possible values. Related classification variable is synonymous with categorical variable and, in reality, the two terms are used interchangeably.

Independent variable values in terms of quantitative amounts could be package size (*e.g.*, 2 ounces and 8 ounces), number of salespeople to employ to cover a particular territory (*e.g.*, 10 and 25), or the amount of advertising budget to spend on print media during a certain period of time.

In an experiment for Crest toothpaste, the quantitative values of an independent variable involving advertising budgets could be, for example, \$200,000 and \$500,000. Such a variable represents a continuous variable — an independent variable with an unlimited number of possible values.

PROTOTYPE TABLES

The figure serves a second purpose in that it also illustrates a valuable research tool referred to as a prototype table (or dummy table). Prototype table is a visual aide for understanding what data are to be collected and how these data then will be tabulated, analyzed, and presented.

Since several stages of all research projects can benefit by a prototype table (*e.g.*, data collection, data analysis, and report presentation), constructing prototype tables is an important activity that should be conducted thoroughly early in a marketing research project, such as at the research design stage.

The prototype tables should be complete with the variables and measures that will comprise the table, the table number, and the table's precise title and headings. The only items that should remain to be filled in after the research design stage are the actual statistics for the data that are collected.

The prototype uses asterisks to designate cells. A cell is a location in a table or chart in which data are entered. As the table title and column headings indicate, data regarding intent to purchase the product in a red package would be entered in cell #1, for the green package in cell #2, and for the yellow package in cell #3.

Similarly, actual purchase data for a product might be entered. Consider an experiment conducted over a one-month time period for Crest toothpaste. Measuring the sales in one neighbourhood that stocked three different container Colours in each store showed that consumers purchased 1200 tubes of Crest toothpaste in red containers, 900 in green containers, and 1500 in yellow containers.

These purchase quantities could then be entered in the table accordingly, which would provide a general visual understanding of how the data (sales and package Colour) relate to each other.

Prototype tables are not limited to sales data. Measures differ according to research objectives, and all the many measures from experiments that differ according to research objectives can be placed into prototype tables. Instead of sales of Crest toothpaste, an experiment could measure consumer attitude, product perception, awareness, and/or intent to purchase, and so on.

As this exhibit indicates, after data from all 150 customers are collected, one mean value representing each of the three respective groups of customers would be entered in the respective cells. If the mean attitude (on a 10-point scale) is 8.2 for the red container, 7.3 for the green container, and 9.0 for the yellow container, these data values then would be entered into the table accordingly.

In this latter prototype table, a cell still represents a location in which data values are entered, but now that location is a combination of two or more variables, such as package Colour, product price, and subject gender.

Experimental Group and Control Group

Company management often becomes interested in distributing new versions of a product, and will turn to marketing research with related questions. An experiment permits management, with the assistance of the researchers, to determine the effectiveness or impact of each of these versions in their attempt to identify the best to market.

But before making a change in their existing product, the company should know if the proposed changes are likely to have a positive or negative impact on consumers, and to what extent, compared to their current product version.

Changing from a successful product version may cause detrimental effects if the new version is less well received by the consumer. As a result, marketing researchers should always be interested to determine the effects of potential changes in a marketing mix compared with the status quo. To permit this comparison, two types of subjects exist in most experiments: the experimental group and the control group. An experimental group is the group of subjects who receive an experimental treatment.

A control group is the group of subjects who do not receive an experimental treatment. The purpose of the control group is to serve as a standard against which possible new marketing actions are compared with the actions currently being performed, or not performed. Therefore, during an experiment, subjects in the control group are not exposed to any of the independent variable values and are treated in every way possible the same as in the past, which is to maintain the status quo for these subjects.

The Crest toothpaste example illustrated three experimental treatments that were tested: red container, green container, and yellow container. Crest toothpaste was already successfully marketed for many years in a primarily white container. In this situation, management at Procter and Gamble would definitely question the impact of the new proposed Colours (*e.g.*, perception of the product) relative to Crest toothpaste in the traditional white container.

The respective experiment might involve four different cities or markets. In three of the markets, Crest toothpaste would be sold in one of the three new container Colours (red, green, or yellow), but in the fourth market the product would continue to be sold in its traditional white container. The three markets with the new container Colours (*i.e.*, those subjects receiving an experimental treatment) are the experimental groups. The one market with the traditional white container (*i.e.*, those not receiving an experimental treatment) is the control group.

During the experiment, this fourth group is treated the same as in the past, which is to provide the package in the traditional white Colour. Purchases of the product during the time period of the experiment are recorded for this control group, as well as the experimental groups. All these data are then compared in the data analysis stage to determine which experimental treatment, or more precisely which experimental condition, causes the greatest sales.

MULTIPLE INDEPENDENT VARIABLES

The independent variable in an experiment can have more than one value. An experiment also can have more than one independent variable and, in fact, is comprised commonly of more than one independent variable. A reason for multiple independent variables is that experiments allow researchers the ability to test the effect caused by multiple independent variables, individually and collectively. For example, in addition to an independent variable such as package

Colour, company management also might be interested in such independent variables as product price and advertising message.

Another example could be company management at Procter and Gamble who may have questions about which of three variables or four variables is most effective. These variables could be container Colour, product price, package shape, and version of advertisement.

While the number of independent variables in an experiment is theoretically unlimited, the difficulty of conducting an experiment increases as the number of variables increase. The reason is that more participants (subjects) are required, which translates into increased difficulty in collecting and analyzing the data and interpreting the results. Therefore, for practical purposes, experiments are typically conducted with a maximum of about four independent variables.

MULTIPLE VARIABLES AND MULTIPLE VALUES

An experiment can be conducted to investigate independent variables and accompanying values at the same time. In other words, both multiple independent variables and multiple values for each variable can be investigated in one experiment.

A strength of an experiment is that it can identify differences in effects caused by different independent variables and different independent variable values. An even greater strength is the ability to identify differences between the independent variables while at the same time identifying differences between each value of each variable. Variables to be investigated stem from research questions to be answered. Related, these questions that are delineated in the problem definition stage of the marketing research process are practically limitless. As a consequent, a large number of hypothesized relationships can stem from questions pertaining to, say, only three independent variables such as package Colour, product price, and commercial length.

Company management might question which of three package Colours is best (*e.g.*, red, green, yellow, and so forth), which product price is best, and which commercial length is best (*e.g.*, a 60-second commercial, 30-second commercial, 15-second commercial, and so on).

DEPENDENT VARIABLES

Up to this point, causality has been discussed in terms of cause and effect. The independent variable regards the cause, and it is hypothesized to cause an effect which regards the dependent variable. A dependent variable is a variable that is responsive to (*i.e.*, depends on) an independent variable. This response is the effect that is caused by an independent variable.

The prior prototype tables illustrate the relationship between independent and dependent variables. In these figures, the cells are the locations where the dependent variable values are recorded. A dependent variable value is a numerical measure used for purposes of analysis relative to an independent variable.

Two common dependent variable values in marketing research are sales volume figures and attitude scale numbers assessed before and/or after participants in an experiment are exposed to an experimental treatment.

The dependent variable in marketing research experiments commonly pertains to response aspects of consumer behaviour and market behaviour. The reason is that the dependent variable typically involves the response portion of research questions posed in the problem definition stage. In other words, questions about consequences or effects in response to various marketing variables that arise from the problem definition stage.

Furthermore, when the problem definition stage focuses on aspects of marketplace responses (such as attitudes, purchase decisions, and sales volumes), the logical choice of a research methodology is an experiment.

Dependent variables are then inherent in this methodology. In fact, the importance of dependent variables is heightened, since no other research methodology permits the same level of certainty for making conclusions about hypothesized effects that an independent variable has on a dependent variable.

SUBJECTS

Marketing research experiments hypothesize relationships between independent and dependent variables. Integral to the dependent variable are the entities on which the hypothesized effect occurs and is measured. These entities are referred to as subjects. Formally defined, a subject is a participant in an experiment. Like all marketing research, the subjects in an experiment are a sample or a subset of the population of interest, which is typically a company's target market about which a marketing decision must be made.

Subjects in marketing research experiments are usually people, but subjects also can be non-human entities and inanimate entities. Non-human entities are animals such as dogs or cats that could be subjects in a marketing research experiment when, for example, the research focus is on the response of pets rather than their owners. Inanimate entities used in marketing research are items such as stores and sales territories, in which case they are commonly referred to as test units.

A test unit is the term usually reserved to describe non-human, inanimate participants in a research project. However, researchers on occasion also use the term "test unit" to describe human subjects. In reality, the two terms — subject and test unit — are synonymous and can be used interchangeably when it is grammatically appropriate. Regardless of descriptive label, measures of dependent variables are collected, recorded, and analyzed from both subjects and test units.

TREATMENT GROUPS AND CONTROL GROUPS

Two broad categories of subjects exist in an experiment: (1) those in the treatment group and (2) those in the control group. Treatment group subjects are those subjects exposed to one or more of the experimental treatments. Generally, there is more than one treatment group of subjects, since a different group is assigned to each of the different independent variable values.

Control group subjects are those subjects who are not exposed to any of the experimental treatments and are included in the experiment for comparison purposes. Generally, there is one control group of subjects who serve an essential experimental function of providing baseline measures.

A baseline measure is the results of measures under normal conditions. In an experiment, measures of a dependent variable for a control group of subjects (*i.e.*, those who receive no experimental treatment) are the values against which measures of the dependent variable for a treatment group are compared, to determine the treatment's effect. Because baseline measures by definition refer to normal conditions, as opposed to experimental conditions, these measures are often abbreviated and simply referred to as the norm or norms. Norm is synonymous with baseline measure and, in reality, these two terms are used interchangeably.

ASSIGNMENT PROCEDURES

Subjects selected for an experiment often are divided two times. The first time subjects are divided is to assign them, through either a random or matched procedure, to the control group or experimental group. Assuming there is not more than one experimental condition, the second level division is to then assign subjects to particular experimental treatments (or experimental conditions). At both times, subject assignment is a systematic division of subjects among experimental groups.

A systematic division is used because subjects that comprise the sample of an experiment are not treated the same. It is therefore necessary to determine which subjects receive which treatments. To make this determination, the total sample is divided through a process of either a random assignment or matching assignment, and much less frequently through a repeated measures process.

When the experiment has more than one experimental group, those subjects assigned initially to the experimental group are divided a second time, again through either a random or matched procedure, to one of the experimental treatment groups.

RANDOM ASSIGNMENT

Random assignment divides subjects among experimental treatments based on a random process. Formally defined, random process is a procedure to select objects, in which all objects have an equal chance to be selected. There is no pattern in which individual objects are selected. A common two-step procedure to perform a random process is (1) assign a number to each object, person, entity, and so on, and then (2) go to any location in a random numbers table to determine the order of selecting the objects for the desired purpose.

Through this "control by chance," certain types of subjects are distributed equally among the experimental treatments so that subjects comprising each of the different experimental conditions are the same. Therefore, if different experimental conditions yield different results, the results can be attributed to differences of effects caused by experimental treatments, rather than differences in subjects who comprised the different groups.

Consider an experiment for Bounty paper towels. The independent variable is towel design, experimental treatments are "fancy" and "plain," and the subjects are 100 housewives from Columbus, Ohio. The random assignment procedure first identifies each of these subjects with a number. Then, using a random digit table, individual subjects are assigned to the "fancy" package condition and to the "plain" package condition.

Generally, less-than-perfect information is better than no information. But consider the alternative assignment procedure for Bounty paper towels. In this situation, less-than-perfect information is worse than no information, since it likely will mislead the decision maker.

MATCHING ASSIGNMENT

In some situations, a researcher makes an informed decision not to use random assignment. This alternative to random assignment is matching assignment. Matching assignment divides subjects among experimental groups based on an identifiable factor, believed to produce a consistent effect in response to the independent variable.

Rather than assign a subject to an experimental treatment based entirely on equal probability, subjects are assigned based on a specific factor or characteristic. This factor is a characteristic that can be identified by the experimenter and is one which the experimenter believes has a consistent effect in response to the independent variable.

Consider again the Bounty paper towels experiment. The experimenter may know that women working outside the home strongly prefer "plain" designs rather than "fancy" designs. It is then best to control their assignment, to ensure that an equal number of these subjects are assigned to the "fancy" condition and to the "plain" condition.

This control does not determine which individual subject or group of subjects is assigned to a specific condition. It only determines that an equal number of this type of woman is assigned to the different conditions.

In the Bounty paper towel experiment, subjects would first be identified as belonging to one of two groups: Either working outside the home or not working outside the home. Then within these groups, an equal number are assigned by a random process to either the fancy condition or the plain condition. Random assignment is therefore not omitted from the matching assignment process. It is performed, rather, as a second stage of subject assignment.

Repeated Measures Assignment

A third procedure for subject assignment, which is used on a limited basis, is repeated measures assignment. Repeated measures assignment assigns subjects to more than one treatment condition in the same experiment.

Rather than divide subjects among the different experimental treatments, as with the random and matching assignment procedures, the same subjects are assigned to different experimental treatments. Subjects are assigned to the control group or experimental group through either a random or matched procedure. Once assigned to the experimental group, these subjects are exposed to all, or at least more than one, of the experimental treatments.

There are pros and cons for using a repeated measures assignment procedure. One advantage is that particular treatments are not disproportionate or inappropriately comprised of a certain type of subject. In this way, repeated measures achieve the goals of both random assignment (for proportionate composition of subject types) and matching assignment (for appropriate composition of subject types).

A second advantage is that fewer subjects are necessary to conduct an experiment. To obtain 50 responses to the "fancy" package design and 50 responses to the "plain" package design in the above Bounty paper towel experiment, 100 subjects are needed. But if repeated measures are assessed, 50 responses to each experimental condition can be obtained by utilizing the same 50 subjects for both treatments.

The major disadvantage of repeated measures is that, by definition, subjects are exposed to more than one experimental treatment. This multiple exposure defeats a major strength of experiments. Specifically, research control that permits the research purpose to be disguised is very likely to be lost. Integral to an experiment is the fact that only the independent variable changes between experimental treatments.

With repeated measures assignment, subjects are first shown one experimental condition and then the second. The independent variable (*i.e.*, the research purpose) then becomes apparent to the subjects, and their responses may be affected accordingly. Ultimately, the loss of this research control, which is an experiment's strength, severely reduces the ability to make conclusions about cause-and-effect relationships.

The disadvantage of repeated measures translates into reduced certainty about cause-and-effect relationships. In the Bounty paper towels experiment, all subjects would be exposed to both the fancy design and the plain design. It would be obvious that the research purpose pertains to the paper design, and any related measurements of a subject's attitude would be influenced accordingly. It would be difficult to conclude that differences in the responses of subjects were due to the experimental treatments.

The differences could instead be due to a comparison effect where exposure to the one paper design results in the subjects comparing that design to the second. Also, subjects may give a more favorable response to the design type they feel is the most socially desirable.

For example, subjects may wish to appear environmentally conscious and therefore express a preference for a functional (plain) paper towel. But in the actual marketplace, these same subjects may purchase the less functional (fancy) paper towel.

DEFINITION OF EXPERIMENTS

An experiment involves the creation of a contrived situation in order that the researcher can manipulate one or more variables whilst controlling all of the others and measuring the resultant effects. For instance, when United Fruits were considering replacing their Gros Michel variety of banana with the Valery variety, a simple experiment was first carried out. In selected retail outlets, the two varieties were switched on different days of the week and sales data examined to determine what effect the variety had on sales volumes. That is, the variety was being manipulated whilst all other variables were held constant.

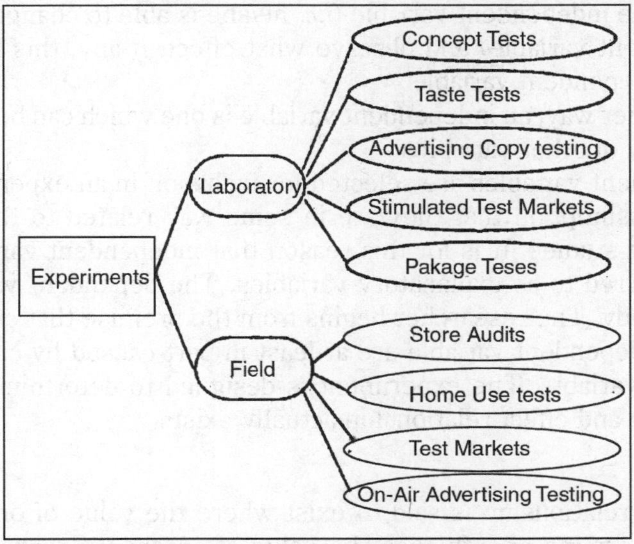

Fig. Types of Experiment Used in Marketing Research.

Experiments can be conducted either in the field or in a laboratory setting. When operating within a laboratory environment, the researcher has direct control over most, if not all, of the variables that could impact upon the outcome of the experiment. For example, an agricultural research station may wish to compare the acceptability of a new variety of maize.

Since the taste characteristics are likely to have a major influence on the level of acceptance, a blind taste panels might be set up where volunteers are given small portions of maize porridge in unmarked bowls.

The participants would perhaps be given two porridge samples and the researcher would observe whether they were able to distinguish between the maize varieties and which they preferred. In addition to taste testing, laboratory experiments are widely used by marketing researchers in concept testing, package testing, advertising research and test marketing.

When experiments are conducted within a natural setting then they are termed field experiments. The variety test carried out by United Fruits on their Gros Michel and Valery bananas is an example of a field experiment. The researcher obviously has less control over variables likely to have an effect upon the experimental variable but will strive to exert whatever control is possible.

BASIC CONCEPTS IN EXPERIMENTATION

Dependency

Experiments allow marketing researchers to study the effects of an independent variable on a dependent variable. The researcher is able to manipulate the independent variable (*i.e.* he/she is able to change the value of the independent variable) and observe what effect, if any, this has upon the value of the dependent variable.

Put another way, an independent variable is one which can be manipulated independently of other variables.

Independent variables are selected for inclusion in an experiment on the basis of an assumption that they are in some way related to the dependent variable being studied. It is for this reason that independent variables are on occasion referred to as explanatory variables. The dependent variable is the one under study. The researcher begins from the premise that changes in the value of the dependent variable are at least in part caused by changes in the independent variable. The experiment is designed to determine whether or not this cause and effect relationship actually exists.

Causality

A causal relationship is said to exist where the value of one variable is known to determine or influence the value of another. Green et al. draw a distinction between two types of causation: deterministic and probabilistic.

Where the independent variable (X) wholly explains changes in the value of the dependent variable (Y) and the researcher is able to establish the functional relationship between the two variables then this can be expressed as follows:

$$y = f(x)$$

In this case, it is said that X is both a necessary and a sufficient condition for Y to occur. The value of Y is determined by X, and X alone. Thus it can be said, in these circumstances, that X is a deterministic cause of Y. An illustrative example would be where the demand for agricultural commodities, say sugar, is dependent upon the world price. Further suppose that the functional relationship between sugar demand and world prices is known, then the formula becomes:

Changes in demand for sugar (grade No. 6) = f (World Price) Whilst this example serves to illustrate the point it is rare to find such relationships when studying marketing problems.

In most instances, the value of the dependent variable will be a function of several variables. For instance, only in exceptional cases would the demand for a product, even a commodity, depend solely upon price movements. Factors such as the reputation of the supplier, terms of sale, promotional activities, packaging etc., are likely to have an impact on demand as well.

A more common causal model is one where the value of the dependent variable is a function of several independent variables.

Marketing problems are more often multivariate than univariate and so the relationship between dependent and independent variables is more often probabilistic than deterministic. A probabilistic relationship could be expressed as:

$$y = f(x_1, x_2...x_n).$$

What is depicted here is a situation where the dependent variable (y) is a function of several variables ($x_1, x_2...x_n$). If marketing research can establish the form of the relationship (f) between the independent variables and also between the independent and dependent variables then the value of y can be predicted.

In this instance x_1, for example, is a necessary but not sufficient condition for y to occur. The same is true of each of the other independent variables. Rather, each individual independent variable is said to be a probabilistic cause of the value of y.

INFERRING CAUSAL RELATIONSHIPS

The evidence for drawing inferences about causal relationships can take three forms: associative variation, consistent ordering of events and the absence of alternative causes.

Associative variation:

Causality cannot be established unless there is associative, or concomitant, variation. That is, the data must show that a change in one variable is almost always accompanied by a change in the other.

Consistent order of events: If variable A causes variable B, then variable A must occur before or simultaneously with B, and not after it. It can happen that two events cause and effect one another. For example, the uptake of marketing innovations among farmers may show a high correlation with the number of visits by extension personnel. Closer study could reveal that extension personnel visit farmers who are immediately responsive to them more frequently than they do other farmers.

Absence of other Causes

Before inferring causation researchers should check for equally plausible alternative explanations for the phenomenon under study. A vegetable trader might, for example, assume that the increase in her sales is due to improved grading procedures which she has introduced. However, there may be several other factors that act individually, or in combination, to bring about the sales increase. The trader might find her competitors are experiencing similar sales increases and that this is actually due to upward shifts in disposable incomes.

It should be noted that none of these forms of evidence, nor all three in combination, can unequivocally prove that a relationship exists. Rather, they help put the notion that a relationship exists beyond reasonable doubt. If all evidence points towards the same conclusion then the conclusion that a relationship exists is all the more compelling.

IMPEDIMENTS TO RESULTS

The validity of experimental results, *i.e.* the extent to which results reflect the truth, is obviously a matter of importance. There are two distinct forms of validity which marketing researchers are concerned about when using experimentation: internal and external validity.

Internal validity: The question being asked is whether the experimental treatment is actually responsible for changes in the value of the dependent variable or if confounding factors have been in operation. Since laboratory experiments afford greater opportunities for controlling extraneous or confounding variables than do field experiments, internal validity is a bigger problem in the case of the latter.

External validity: External validity has to do with the extent to which experimental findings can be generalised to the population from which the participants in the experiment were drawn. In other words, the issue is the degree to which the sample represents the population. Given the naturalistic setting of field experiments, this category generally provides greater external validity than do those experiments conducted within a laboratory environment.

In some cases the marketing researcher seeks to exclude extraneous factors that can confound the results of an experiment. However, this is not always possible since it is difficult to determine when certain types of extraneous variable is in operation and even more difficult to measure them. In these circumstances, the researcher will seek to control confounding variables in a different way. Examples of confounding are:

Table. Internal Validity.

History	Events taking place at the same time as the experiment is underway
Pre-testing	Errors arising from the process of taking "before" and "after" measures from the same sample as that providing "after" measures
Maturation	Biological and/or psychological changes in participants
Instrumentation	Changes in the calibration of measurement instruments, questionnaires, interviewers or interviewing technique
Sampling bias	Assignment of participants to experimental groups in a way likely to prejudice outcomes
Mortality	Differential loss of participants from experimental groups

Table. External validity.

Interactive effects of testing	Pre-exposure measurements going rise to heightened awareness
Interactive effects of sampling bias	Non-random assignment of participants to experimental groups leading to differing responses to the experimental treatment
Contrived situations	Experimental setting elicits responses that differ from those which would be obtained in the real world.

INTERNAL VALIDITY

History

The term 'history' has been used to describe events that happen whilst the experiment is underway and serve to distort experimental results. A common occurence is when a commercial organisation is testing a new product within a small geographical area, prior to launching the product nationwide, and competitors intentionally set out to distort test results by giving additional promotional support to their own competing product and/or by cutting the price of their product.

Pretest Effect

It is sometimes considered necessary to take some preliminary measures before the main experiment is carried out. For instance, a company wishing to promote monogerm sugar beet seed in Pakistan wanted to first establish how much farmers already knew about the different types of seed available. A particular district was chosen as a test area and a pretest was undertaken where a sample of farmers from that area were asked to list the types of seed of which they were aware. The farmers were also asked to list the brands of sugar beet seed with which they were familiar. This constituted the 'before' measure. A little later a promotional campaign was launched within the test area and after a period of time the sample of farmers were again visited and asked to identify the brands of seed with which they were familiar. It is likely that any increase in awareness of the company's brand was due, in part at least, to the heightened awareness of issues relating to seeds caused by the pretest activity.

Maturation

Maturation refers to biological and/or psychological changes to respondents that occur in the period between the 'before' and 'after' measurements and consequently affect the information which they provide.

Experiments requiring the cooperation of respondents over a substantial period of time are most likely to suffer from maturation effects. Consumer and farmer panels are examples of experimental instruments that demand longer term participation by panel members.

Suppose that a farmer panel were established to measure the level of adoption of new marketing practices or technologies promoted by agricultural extension officers. As the years pass the marketing extension officer has noted that farmers on the panel appear to be adopting fewer of the innovations being proposed by the extension service.

However, the lower rates of adoption may not be explained by either the marketing extension service becoming less effective in communicating the benefits of innovative marketing practices and technologies nor by current innovations being somehow less appropriate or offering more marginal benefits.

Rather, the explanation may be that the panel itself is aging and as farmers get older they may become more resistant to change. Certainly as people get older their needs and attitudes are subject to change. In these circumstances the data drawn from the panel is a function of the maturation of the panel rather than the experimental variables (*i.e.* the efforts of the marketing extension officers and the characteristics of the marketing innovations).

Whilst it is not always possible to adjust the experimental design so as to eliminate each of these potential threats to the validity of results, it is always possible to measure their impact upon results. The chief device for doing so is to include a 'control group'.

Instrumentation

From time to time, measurement instruments have to be recalibrated or their readings become suspect. Although marketing research does make use of a wide range of mechanical, electrical and electronic instruments in experiments that clearly require periodic readjustment, (*e.g.* tachistoscopes, pupilometers, audiometer) there are other, more commonly used, marketing research test instruments that also need to be checked for consistency, such as, questionnaires, interviewers, interviewing procedures.

Questionnaires may contain standardised questions with the challenge to consistency coming from the interpretation of the meaning of the question. Consider the apparently straight-forward question, "How big is your farm?" There are several equally valid responses to this question that could combine to give a totally misleading set of data. The variation is due to farmers' interpretation of what the researcher really wants to know.

Some farmers will include only the land area that they had under crop in the year of the survey whilst others will include both productive and non-productive land. In other instances, farmers may understand the question to mean the area of land they actually own. Some farmers may believe it is the farmland that they own and/or rent.

Another aspect is that of consistency in the conduct of interviews. There can be variation in the data collected during an experiment if either different interviewers are used to collect data after the experiment from those who conducted interviews before the experiment; or interviewers change the way questions are put to participants as they become more familiar with the content of the questionnaire.

Mortality

Over time there is a danger that some participants will drop out of an experiment. This can happen when people literally die or decide withdraw from an experimental group for one reason or another.

This obviously changes the composition of the experimental group. Where the effects of a marketing variable are being studied by comparing data drawn either from two groups that have been matched to ensure that their composition is identical or the same group at different points in time then mortality can confound the results.

Sampling Bias

Sampling bias occurs when the method of assigning participants to experimental groups results in groups whose behaviour cannot be compared to one another because they differ in some important respect(s).

Consider the task of evaluating the implementation of new weighing and grading practices within a municipal grain market. It could be that it is easier for larger grain traders to adopt the new practices since they are better able to afford the grading and weighing equipment required.

If during a field experiment conducted to study the rate of adoption two groups are established with a view to comparing the rate of adoption within them and one of those groups is predominantly comprised of larger (or smaller) traders then this is likely to distort the results.

EXTERNAL VALIDITY

Interactive Effects of Testing

The design of the experiment itself may give rise to measurement variations between the "before" and "after" phases of the research.

Consider a test of consumer acceptance involving two exotic rice varieties being evaluated as possible replacements for a popular indigenous variety which is suffering from a disease and is therefore in short supply.

The experimental design involves leaving a trial pack of rice A with a sample of households and returning a few weeks later to interview members of the household about rice A and to deliver a second trial pack containing rice B. A third visit is subsequently made during which household members are asked questions about rice B.

Respondents' assessment of rice B is not made under the same conditions as their assessment of rice A. When trying rice A the respondents are likely to have made comparisons, perhaps only subconsciously, with existing rice varieties that they already use.

However, when evaluating rice B the respondents will also be making comparisons with rice A. This problem can be overcome, to some extent, by splitting the sample so that half are given the trial varieties in the order rice A then rice B; the remaining half are given the two varieties in the reverse order of rice B then rice A.

A more difficult problem to overcome is that whatever the sequence of presentation, by the time household members are asked about the second trial variety, they have become more 'experienced' interviewees and respond differently simply because they feel they better understand what the interviewer wants and how to answer the questions.

By the same measure, the interviewer becomes more experienced the second time around, having become more familiar with the product, the interviewing process, and the questionnaire (or interview schedule), and may pose the questions in a different way.

As a result, the interviewer may elicit different information on the third call from that which was obtained on the second visit.

Interactive Effects of Sampling Bias

It can happen that participants are assigned to an experimental group without due concern for possible bias and this then interacts with the experimental treatment producing a spurious outcome.

Such an interactive sampling bias would result from unknowingly assigning heavy users of a particular product category to one experimental group and using favourable responses to a new formulation within the category as the basis for projecting national demand.

Contrived Situations

Any laboratory experiment is, by definition, unlike the real world. Typically, the researcher manipulates the situation so that only those variables in which he/she is immediately interested in studying are allowed to operate as they would in the real world.

On occasion this leads to experimental results which are not replicated in the real world. An outstanding example of this set of circumstances is that of Coca Cola's infamous blind taste panels.

Coca Cola was concerned at the creeping increases in market share of Coke's main competitor Pepsi. Coca Cola decided to conduct sensory analysis tests where participants were asked to score two colas on taste preference.

The participants were given the colas in unmarked cups (*i.e.* a 'blind' tasting) before being asked which they preferred. On balance, the preference was of Pepsi's slightly sweeter cola. Coca Cola reacted in a way seldom seen anywhere in the world.

The brand leader was removed from the market and a new, slightly sweeter formulation was launched under the Coca Cola brand name.

It was to prove a costly mistake. Coca Cola were inundated by calls from consumers who were irate over the company's tampering with a product that has almost become a national institution. Most Americans have grown up with Coca Cola and could not accept that it could be changed. The company was forced to reintroduce the original formulation under the title of Coke Classic.

Coca Cola's taste panels were conducted in an artificial environment in which such variables as the brand name, the packaging and all the associations which go along with these were not allowed to operate. The research focused only on the taste characteristics of the product and a particular result was obtained.

However, in the real world people consume Coca Cola for many reasons, many of them having little to do with the taste.

EXPERIMENTAL DESIGNS

The process of experimentation is one of subjecting participants (*e.g.* target consumers, farmers, distributors etc.) to an independent variable such as an advertisement, a packaging design or a new product, and measuring the effect on a dependent variable (*e.g.* level of recall, sales or attitude scores).

"After-only" Designs

As the name suggests, with after-only experimental designs measures of the independent variable are only taken after the experimental subjects have been exposed to the independent variable.

This is a common approach in advertising research where a sample of target customers are interviewed following exposure to an advertisement and their recall of the product, brand, or sales features is measured. The advertisement could be one appearing on national television and/or radio or may appear in magazines, newspapers or some other publication. The amount of information recalled by the sample is taken as an indication of the effectiveness of the advertisement.

Fig. An Example of an After-only Design.

The chief problem with after-only designs is that they do not afford any control over extraneous factors that could have influenced the post-exposure measurements. For example, marketing extension personnel might have completed a trial campaign to persuade small-scale poultry producers, in a localised area, to make use of better quality feeds in order to improve the marketability and price of the end product. The decision to extend the campaign to other districts will depend on the results of this trial.

After-only measures are taken, following the campaign, by checking poultry feed sales with merchants operating within the area. Suppose a rise in sales of good quality poultry feed mixes occurs four weeks after the campaign ends. It would be dangerous to assume that this sales increase is wholly due to the work of the marketing extension officers. A large part of the increase may be due to other factors such as promotional activity on the part of feed manufacturers and merchants who took advantage of the campaign, of which they were forewarned, and timed their marketing programme to coincide with the extension campaign.

If the extension service erroneously drew the conclusion that the sales increase was entirely due to their own promotional activity, then they might be misled into repeating the same campaign in other areas where there would not necessarily be the same response from feed manufacturers and merchants.

Before-afterDesigns

A before-after design involves the researcher in measuring the dependent variable both before and after the participants have been exposed to the independent variables.

The before-after design is an improvement upon the after-only design, in that the effect of the independent variable, if any, is established by observing differences between the value of the dependent variable before and after the experiment. Nonetheless, before-after designs still have a number of weaknesses.

Consider the case of the vegetable packer who is thinking about sending his/her produce to the wholesale market in more expensive, but more protective, plastic crates, instead of cardboard boxes. The packer is considering doing so in response to complaints from commissioning agents that the present packaging affords little protection to produce from handling damage. The packer wants to be sure that the economics of switching to plastic crates makes sense. Therefore, the packer introduces the plastic crates for a trial period. Before introducing these crates, the packer records the prices received for his/her top grade produce. Unless prices increase by more than the additional cost of plastic crates then there is no economic advantage to using the more expensive packaging.

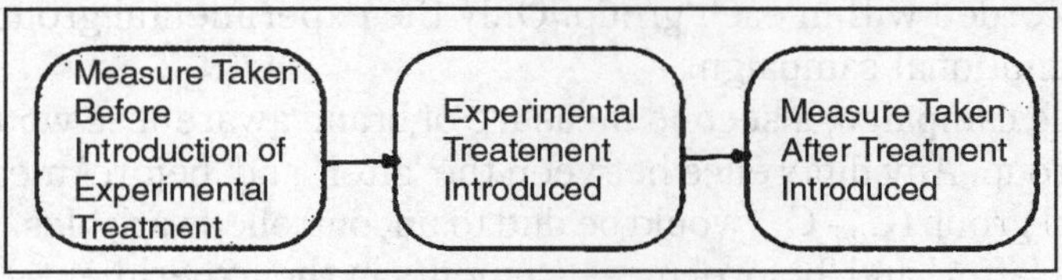

Fig. Before-After Designs.

Suppose, for instance, that the packer was receiving $15 per crate, when these were of the cardboard type, but that the price after the introduction of plastic crates had risen to $17 per crate.

The $2 difference would be attributed to better quality produce reaching the market as a result of the protection afforded by the plastic crates. However, there are several equally plausible explanations for the upward drift in produce prices including a shortfall in supply, a fall in the quality of produce supplied by competitors who operate in areas suffering adverse weather conditions, random fluctuation in prices, etc.

Before-After With Control Group Design

This design involves establishing two samples or groups of respondents: an experimental group that would be exposed to the marketing variable and a control group which would not be subjected to the marketing variable under study. The two groups would be matched.

That is, the two samples would be identical in all important respects. The idea is that any confounding factors would impact equally on both groups and therefore any differences in the data drawn from the two groups can be attributed to the experimental variable.

Study figure which depicts how an experiment involving the measurement of the impact of a sugar beet seed promotional campaign on brand awareness might be configured with a control group.

Before-After with Control Group Design

First, the two groups would be matched: attributes such as age distribution of group members, spread of sizes of farms operated, types of farms operated, ratio of dependence on hand tools, animal drawn tools and tractor mounted equipment, etc. would be matched within each group so that the groups are interchangeable for the purposes of the test.

	Experimental Group	Control Group
Before measure:% recalling Brand X sugarbeet seed	25.5%	25.5%
Exposed to promotional campaign	Yes	No
'After' measure:% recalling Brand X sugarbeet seed	34.5%	24,5%

As figure conveys, the initial level of awareness of the sugar beet brand would be recorded within each group. Only the experimental group would see the test promotional campaign.

After the campaign, a second measure of brand awareness would be taken from each group. Any difference between the 'after' and 'before' measurements of the control group (C_2 - C_1) would be due to uncontrolled variables. Differences between the 'after' and 'before' measurements in the experimental group (E_2 - E_1) would be the result of the experimental variable plus the same uncontrolled variables affecting the control group.

Isolating the effect of the experimental variable is simply a matter of subtracting the difference in the two measurements of the control group from the difference in the two measures taken from the experimental group. To illustrate the computation consider the following hypothetical figures.

Awareness of the brand within the experimental group has increased by 9 per cent. At the same time, the awareness level, within the control group, appears to have fallen by 1 per cent.

This could be due to random fluctuations or a real lowering of awareness due to some respondents forgetting the brand in the absence of any supporting advertisements/promotions. Thus the effects of the test campaign would seem to have been:

$$\text{Effect of experimental variable} = (34.5 - 25.5) - (24.5 - 25.5)$$
$$= (9\%) - (-1\%) = 10\%$$

If a "before and after with control group" experiment is properly designed and executed then the effects of maturation, pretesting and measurement variability should be the same for the experimental group as for the control group. In this case. these factors appear to have had a negative effect on awareness of one per cent. Had it not been for the experimental variable, the experimental group would have shown a similar fall in awareness over the period of the test. Instead of recording a fall in the level of awareness of the sugar beet brand, the experimental group actually showed a nine per cent increase in brand awareness. However, the design is not guaranteed to be unflawed. The accurate matching of the two groups is a difficult, some would say impossible, task. Moreover, over time the rate and extent of mortality, or drop out, is likely to vary between the groups and create additional problems in maintaining a close match between groups.

EXPERIMENTAL DESIGN

Again, this design involves establishing two matched samples or groups of respondents. There is no measurement taken from either group before the experimental variable is introduced and the control group is not subsequently subjected to the experimental variable. Afterwards measures are taken from both groups and the effect of the experimental variable is established by deducting the control group measure from the experimental group measure. An illustrative example will help clarify the procedures followed.

A Sri Lankan food technology research institute was trying to convince small-scale food processors to adopt solar dryers to produce dried plantain and other dehydrated vegetables. Much of the initial resistance to the adoption of this technology was due to the belief that the taste characteristics of this snack food would be altered from those of traditional sun-dried plantain. The research institute was able to convince the food manufacturers that there would be no perceptible changes in the taste characteristics by carrying out an "after-only with control group" experiment. Sensory analysis experiments conclusively showed that almost none of the participants was able to discriminate between plantain dehydrated by means of the solar powered dryer and that which was sun-dried.

Many product tests are of the "after-only with control group" type. This design escapes the problems of pretesting, history and maturation. However, this form of "after-only design" does not facilitate an analysis of the process of change, whereas a comparable "before-after design" would. The attitudes, opinions and/or behaviour of individual participants can be recorded both before and afterwards and changes noted. For instance, the effect of the experimental variable on those participants who held unfavourable attitudes can be compared with those they held in the "before" measurement. Changes in those that held favourable attitudes in the "before" measurement can also be assessed after exposure to the experimental variable.

EX POST FACTO DESIGN

The ex post facto design is a variation of the "after-only with control group" experimental design. The chief difference is that both the experimental and control groups are selected after the experimental variable is introduced rather than before. This approach eliminates the possibility that participants will be influenced by an awareness that they are being tested.

Following market liberalisation in Zimbabwe a number of maize meal producers, using hammer mill technology, came into the industry to compete against millers using roller mill technology. The hammer milled product was much coarser than the highly refined roller milled maize meal to which most urban consumers had grown accustomed. The hammer milled product, however, had superior nutritional benefits since meal produced in this way retained a much larger amount of the germ, bran and endosperm.

One production miller sought to communicate the nutritional advantages of hammer milled meal through point-of-sale material in stores and provisions merchants. A sample of consumers who claimed to have seen the point-of-sale material was subsequently assigned to an experimental group and a matching selection of consumers who denied having seen the point-of-sale material comprised the control group. It was hypothesised that those who had seen the point-of-sale material would suggest that hammer milled maize meal had superior nutritional properties to that of roller meal to a far greater extent than would those who had not seen the point-of-sale aids.

The results supported the hypothesis in as much as 68 per cent of those recalling having seen the point-of-sale promotional aids reported hammer milled meal as nutritionally superior whilst only 43 per cent of those unaware of the point-of-sale aids said that hammer mill was more nutritious than roller meal. However, some care has to be taken in making the conclusion that the point-of-sale campaign was an unqualified success.

It is to be remembered that participants were assigned to the two groups on the basis of self-selection. Those reporting having seen the promotional material were probably those on whom the campaign had made most impression. It is quite likely that some of those in the control group also saw the material but do not recall having done so.

Where exposure to the experimental variable can be determined objectively, on an ex post facto basis, the bias introduced by self-selection can be eliminated and the design, in essence, becomes identical to the "after-only with control group" design. In these circumstances, the ex post facto design is an improvement upon the "after-only with control group" design since the experimental variable would have its impact in a natural situation. Suppose, for example, that government has been using radio to communicate thy benefits of giving vitamin supplements to children under two years of age and that these are available in tablet form, free-of-charge, in local clinics. Ownership, and access, to a radio can be established objectively.

Experimentation offers the possibility of establishing a caue and effective relationship between variables and this maes it an attractive methodology to marketing researchers. An experiment is a contrived situation that allows a researcher to manipulate one or more variables whilst controlling all of the others and measuring the resultant effects on some independent variable.

Experiments are of two types: those conducted in a laboratory setting and those which are executed in natural settings; these are referred to as field experiments. Laboratory experiments give the researcher direct control over most, if not all, of the variables that could affect the outcome of the experiment. The evidence for drawing inferences about causal relationships takes three forms: associative variation, consistent ordering of events and the absence of alternative causes.

There are a number of potential impediments to obtaining valid results from experiments. These may be categorised according to whether a given confounding factor has internal validity, external validity, or both. Internal validity is called into question when there is doubt that the experimental treatment is actually responsible for changes in the value of the dependent variable. External validity becomes an issue when there is uncertainty as to whether experimental findings can be generalised to a defined population. The impediments to internal validity are history, pre-testing, maturation, instrumentation, sampling bias and mortality. Impediments to external validity are: the interactive effects of testing, the interactive effects of sampling bias and errors arising from making use of contrived situations.

The main forms of experimental design differ according to whether or not a measure is taken both before and after the introduction of the experimental variable or treatment, and whether or not a control group is used alongside the experimental group. The designs are: after-only, before-after, before-after with control group, after-only with control group and ex post factodesigns.

DECISION ON DATA COLLECTION METHOD

The next set of decisions concerns the method(s) of data gathering to be employed. The main methods of data collection are secondary data searches, observation, the survey, experimentation and consumer panels. Each of these topics is dealt with later on, so they are simply noted here.

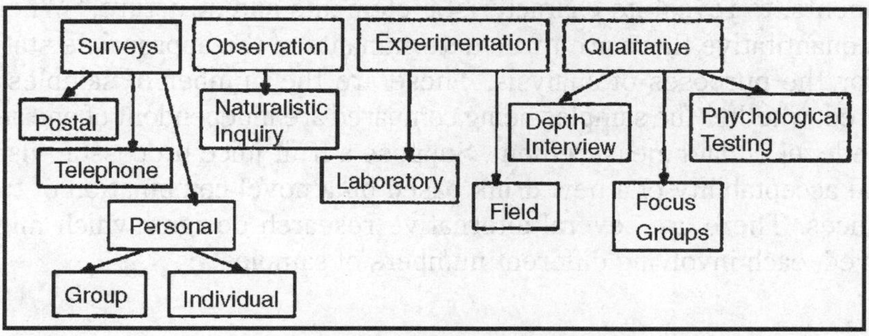

Fig. Data Collection Methods.

Those new to marketing research often intuitively believe that decisions about the techniques of analysis to be used can be left until after the data has been collected. Such an approach is ill-advised.

Before interviews are conducted the following checklist should be applied:

- Is it known how each and every question is to be analyzed? (*e.g.* which univariate or bivariate descriptive statistics, tests of association, parametric or non-parametric hypotheses tests, or multivariate methods are to be used?)

- Does the researcher have a sufficiently sound grasp of these techniques to apply them with confidence and to explain them to the decision-maker who commissioned the study?
- Does the researcher have the means to perform these calculations? (*e.g.* access to a computer which has an analysis programme which he/she is familiar with? Or, if the calculations have to be performed manually, is there sufficient time to complete them and then to check them?)
- If a computer programme is to be used at the data analysis stage, have the questions been properly coded?
- Have the questions been scaled correctly for the chosen statistical technique? (*e.g.* a t-test cannot be used on data which is only ranked)

There is little point in spending time and money on collecting data which subsequently is not or cannot be analysed. Therefore consideration has to be given to issues such as these before the fieldwork is undertaken.

DATA COLLECTION

At this stage the researcher is ready to go into the field and collect data. The various issues relating to data collection constitute the main body of the text and therefore, are not dwelt upon here.

Analysis of Data

The word 'analysis' has two component parts, the prefix 'ana' meaning 'above' and the Greek root 'lysis' meaning 'to break up or dissolve'. Thus data analysis can be described as: "A process of resolving data into its constituent components, to reveal its characteristic elements and structure." Where the data is quantitative there are three determinants of the appropriate statistical tools for the purposes of analysis. These are the number of samples to be compared, whether the samples being compared are independent of one another and the level of data measurement. Suppose a fruit juice processor wishes to test the acceptability of a new drink based on a novel combination of tropical fruit juices. There are several alternative research designs which might be employed, each involving different numbers of samples.

Test A

Comparing sales in a test market and the market share of the product it is targeted to replace. Number of samples = 1

Test B

Comparing the responses of a sample of regular drinkers of fruit juices to those of a sample of non-fruit juice drinkers to a trial formulation. Number of samples = 2.

Test C

Comparing the responses of samples of heavy, moderate and infrequent fruit juice drinkers to a trial formulation. Number of samples = 3

The next consideration is whether the samples being compared are dependent (*i.e.* related) or independent of one another (*i.e.* unrelated). Samples are said to be dependent, or related, when the measurement taken from one sample in no way affects the measurement taken from another sample. Take for example the outline of test B above.

The measurement of the responses of fruit juice drinkers to the trial formulation in no way affects or influences the responses of the sample of non-fruit juice drinkers. Therefore, the samples are independent of one another. Suppose however a sample were given two formulations of fruit juice to taste. That is, the same individuals are asked first to taste formulation X and then to taste formulation Y.

The researcher would have two sets of sample results, *i.e.* responses to product X and responses to product Y. In this case, the samples would be considered dependent or related to one another. This is because the individual will make a comparison of the two products and his/her response to one formulation is likely to affect his/her reaction or evaluation of the other product.

The third factor to be considered is the levels of measurement of the data being used. Data can be nominal, ordinal, interval or ratio scaled. Table summarises the mathematical properties of each of these levels of measurement.

Once the marketing researcher knows how many samples are to be compared, whether these samples are related or unrelated to one another and the level of measurement then the selection of the appropriate statistical test is easily made. To illustrate the importance of understanding these connections consider the following simple, but common, question in marketing research. In many instances the age of respondents will be of interest.

KEY TERMS

- Analysis plan,
- Causal research,
- Continuous research,
- Descriptive research,
- Exploratory research,
- Hypotheses,
- Interval scales,
- Nominal scales,
- Ordinal Scales,
- Primary research,
- Ratio scales,

- Research brief,
- Research design,
- Research proposal,
- Secondary research.

CAPABILITIES AND LIMITATIONS

If your company is like many, there's some natural tension between marketing and product. One often controversial topic is the appropriate role in product creation of market research tools and techniques such as focus groups, customer surveys, site analytics, site visits, usability testing/field testing and competitive analysis.

Unfortunately I think this is an area of significant confusion, fueled in part by the various camps – those from a marketing background that may see the benefits of these tools, and those from product that see the limitations. The results is that some product teams miss out because they don't take advantage of the information these tools and techniques can offer, and other teams go astray because they depend on these techniques to answer questions the tools are incapable of.

LIMITATIONS AND CONSTRAINTS

Accurate, up-to-date information obtained by marketing research can be of enormous value to an organisation in gaining and/or maintaining its competitive edge. However, there are a number of reasons why, in reality, these potential benefits may not be realized:

Budgetary Constraints

Gathering and processing data can be very expensive. Many organizations may lack the expertise to conduct extensive surveys to gather primary data, whatever the potential benefits, and also lack the funds to pay specialist market research agencies to gather such data for them. In these cases, organizations may be forced to rely on data that is less than 'perfect' but that can be accessed more cheaply, *e.g.*, from secondary sources

Time Constraints

Organizations are often forced to balance the need to build up as detailed a picture as possible regarding customer needs etc. against the desire to make decisions as quickly as possible, in order to maintain or improve their position in the market

Reliability Of The Data

The value of any research findings depend critically on the accuracy of the data collected. Data quality can be compromised via a number of potential routes, *e.g.*, leading questions, unrepresentative samples, biased interviewers etc. Efforts to ensure that data is accurate, samples are representative and interviewers are objective will all add to the costs of the research but such costs are necessary if poor decisions and expensive mistakes are to be avoided.

Legal and Ethical Constraints

The Data Protection Act is a good example of a law that has a number of implications for market researchers collecting and holding personal data. For instance, researchers must ensure that the data they obtain is kept secure, is only used for lawful purposes and is only kept for as long as it is necessary. It must be made clear as to why data is being collected and the consent of participants must be obtained.

In addition to this, there are a number of guidelines, laid down by such organisations as the Market Research Society, that, although not legally binding, encourage organisations to behave ethically when dealing with members of the public.

DIFFERENT RESEARCH METHODS

TRUE EXPERIMENTAL DESIGN

True experimental design is regarded as the most accurate form of experimental research, in that it tries to prove or disprove a hypothesis mathematically, with statistical analysis.

For some of the physical sciences, such as physics, chemistry and geology, they are standard and commonly used. For social sciences, psychology and biology, they can be a little more difficult to set up.

For an experiment to be classed as a true experimental design, it must fit all of the following criteria.

- The sample groups must be assigned randomly.
- There must be a viable control group.
- Only one variable can be manipulated and tested. It is possible to test more than one, but such experiments and their statistical analysis tend to be cumbersome and difficult.
- The tested subjects must be randomly assigned to either control or experimental groups.

Advantages

The results of a true experimental design can be statistically analyzed and so there can be little argument about the results.

It is also much easier for other researchers to replicate the experiment and validate the results.

For physical sciences working with mainly numerical data, it is much easier to manipulate one variable, so true experimental design usually gives a yes or no answer.

Disadvantages

Whilst perfect in principle, there are a number of problems with this type of design. Firstly, they can be almost too perfect, with the conditions being under complete control and not being representative of real world conditions.

For psychologists and behavioural biologists, for example, there can never be any guarantee that a human or living organism will exhibit 'normal' behaviour under experimental conditions.

True experiments can be too accurate and it is very difficult to obtain a complete rejection or acceptance of a hypothesis because the standards of proof required are so difficult to reach.

True experiments are also difficult and expensive to set up. They can also be very impractical.

While for some fields, like physics, there are not as many variables so the design is easy, for social sciences and biological sciences, where variations are not so clearly defined it is much more difficult to exclude other factors that may be affecting the manipulated variable.

True experimental design is an integral part of science, usually acting as a final test of a hypothesis. Whilst they can be cumbersome and expensive to set up, literature reviews, qualitative research and descriptive research can serve as a good precursor to generate a testable hypothesis, saving time and money.

Whilst they can be a little artificial and restrictive, they are the only type of research that is accepted by all disciplines as statistically provable.

Quasi-experimental Design

Quasi-experimental design is a form of experimental research used extensively in the social sciences and psychology

Whilst regarded as unscientific and unreliable, by physical and biological scientists, the method is, nevertheless, a very useful method for measuring social variables.

The inherent weaknesses in the methodology do not undermine the validity of the data, as long as they are recognized and allowed for during the whole experimental process. Quasi experiments resemble quantitative and qualitative experiments, but lack random allocation of groups or proper controls, so firm statistical analysis can be very difficult.

Design

Quasi-experimental design involves selecting groups, upon which a variable is tested, without any random pre-selection processes.

For example, to perform an educational experiment, a class might be arbitrarily divided by alphabetical selection or by seating arrangement. The division is often convenient and, especially in an educational situation, causes as little disruption as possible.

After this selection, the experiment proceeds in a very similar way to any other experiment, with a variable being compared between different groups, or over a period of time.

Advantages

Especially in social sciences, where pre-selection and randomization of groups is often difficult, they can be very useful in generating results for general trends.

E.g. if we study the effect of maternal alcohol use when the mother is pregnant, we know that alcohol does harm embryos.

A strict experimental design would include that mothers were randomly assigned to drink alcohol. This would be highly illegal because of the possible harm the study might do to the embryos.

So what researchers does is to ask people how much alcohol they used in their pregnancy and then assign them to groups.

Quasi-experimental design is often integrated with individual case studies; the figures and results generated often reinforce the findings in a case study, and allow some sort of statistical analysis to take place.

In addition, without extensive pre-screening and randomization needing to be undertaken, they do reduce the time and resources needed for experimentation.

Disadvantages

Without proper randomization, statistical tests can be meaningless. For example, these experimental designs do not take into account any pre-existing factors (as for the mothers: what made them drink or not drink alcohol), or recognize that influences outside the experiment may have affected the results. A quasi experiment constructed to analyse the effects of different educational programmes on two groups of children, for example, might generate results that show that one programme is more effective than the other.

These results will not stand up to rigorous statistical scrutiny because the researcher also need to control other factors that may have affected the results. This is really hard to do properly.

One group of children may have been slightly more intelligent or motivated. Without some form of pre-testing or random selection, it is hard to judge the influence of such factors.

Disadvantages aside, as long as the shortcomings of the quasi-experimental design are recognized, these studies can be a very powerful tool, especially in situations where 'true' experiments are not possible.

They are very good way to obtain a general overview and then follow up with a case study or quantitative experiment, to focus on the underlying reasons for the results generated.

Double Blind Experiment

A double blind experiment is an experimental method used to ensure impartiality, and avoid errors arising from bias. It is very easy for a researcher, even subconsciously, to influence experimental observations, especially in behavioural science, so this method provides an extra check. For example, imagine that a company is asking consumers for opinions about its products, using a survey.

There is a distinct danger that the interviewer may subconsciously emphasize the company's products when asking the questions. This is the major reason why market research companies generally prefer to use computers, and double blind experiments, for gathering important data.

The Blind Experiment

The blind experiment is the minimum standard for any test involving subjects and opinions, and failure to adhere to this principle may result in experimental flaws. The idea is that the groups studied, including the control, should not be aware of in which group they are placed. In medicine, when researchers are testing a new medicine, they ensure that the placebo looks, and tastes, the same as the actual medicine.

There is strong evidence of a placebo effect with medicine, where, if people believe that they are receiving a medicine, they show some signs of improvement in health. A blind experiment reduces the risk of bias from this effect, giving an honest baseline for the research, and allowing a realistic statistical comparison.

The Double Blind E–xperiment

The double blind experiment takes this precaution against bias one-step further, by ensuring that the researcher does not know in which group a patient falls. Whilst the vast majority of researchers are professionals, there is always a chance that the researcher might subconsciously tip off a patient about the pill they were receiving. They may even favour giving the pill to patients that they thought had the best chance of recovery, skewing the results.

Whilst nobody likes to think of scientists as dishonest, there is often pressure, from billion dollar drug companies and the fight for research grants, to generate positive results.

This always gives a chance that a scientist might manipulate results, and try to show the research in a better light. Proving that the researcher carried out a double blind experiment reduces the chance of criticism.

Other Applications

Whilst better known in medicine, double blind experiments are often used in other fields. Surveys, questionnaires and market research all use this technique to retain credibility.

If you wish to compare two different brands of washing powder, the samples should be in the same packaging.

A consumer might have an inbuilt brand identity awareness, and preference, which will lead to favouritism and bias.

An example of the weakness of single blind techniques is in police line-ups, where a witness picks out a suspect from a group. Many legal experts are advocating that these line-ups should be unsupervised, and unprompted.

If the police are fixed on bringing a particular subject to justice, they may consciously, or subconsciously, tip off the witness. Humans are very good at understanding body language and unconscious cues, so the chance of observer's bias should be minimized.

Descriptive Research Design

Descriptive research design is a scientific method which involves observing and describing the behaviour of a subject without influencing it in any way. Many scientific disciplines, especially social science and psychology, use this method to obtain a general overview of the subject.

Some subjects cannot be observed in any other way; for example, a social case study of an individual subject is a descriptive research design and allows observation without affecting normal behaviour. It is also useful where it is not possible to test and measure the large number of samples needed for more quantitative types of experimentation.

These types of experiments are often used by anthropologists, psychologists and social scientists to observe natural behaviours without affecting them in any way.

It is also used by market researchers to judge the habits of customers, or by companies wishing to judge the morale of staff. The results from a descriptive research can in no way be used as a definitive answer or to disprove a hypothesis but, if the limitations are understood, they can still be a useful tool in many areas of scientific research.

Advantages

The subject is being observed in a completely natural and unchanged natural environment. A good example of this would be an anthropologist who wanted to study a tribe without affecting their normal behaviour in any way. True experiments, whilst giving analyzable data, often adversely influence the normal behaviour of the subject.

Descriptive research is often used as a pre-cursor to more quantitatively research designs, the general overview giving some valuable pointers as to what variables are worth testing quantitatively.

Quantitative experiments are often expensive and time-consuming so it is often good sense to get an idea of what hypotheses are worth testing.

Disadvantages

Because there are no variables manipulated, there is no way to statistically analyse the results. Many scientists regard this type of study as very unreliable and 'unscientific'. In addition, the results of observational studies are not repeatable, and so there can be no replication of the experiment and reviewing of the results.

Descriptive research design is a valid method for researching specific subjects and as a precursor to more quantitative studies. Whilst there are some valid concerns about the statistical validity, as long as the limitations are understood by the researcher, this type of study is an invaluable scientific tool. Whilst the results are always open to question and to different interpretations, there is no doubt that they are preferable to performing no research at all.

Literature Review

Many students are instructed, as part of their research programme, to perform a literature review, without always understanding what a literature review is.

Most are aware that it is a process of gathering information from other sources and documenting it, but few have any idea of how to evaluate the information, or how to present it.

A literature review can be a precursor in the introduction of a research paper, or it can be an entire paper in itself, often the first stage of large research projects, allowing the supervisor to ascertain that the student is on the correct path.

A literature review is a critical and in depth evaluation of previous research. It is a summary and synopsis of a particular area of research, allowing anybody reading the paper to establish why you are pursuing this particular research programme. A good literature review expands upon the reasons behind selecting a particular research question.

What is a Literature Review Not

It is not a chronological catalog of all of the sources, but an evaluation, integrating the previous research together, and also explaining how it integrates into the proposed research programme. All sides of an argument must be clearly explained, to avoid bias, and areas of agreement and disagreement should be highlighted.

It is not a collection of quotes and paraphrasing from other sources. A good literature review should also have some evaluation of the quality and findings of the research. A good literature review should avoid the temptation of impressing the importance of a particular research programme. The fact that a researcher is undertaking the research programme speaks for its importance, and an educated reader may well be insulted that they are not allowed to judge the importance for themselves. They want to be re-assured that it is a serious paper, not a pseudo-scientific sales advertisement.

Whilst some literature reviews can be presented in a chronological order, it is best avoided. For example, a review of Victorian Age Physics, could present J.J. Thomson's famous experiments in a chronological order. Otherwise, this is usually perceived as being a little lazy, and it is better to organize the review around ideas and individual points.

As a general rule, certainly for a longer review, each paragraph should address one point, and present and evaluate all of the evidence, from all of the differing points of view.

Conducting a Literature Review

Evaluating the credibility of sources is one of the most difficult aspects, especially with the ease of finding information on the internet. The only real way to evaluate is through experience, but there are a few tricks for evaluating information quickly, yet accurately.

There is such a thing as 'too much information,' and Google does not distinguish or judge the quality of results, only how search engine friendly a paper is. This is why it is still good practice to begin research in an academic library. Any journals found there can be regarded as safe and credible.

The next stage is to use the internet, and this is where the difficulties start. It is very difficult to judge the credibility of an online paper. The main thing is to structure the internet research as if it were on paper. Bookmark papers, which may be relevant, in one folder and make another subfolder for a 'shortlist.'

The easiest way is to scan the work, using the abstract and introduction as guides. This helps to eliminate the non-relevant work and also some of the lower quality research.

If it sets off alarm bells, there may be something wrong, and the paper is probably of a low quality. Be very careful not to fall into the trap of rejecting research just because it conflicts with your hypothesis. Failure to do this will completely invalidate the literature review and potentially undermine the research project. Any research that may be relevant should be moved to the shortlist folder.

The next stage is to critically evaluate the paper and decide if the research is sufficient quality. Think about it this way: The temptation is to try to include as many sources as possible, because it is easy to fall into the trap of thinking that a long bibliography equates to a good paper. A smaller number of quality sources is far preferable than a long list of irrelevance.

Check into the credentials of any source upon which you rely heavily for the literature review. The reputation of the University or organization is a factor, as is the experience of the researcher.

If their name keeps cropping up, and they have written many peoples, the source is usually OK. Look for agreements. Good research should have been replicated by other independent researchers, with similar results, showing that the information is usually fairly safe to use.

If the process is proving to be difficult, and in some fields, like medicine and environmental research, there is a lot of poor science, do not be afraid to ask a supervisor for a few tips. They should know some good and reputable sources to look at. It may be a little extra work for them, but there will be even more work if they have to tear apart a review because it is built upon shaky evidence.

Conducting a good literature review is a matter of experience, and even the best scientists have fallen into the trap of using poor evidence. This is not a problem, and is part of the scientific process; if a research programme is well constructed, it will not affect the results.

Case Study Research Design

The case study research design have evolved over the past few years as a useful tool for investigating trends and specific situations in many scientific disciplines, especially social science, psychology, anthropology and ecology.

This method of study is especially useful for trying to test theoretical models by using them in real world situations. For example, if an anthropologist were to live amongst a remote tribe, whilst their observations might produce no quantitative data, they are still useful to science.

What is a Case Study

Basically, a case study is an in depth study of a particular situation rather than a sweeping statistical survey. It is a method used to narrow down a very broad field of research into one easily researchable topic. Whilst it will not answer a question completely, it will give some indications and allow further elaboration and hypothesis creation on a subject.

The case study research design is also useful for testing whether scientific theories and models actually work in the real world. You may come out with a great computer model for describing how the ecosystem of a rock pool works but it is only by trying it out on a real life pool that you can see if it is a realistic simulation.

For psychologists, anthropologists and social scientists they have been regarded as a valid method of research for many years. Scientists are sometimes guilty of becoming bogged down in the general picture and it is sometimes important to understand specific cases and ensure a more holistic approach to research.

Case Study Research Design

Some argue that because a case study is such a narrow field that its results cannot be extrapolated to fit an entire question and that they show only one narrow example. On the other hand, it is argued that a case study provides more realistic responses than a purely statistical survey.

The truth probably lies between the two and it is probably best to try and synergize the two approaches. It is valid to conduct case studies but they should be tied in with more general statistical processes.

For example, a statistical survey might show how much time people spend talking on mobile phones, but it is case studies of a narrow group that will determine why this is so.

The other main thing to remember during case studies is their flexibility. Whilst a pure scientist is trying to prove or disprove a hypothesis, a case study might introduce new and unexpected results during its course, and lead to research taking new directions.

The argument between case study and statistical method also appears to be one of scale. Whilst many 'physical' scientists avoid case studies, for psychology, anthropology and ecology they are an essential tool. It is important to ensure that you realise that a case study cannot be generalized to fit a whole population or ecosystem.

Finally, one peripheral point is that, when informing others of your results, case studies make more interesting topics than purely statistical surveys, something that has been realized by teachers and magazine editors for many years. The general public has little interest in pages of statistical calculations but some well placed case studies can have a strong impact.

How to Design and Conduct a Case Study

The advantage of the case study research design is that you can focus on specific and interesting cases. This may be an attempt to test a theory with a typical case or it can be a specific topic that is of interest. Research should be thorough and note taking should be meticulous and systematic.

The first foundation of the case study is the subject and relevance. In a case study, you are deliberately trying to isolate a small study group, one individual case or one particular population.

For example, statistical analysis may have shown that birthrates in African countries are increasing. A case study on one or two specific countries becomes a powerful and focused tool for determining the social and economic pressures driving this. In the design of a case study, it is important to plan and design how you are going to address the study and make sure that all collected data is relevant. Unlike a scientific report, there is no strict set of rules so the most important part is making sure that the study is focused and concise; otherwise you will end up having to wade through a lot of irrelevant information.

It is best if you make yourself a short list of 4 or 5 bullet points that you are going to try and address during the study. If you make sure that all research refers back to these then you will not be far wrong.

With a case study, even more than a questionnaire or survey, it is important to be passive in your research. You are much more of an observer than an experimenter and you must remember that, even in a multi-subject case, each case must be treated individually and then cross case conclusions can be drawn.

How to Analyse the Results

Analyzing results for a case study tends to be more opinion based than statistical methods. The usual idea is to try and collate your data into a manageable from and construct a narrative around it.

Use examples in your narrative whilst keeping things concise and interesting. It is useful to show some numerical data but remember that you are only trying to judge trends and not analyse every last piece of data. Constantly refer back to your bullet points so that you do not lose focus.

It is always a good idea to assume that a person reading your research may not possess a lot of knowledge of the subject so try to write accordingly. In addition, unlike a scientific study which deals with facts, a case study is based on opinion and is very much designed to provoke reasoned debate. There really is no right or wrong answer in a case study.

Survey Research Design

The survey research design is often used because of the low cost and easy accessible information. Conducting accurate and meaningful surveys is one of the most important facets of market research in the consumer driven 21st century.

Businesses, governments and media spend billions of dollars on finding out what people think and feel.

Accurate research can generate vast amounts of revenue; bad or inaccurate research can cost millions, or even bring down governments. The survey research design is a very valuable tool for assessing opinions and trends. Even on a small scale, such as local government or small businesses, judging opinion with carefully designed surveys can dramatically change strategies.

Television chat-shows and newspapers are usually full of facts and figures gleaned from surveys but often no information is given as to where this information comes from or what kind of people were asked.

A cursory examination of these figures usually shows that the results of these surveys are often manipulated or carefully sifted to try and reflect distort the results to match the whims of the owners.

Businesses are often guilty of carefully selecting certain results to try and portray themselves as the answer to all needs. When you decide to enter this minefield and design a survey, how do you avoid falling into the trap of inaccuracy and bias? How do you ensure that your survey research design reflects the views of a genuine cross-section of the population?

The simple answer is that you cannot; even with unlimited budget, time and resources, there is no way of achieving 100 per cent accuracy. Opinions, on all levels, are very fluid and can change on a daily or even hourly basis.

Despite this, surveys are still a powerful tool and can be an extremely powerful research tool. As long as you design your survey well and are prepared to be self-critical, you can still obtain an accurate representation of opinion.

Establishing the Aims of Your Research

This is the single most important step of your survey research design and can make or break your research; every single element of your survey must refer back to this design or it will be fatally flawed.

If your research is too broad, you will have to ask too many questions; too narrow and you will not be researching the topic thoroughly enough.

Researching And Determining Your Sample Group

This is the next crucial step in determining your survey and depends upon many factors.

The first is accuracy; you want to try and interview as broad a base of people as possible. Quantity is not always the answer; if you were researching a detergent, for example, you would want to target your questions at those who actually use such products.

For a political or ethical survey, about which anybody can have a valid opinion, you want to try and represent a well balanced cross section of society.

It is always worth checking beforehand what quantity and breadth of response you need to provide significant results or your hard work may be in vain.

Before you start the planning, it is important that you consult somebody about the statistical side of your survey research design. This way, you know what number and type of responses you need to make it a valid survey and prevent inaccurate results.

Methodology

How do you make sure that your questionnaire reaches the target group? There are many methods of reaching people but all have advantages and disadvantages. For a college or university study it is unlikely that you will have the facilities to use internet, e-mail or phone surveying so we will concentrate on only the likely methods you will use.

Face to Face

This is probably the most traditional method of the survey research design. It can be very accurate. It allows you to be selective about to whom you ask questions and you can explain anything that they do not understand.

In addition, you can make a judgement about who you think is wasting your time or giving stupid answers.

There are a few things to be careful of with this approach; firstly, people can be reluctant to give up their time without some form of incentive. Another factor to bear in mind is that is difficult to ask personal questions face to face without embarrassing people. It is also very time consuming and difficult to obtain a representative sample.

Finally, if you are going to be asking questions door-to-door, it is essential to ensure that you have some official identification to prove who you are.

Mail

This does not necessarily mean using the postal service; putting in the legwork and delivering questionnaires around a campus or workplace is another method.

This is a good way of targeting a certain section of people and is excellent if you need to ask personal or potentially embarrassing questions. The problems with this method are that you cannot be sure of how many responses you will receive until a long time period has passed.

You must also be wary of collecting personal data; most countries have laws about how much information you can keep about people so it is always wise to check with somebody more knowledgeable.

Structuring and Designing the Questionnaire

The design of your questionnaire depends very much upon the type of survey and the target audience.

If you are asking questions face to face it is easy to explain if people are unsure of a question. On the other hand, if your questionnaire is going to include many personal questions then mailing methods are preferable (but may violate local legislation).

You must keep your questionnaire as short as possible; people will either refuse to fill in a long questionnaire or get bored halfway through.

Cover Note

It is also polite, especially with mailed questionnaires, to send a short cover note explaining what you are doing and how the subject should return the surveys to you.

You should introduce yourself; explain why you are doing the research, what will happen with the results and who to contact if the subject has any queries.

Types Of Question

Multiple choice questions allow many different answers, including don't know, to be assessed. The main strength of this type of question is that the form is easy to fill in and the answers can be checked easily and quantitatively; this is useful for large sample groups.

Rating, on some scale, is a tried and tested form of question structure. This way is very useful when you are seeking to be a little more open-ended than is possible with multiple choice questions. It is a little harder to analyse your responses. It is important to make sure that the scale allows extreme views.

Questions asking for opinions must be open-ended and allow the subject to give their own response; you should avoid entrapment and appear to be as neutral as possible during the procedure. The major problem is that you have to devise a numerical way of analyzing and statistically evaluating the responses which can lead to a biased view, if care is not taken. These types of question should really be reserved for experienced researchers.

The order in which you ask the questions can be important. Try to start off with the most relevant questions first. Also friendly and non-threatening questions put the interviewee at ease. Questions should be simple and straightforward using everyday language rather than perfect grammar.

Try and group questions about similar topics together; this makes it a lot quicker for people to answer questions more quickly and easily.

Some researchers advocate mixing up and randomizing questions for accuracy but this approach tends to be more appropriate for advanced market research. For this type of survey the researcher is trying to disguise the nature of the research and filter out preconceptions.

It is also a good idea to try out a test survey; ask a small group to give genuine and honest feedback so that you can make adjustments. Common mistakes when doing the survey research design.

Analyzing Your Results

This is where the fun starts and it will depend upon the type of questions used.

For multiple choice questions it is a matter of counting up the answers to each question and using statistics to 'crunch the numbers' and test relevance.

Rating type question require a little more work but the follow broadly the same principle.

For opinion questions you have to devise some way of judging the responses numerically.

The next step is to devise which statistical test you are going to use and start to enter some numbers to judge the significance of your data.

This is where you have to analyse the results. Be self critical whether your results showed what you expected or not. Any survey has flaws in its method so it is always a good idea to show that you are aware of these. For example, a university represents only a narrow cross section of society; as long as you are aware of this then your results are valid. If your survey gave unexpected results explain the possible reasons for why this happened and suggestions for refining the techniques and structure of your survey next time.

Identical Twins Study

The identical twins study has been used for a long time, to study the effects of environment and genetics on human development.

Some studies have tried to determine how genetics and environmental factors contribute to intelligence, aggression or substance addictions.

Most of the twin's studies compare identical twins, having 100 per cent genetic similarity, with non- identical twins, with about 50 per cent genetic similarity. The researcher compares the occurrence of an individual trait between identical and fraternal twins. If the identical twins show more similarity for this trait than the non-identical twins, then the excess is assumed to be down to genetic factors.

This type of analysis would then allow the researchers to estimate the heritability of specific traits and quantify the effect of genetic factors on the individual trait. Psychologists have long known that a twin study is not a true experimental design, but it has led to some interesting insights into the influence of genes on human behaviour.

For this method, a number of assumptions have to be made; that the identical twins share identical DNA profiles, and that the environmental factors are the same for all participants.

Criticisms

There have been few criticisms of identical twin studies over the years. By their nature, and because of small sample sizes, it is very difficult to quantitatively analyse the results and so all experimentation tends to be observational; the sample groups cannot be random so statistical analysis is impossible.

The experimental methods assume that there is little difference in the environmental factors between fraternal and identical twins, but there is a criticism that the tendency of adults to treat identical twins in exactly the same way makes this assumption invalid. Parents tend to dress identical twins the same way and encourage them to pursue the same interests.

The distinction between environmental factors and genetic influences may not be as black and white as the identical twins study assumes. There is probably an interaction between genes and environment and so the whole picture may be a lot more complex.

In addition, the experiment tends to assume that one gene affects one behavioural trait. Modern genetic research is showing that many different genes can influence behaviour.

The above criticisms all have some validity, but the main point is that twin studies have never claimed to be anything other than observational, identifying and trying to explain trends rather than prove a hypothesis.

Whilst there are some concerns about the validity of the identical twins study, such experiments are certainly better than performing no research at all.

Twins studies are now trying to analyse the environmental factors more. Instead of assuming that the environmental factors are the same, they are now contrasting shared family environment with the individual events suffered by the individual twin.

In addition, identical twins study is constantly evolving into more complex forms, now taking into account whole families and other siblings in addition to the twins.

Research into the human genome is now resurrecting the studies of twins; hereditary trends observed in an identical twins study can now be studied quantitatively in the laboratory. It is now standard practice, when conducting twin's research to analyse DNA from all participants and this is bypassing many of the concerns about the twin study.

Meta Analysis

Meta analysis is a statistical technique developed by social scientists, who are very limited in the type of experiments they can perform.

Social scientists have great difficulty in designing and implementing true experiments, so meta-analysis gives them a quantitative tool to analyse statistically data drawn from a number of studies, performed over a period of time.

Medicine and psychology increasingly use this method, as a way of avoiding time-consuming and intricate studies, largely repeating the work of previous research.

What is meta-analysis

Social studies often use very small sample sizes, so any statistics used generally give results containing large margins of error.

This can be a major problem when interpreting and drawing conclusions, because it can mask any underlying trends or correlations. Such conclusions are only tenuous, at best, and leave the research open for criticism. Meta analysis is the process of drawing from a larger body of research, and using powerful statistical analyzes on the conglomerated data. This gives a much larger sample population and is more likely to generate meaningful and usable data.

The Advantages Of Meta Analysis

Meta analysis is an excellent way of reducing the complexity and breadth of research, allowing funds to be diverted elsewhere. For rare medical conditions, it allows researchers to collect data from further afield than would be possible for one research group.

As the method becomes more common, database programmes have made the process much easier, with professionals working in parallel able to enter their results and access the data. This allows constant quality assessments and also reducing the chances of unnecessary repeat research, as papers can often take many months to be published, and the computer records ensure that any researcher is aware of the latest directions and results.

The field of meta study is also a lot more rigorous than the traditional literature review, which often relies heavily upon the individual interpretation of the researcher.

When used with the databases, a meta study allows a much wider net to be cast than by the traditional literature review, and is excellent for highlighting correlations and links between studies that may not be readily apparent as well as ensuring that the compiler does not subconsciously infer correlations that do not exist.

The Disadvantages Of Meta Analysis

There are a number of disadvantages to meta analysis, of which a researcher must be aware before relying upon the data and generated statistics.

The main problem is that there is the potential for publication bias and skewed data.

Research generating results not refuting a hypothesis may tend to remain unpublished, or risks not being entered into the database. If the meta study is restricted to the research with positive results, then the validity is compromised.

The researcher compiling the data must make sure that all research is quantitative, rather than qualitative, and that the data is comparable across the various research programmes, allowing a genuine statistical analysis.

It is important to pre-select the studies, ensuring that all of the research used is of a sufficient quality to be used.

One erroneous or poorly conducted study can place the results of the entire meta analysis at risk. On the other hand, setting almost unattainable criteria and criteria for inclusion can leave the meta study with too small a sample size to be statistically relevant.

Striking a balance can be a little tricky, but the whole field is in a state of constant development, incorporating protocols similar to the scientific method used for normal quantitative research.

Finding the data is rapidly becoming the real key, with skilled meta analysts developing a skill-set of library based skills, finding information buried in government reports and conference data, developing the knack of assessing the quality of sources quickly and effectively.

Conclusions And The Future

Meta analysis is here to stay, as an invaluable tool for research, and is rapidly gaining momentum as a stand-alone discipline, with practitioners straddling the divide between statisticians and librarians.

The conveniences, as long as the disadvantages are taken into account, are too apparent to ignore, and a meta study can reduce the need for long, expensive and potentially intrusive repeated research studies.

Systematic Reviews

Heavily used by the health care sector, systematic reviews are a powerful way of isolating and critically evaluating previous research.

Modern medical research generates so much literature, and fills so many journals, that a traditional literature review could take months, and still be out of date by the time that the research is designed and performed.

In addition, researchers are often guilty of selecting the research best fitting their pre-conceived notions, a weakness of the traditional 'narrative' literature review process.

To help medical professionals, specialist compilers assess and condense the research, entering it into easily accessible research databases. They are an integral part of the research process, and every student of medicine routinely receives a long and extensive training in the best methods for critically evaluating literature.

Addressing the Deficiencies in Narration

The problems with narrative literature came to light a couple of decades ago, when critics realized that reviewers looking at the same body of evidence often generated completely different findings. They drew conclusions based upon their specialty, rather than the compelling evidence contained within the body of research.

It is unclear whether this was a case of conscious or subconscious manipulation (bias), but this particular finding was worrying, especially in a research area where life and death could be at stake. To address this issue, medical authorities developed a new protocol of systematic reviewing, based upon a structure as strict as the scientific method governing empirical research programmes.

The Protocols Underpinning Systematic Reviews

Define a research question, in a similar way to formulating a research question for a standard research design

Locate and select relevant previous research studies, with no attempt at evaluation at this stage. Ideally, research in languages other than English should be used, and the researcher should try to find papers and reports unpublished in journals, such as conference speeches or company reports. Critically evaluate the studies. The reviewer should assess each study upon criteria based upon quality, strength of the findings and validity. For safety, this process should include at least two independent reviewers, although a greater number is advisable. Combine the results. This is the process of combining all of the findings, sometimes qualitatively, but usually quantitatively, using meta-analysis.

Publish the results. As with any research, the results have to be written and published, usually with a system of independent review. Discussion of the conclusions, as with any research, allows the validity of the findings to be verified.

The Reasoning Behind Systematic Reviews

The principle behind the systematic reviews process is that the researcher critically evaluates previous studies, in a much more comprehensive and systematic way than a standard literature review. In many cases, statistical meta-analysis tools are used to give the review a quantitative foundation, allowing correlations to be documented and conclusions to be drawn. Whilst the techniques are mainly used by medicine and psychology, there is a growing trend towards using systematic reviews in other disciplines. Many branches of science are becoming increasingly fragmented and anarchic, so this layer of analysis aggregates all of the disparate elements.

Systematic reviews, and meta-analysis, are regarded as a cornerstone of health care research, essential where it is impractical or unethical to keep repeating old research.

In addition to the potential risks of repeated research upon patients and volunteers, there are now laws in many countries prohibiting excessive research using animals. Systematic reviews are a great way of reducing the amount of suffering caused by vivisection.

Disadvantages Of Systematic Reviews

As with most systems, despite the protocols, systematic reviews do have some inherent weaknesses. The main problem is the rapid advancement of medical research and technology, often meaning that many reviews are out of date before they are even published, forcing researchers to update their findings constantly. The development of specialist organizations for finding and evaluating data minimizes the effects of this particular shortcoming.

As with any subjective review, there is the problem of selection bias, where contradictory research is jettisoned, although most medical researchers are adept at following the proper procedures.

Funding and research grants cause researchers to try to find results that suit their paymasters, a growing problem in many areas of science, not just medicine. The specialist reviewers sidestep this problem, to a certain extent, by producing independent research, uncorrupted by governmental or private health care funding, curbing the worst excesses.

Often, a blind system is used, and reviewers are unaware of where the papers they are reviewing came from, or who they are written by. This lessens allegations of favouritism and judging research by the reputation of the researcher rather than on merit. Ultimately, the onus is on the reader to draw their own assessments, using their own experience to judge the quality of the systematic review. Whilst not a perfect system, systematic reviews are far superior to the traditional narrative approach, which often allows a lot of good research to fall through the cracks.

Observational Study

In the fields of social science, psychology and medicine, amongst others, observational study is an essential tool.

This type of research draws a conclusion by comparing subjects against a control group, in cases where the researcher has no control over the experiment.

A research study comparing the risk of developing lung cancer, between smokers and non-smokers, would be a good example of an observational study.

The main reason for performing any observational research is due to ethical concerns.

With the smoking example, a scientist cannot give cigarettes to non-smokers for 20 years and compare them with a control group. This also brings up the other good reason for such studies, in that few researchers can study the long-term effects of certain variables, especially when it runs into decades.

For this study of long-term and subtle effects, they have to use pre-existing conditions and medical records. The researcher may want to study an extremely small sample group, so it is easier to start with known cases and works backwards. The thalidomide cases, for example, are an example of an observational study where researchers had to work backwards, and establish that the drug was the cause of disabilities.

The main problem with observational studies is that the experimenter has no control over the composition of the control groups, and cannot randomize the allocation of subjects. This can create bias, and can also mask cause and effect relationships or, alternatively, suggest correlations where there are none (error in research).

For example, in the smoking example, if the researcher found that there is a correlation between smoking and increased rates of lung cancer, without knowing the full and complete background of the subjects, there is no way of determining whether other factors were involved, such as diet, occupation or genetics. Randomization is assumed to even out external causal effects, but this is impossible in an observational study. There is no independent variable, so it is dangerous to assume cause and effect relationships, a process often misunderstood by the mass media lauding the next wonder food, or sensationalizing a political debate with unfounded results and pseudo-science.

Despite the limitations, an observational study allows a useful insight into a phenomenon, and sidesteps the ethical and practical difficulties of setting up a large and cumbersome medical research project.

Naturalistic Observation

In many scientific disciplines, naturalistic observation is a useful tool for expanding knowledge about a specific phenomenon or species.

In fields such as anthropology, behavioural biology and ecology, watching a person or organism in a natural environment is essential.

Most naturalistic observation is unobtrusive, such as a researcher setting up a camera to film the behaviour of a badger underground. Most nature documentaries are examples of naturalistic observational study, where days, weeks or even years of film are analyzed and edited, to give an overview of the life cycle of the organism.

There is often little attempt at analysis, quantitative or qualitative, but the observational study does uncover unknown phenomena and behaviours.

Obtrusive naturalistic observational study is often used in anthropology, where a researcher lives with a remote tribe for a period of time and records their behaviour. By living there, she is influencing their social interactions and habits, but can still make some excellent observations.

Often, anthropologists will adopt the lifestyle of a particular group of people, in an attempt to understand why they have certain customs and beliefs.

In technical terms, it would be difficult to follow people without discovery, and it would also be unethical to observe without consent, so obtrusive naturalistic observation is the only method that can be used with human subjects.

Many of the producers of the recent glut of reality shows try to claim that their shows are psychological experiments, based around observational study. This is stretching the idea too far, as there are very few people who would not change their behaviour when they are aware that a camera is watching.

In these cases, it is difficult to make any realistic and valid observations about their lifestyle.

Most criticisms of naturalistic observation are based around this principle, and an anthropologist or social scientist has to ensure that they intervene as little as possible.

Field Experiments

For geologists, social scientists and environmental biologists, amongst others, field experiments are an integral part of the discipline.

As the name suggests, a field study is an experiment performed outside the laboratory, in the 'real' world. Unlike case studies and observational studies, a field experiment still follows all of the steps of the scientific process, addressing research problems and generating hypotheses.

The obvious advantage of a field study is that it is practical and also allows experimentation, without artificially introducing confounding variables.

A population biologist examining an ecosystem could not move the entire environment into the laboratory, so field experiments are the only realistic research method in many fields of science.

In addition, they circumvent the accusation leveled at laboratory experiments of lacking external or ecological validity, or adversely affecting the behaviour of the subject.

Social scientists and psychologists often used field experiments to perform blind studies, where the subject was not even aware that they were under scrutiny.

A good example of this is the Piliavin and Piliavin experiment, where the propensity of strangers to help blood covered 'victims' was measured. This is now frowned upon, under the policy of informed consent, and is only used in rare and highly regulated circumstances.

Field experiments can suffer from a lack of a discrete control group and often have many variables to try to eliminate.

For example, if the effects of a medicine are studied, and the subject is instructed not to drink alcohol, there is no guarantee that the subject followed the instructions, so field studies often sacrifice internal validity for external validity.

For fields like biology, geology and environmental science, this is not a problem, and the field experiment can be treated as a sound experimental practice, following the steps of the scientific method.

A major concern shared by all disciplines is the cost of field studies, as they tend to be very expensive.

For example, even a modestly sized research ship costs many thousands of dollars every day, so a long oceanographical research programme can run into the millions of dollars.

Pilot studies are often used to test the feasibility of any long term or extensive research programme before committing vast amounts of funds and resources. The changeable nature of the external environment and the often-prohibitive investment of time and money mean that field experiments are rarely replicable, so any generalization is always tenuous.

Cohort Study

A cohort study is a research programme investigating a particular group with a certain trait, and observes over a period of time.

Some examples of cohorts may be people who have taken a certain medication, or have a medical condition. Outside medicine, it may be a population of animals that has lived near a certain pollutant or a sociological study of poverty.

A cohort study can delve even further and divide a cohort into sub-groups, for example, a cohort of smokers could be sub-divided, with one group suffering from obesity. In this respect, a cohort study is often interchangeable with the term naturalistic observation.

There are two main sub-types of cohort study, the retrospective and the prospective cohort study. The major difference between the two is that the retrospective looks at phenomena that have already happened, whilst the prospective type starts from the present.

Retrospective Cohort Study

The retrospective case study is historical in nature. Whilst still beginning with the division into cohorts, the researcher looks at historical data to judge the effects of the variable.

For example, it might compare the incidence of bowel cancer over time in vegetarians and meat eaters, by comparing the medical histories. It is a lot easier than the prospective, but there is no control, and confounding variables can be a problem, as the researcher cannot easily assess the lifestyle of the subject.

A retrospective study is a very cheap and effective way of studying health risks or the effects of exposure to pollutants and toxins. It gives results quickly, at the cost of validity, because it is impossible to eliminate all of the potentially confounding variables from historical records and interviews alone.

Prospective Cohort Study

In a prospective cohort study, the effects of a certain variable are plotted over time, and the study becomes an ongoing process. To maintain validity, all of the subjects must be initially free of the condition tested for.

For example, an investigation, over time, into the effects of smoking upon lung cancer must ensure that all of the subjects are free of the disease. It is also possible to subgroup and try to control variables, such as weight, occupation type or social status.

They are preferable to a retrospective study, but are expensive and usually require a long period of time to generate useful results, so are very expensive and difficult.

Some studies have been running for decades, but are generating excellent data about underlying trends in a population. The prospective cohort study is a great way to study long-term trends, allowing the researcher to measure any potential confounding variables, but the potential cost of error is high, so pilot studies are often used to ensure that the study runs smoothly.

Ambidirectional Cohort Study

The ambidirectional cohort study is the ultimate method, combining retrospective and prospective aspects. The researcher studies and analyzes the previous history of the cohorts and then continues the research in a prospective manner.

This gives the most accurate results, but is an extremely arduous undertaking, costing time and a great deal of money.

The ambidirectional study shares one major drawback with the prospective study, in that it is impossible to guarantee that any data can be followed up, as participants may decline to participate or die prematurely. These studies need to look at very large samples to ensure that any attributional losses can be absorbed by the statistics.

Longitudinal Study

A longitudinal study is observational research performed over a period of years or even decades, and allows social scientists and economists to study long-term effects in a human population.

A cohort study is a subset of the longitudinal study because it observes the effect on a specific group of people over time. Quite often, a longitudinal study is an extended case study, observing individuals over long periods, and is a purely qualitative undertaking.

The lack of quantitative data means that any observations are speculative, as with many case studies, but they allow a unique and valuable perspective on some aspects of human culture and sociology.

The 'up' Series

The groundbreaking television documentary 'UP' is probably the most famous example of a long-term longitudinal study, a case study of a group of British people from birth.

The original producer, Michael Apted, proposed the hypothesis that children born into a certain social class would remain entrenched in that class throughout their life.

In 1967, he selected children from the rich, poor and middle classes, and proceeded to interview and film them every seven years. The highly acclaimed series is still running, with the next set of interviews to be performed in 2011/2012, and it has provided a unique insight into the development of British culture since the 1960's. Even this series highlights one of the major flaws of a longitudinal study, the problem that there can be no retesting or restart. Apted, with hindsight, wished that he had used more female subjects, showing the importance of the initial planning stage of a longitudinal study. Once a course of action is decided, the clock cannot be turned back, and the results must stand as tested.

The Cross Sectional Study

The cross sectional study looks at a different aspect than the standard longitudinal study.

The longitudinal study uses time as the main variable, and tries to make an in depth study of how a small sample changes and fluctuates over time.

A cross sectional study, on the other hand, takes a snapshot of a population at a certain time, allowing conclusions about phenomena across a wide population to be drawn. An example of a cross-sectional study would be a medical study looking at the incidence of breast cancer in a population. The researcher can look at a wide range of ages, ethnicities and social backgrounds. If a significant number of women from a certain social background are found to have the disease, then the researcher can investigate further.

This is a relatively easy way to perform a preliminary experiment, allowing the researcher to focus on certain population groups and understand the wider picture. Of course, researchers often use both methods, using a cross section to take the snapshot and isolate potential areas of interest, and then conducting a longitudinal study to find the reason behind the trend.

This is called panel data, or time series cross-sectional data, but is generally a complicated and expensive type of research, notoriously difficult to analyse.

Such programmes are rare, but can give excellent data, allowing a long-term picture of phenomena to be ascertained.

Factorial Design

A factorial design is often used by scientists wishing to understand the effect of two or more independent variables upon a single dependent variable.

Traditional research methods generally study the effect of one variable at a time, because it is statistically easier to manipulate.However, in many cases, two factors may be interdependent, and it is impractical or false to attempt to analyse them in the traditional way.

Social researchers often use factorial designs to assess the effects of educational methods, whilst taking into account the influence of socio-economic factors and background. Agricultural science, with a need for field-testing, often uses factorial designs to test the effect of variables on crops. In such large-scale studies, it is difficult and impractical to isolate and test each variable individually.

Factorial experiments allow subtle manipulations of a larger number of interdependent variables. Whilst the method has limitations, it is a useful method for streamlining research and letting powerful statistical methods highlight any correlations.

The Basics

Imagine an aquaculture research group attempting to test the effects of food additives upon the growth rate of trout.

A traditional experiment would involve randomly selecting different tanks of fish and feeding them varying levels of the additive contained within the feed, for example none or 10 per cent.

However, as any fish farmer knows, the density of stocking is also crucial to fish growth; if there are not enough fish in a tank, then the wasted capacity costs money. If the density is too high, then the fish grow at a slower rate.

Rather than the traditional experiment, the researchers could use a factorial design and co-ordinate the additive trial with different stocking densities, perhaps choosing four groups. The factorial experiment then needs 4 x 2, or eight treatments.

The traditional rules of the scientific method are still in force, so statistics require that every experiment be conducted in triplicate.

This means 24 separate treatment tanks. Of course, the researchers could also test, for example, 4 levels of concentration for the additive, and this would give 4 x 4 or 16 tanks, meaning 48 tanks in total. Each factor is an independent variable, whilst the level is the subdivision of a factor.

Assuming that we are designing an experiment with two factors, a 2 × 2 would mean two levels for each, whereas a 2 × 4 would mean two subdivisions for one factor and four for the other.

It is possible to test more than two factors, but this becomes unwieldy very quickly. In the fish farm example, imagine adding another factor, temperature, with four levels into the mix. It would then be 4 × 4 × 4, or 64 runs. In triplicate, this would be 192 tanks, a huge undertaking.

There are a few other methods, such as fractional factorial designs, to reduce this, but they are not always statistically valid.

This lies firmly in the realm of advanced statistics and is a long, complicated and arduous undertaking.

The Pros and Cons of Factorial Design

Factorial designs are extremely useful to psychologists and field scientists as a preliminary study, allowing them to judge whether there is a link between variables, whilst reducing the possibility of experimental error and confounding variables.

The factorial design, as well as simplifying the process and making research cheaper, allows many levels of analysis. As well as highlighting the relationships between variables, it also allows the effects of manipulating a single variable to be isolated and analyzed singly.

The main disadvantage is the difficulty of experimenting with more than two factors, or many levels. A factorial design has to be planned meticulously, as an error in one of the levels, or in the general operationalization, will jeopardize a great amount of work.

Other than these slight detractions, a factorial design is a mainstay of many scientific disciplines, delivering great results in the field.

Case Control Study

A case control study is a method extensively used by the medical profession, as an easy and quick way of comparing treatments, or investigating the causes of disease.

Longitudinal studies are the preferred method, but are often expensive, time consuming and difficult. Whilst this method does suffer from some weaknesses, it is quick, and delivers results quickly.

The case control study uses groups of patients stricken with a disease, and compares them with a control group of patients not suffering symptoms. Medical records and interviews are used to try to build up a historical picture of the patient's life, allowing cross-reference between patients and statistical analysis. Any trends can then be highlighted and action can be taken.

Statistical analysis allows the researcher to draw a conclusion about whether a certain situation or exposure led to the medical condition. For example, a scientist could compare a group of coal miners suffering from lung cancer with those clear of the disease, and try to establish the underlying cause. If the majority of the cases arose in collieries owned by one company, it might indicate that the company's safety equipment and procedures were at fault.

Possibly the most famous case control study using this method was a study into whether bicycle helmets reduce the chance of cyclists receiving bad head injuries in an accident.

Obviously, the researcher could not use standard experimentation and compare a control group of non-helmet wearers with helmet wearers, measuring the chances of head injury, as this would be unethical.

A case study control was utilized, and the researchers looked at medical records, comparing the number of head injury sufferers wearing helmets against those without. This generated a statistical result, showing that wearing a cycle helmet made it 88 per cent less likely that head injury would be suffered in an accident.

The main weakness of the case control study is that it is very poor at determining cause and effect relationships.

In the cycle helmet example, it could be argued that a cyclist who bothered wearing a helmet may well have been a safer cyclist anyway, and less likely to have accidents. Evidence showed that children wearing helmets were more likely to be from a more affluent class, more used to cycling through parks than city streets. The study also showed that helmets were of little use to adults.

Whilst most agree that cycle helmets are probably a good thing for children, there is not enough evidence to suggest that they should be mandatory for adults outside extreme cycling.

These problems serves as a warning that the results of any case control study should not be relied upon, instead acting as a guide, possibly allowing deeper and more rigorous methods to be utilized.

Pilot Study

A pilot study is a standard scientific tool for 'soft' research, allowing scientists to conduct a preliminary analysis before committing to a full-blown study or experiment. A small chemistry experiment in a college laboratory, for example, costs very little, and mistakes or validity problems easily rectified. At the other end of the scale, a medical experiment taking samples from thousands of people from across the world is expensive, often running into the millions of dollars. Finding out that there was a problem with the equipment or with the statistics used is unacceptable, and there will be dire consequences.

A field research project in the Amazon Basin costs a lot of time and money, so finding out that the electronics used do not function in the humid and warm conditions is too late. To test the feasibility, equipment and methods, researchers will often use a pilot study, a small-scale rehearsal of the larger research design. Generally, the pilot study technique specifically refers to a smaller scale version of the experiment, although equipment tests are an increasingly important part of this sub-group of experiments.

For example, the medical researchers may conduct a smaller survey upon a hundred people, to check that the protocols are fine. The Amazon Researchers may perform an experiment, in similar conditions, sending a small team either to the Amazon to test the procedures, or by using something like the tropical bio-dome at the Eden Project.

Pilot studies are also excellent for training inexperienced researchers, allowing them to make mistakes without fear of losing their job or failing the assignment. Logistical and financial estimates can be extrapolated from the pilot study, and the research question, and the project can be streamlined to reduce wastage of resources and time. Pilots can be an important part of attracting grants for research as the results can be placed before the funding body.

Generally, most funding bodies see research as an investment, so are not going to dole out money unless they are certain that there is a chance of a financial return. Unfortunately, and paper reporting the preliminary pilot study, especially if problems were reported, is often stigmatized and sidelined. This is unfair, and punishes researchers for being methodical, so these attitudes are under a period of re-evaluation. Discouraging researchers from reporting methodological errors, as found in pilot studies, means that later researchers may make the same mistakes.

The other major problem is deciding whether the results from the pilot study can be included in the final results and analysis, a procedure that varies wildly between disciplines. Pilots are rapidly becoming an essential pre-cursor to many research projects, especially when universities are constantly striving to reduce costs. Whilst there are weaknesses, they are extremely useful for driving procedures in an age increasingly dominated by technology, much of it untested under field conditions.

5

Market Research Process

Market research, like many other components of marketing, can be quite simple or very complex. You might conduct simple market research such as including a questionnaire in your customer bills to gather demographic information about your customers. On the more complex side, you might engage a professional market research firm to conduct primary research to aid you in developing a marketing strategy to launch a new product.

Regardless of the simplicity or complexity of your marketing research project, you will benefit by reviewing the following seven steps in the market research process.

RESEARCH PROCESS

We understand the world by asking questions and searching for answers. Our construction of reality depends on the nature of our enquiry.

Until the sixteenth century, human enquiry was primarily based on introspection. The way to know things was to turn inward and use logic to seek the truth. This paradigm had endured for a millennium and was a well-established conceptual framework for understanding the world. The seeker of knowledge was an integral part of the enquiry process.

A profound change occurred during the sixteenth and seventeenth centuries. Copernicus, Kepler, Galileo, Descartes, Bacon, Newton, and Locke presented new ways of examining nature. Our method of understanding the world came to rely on measurement and quantification. Mathematics replaced introspection as the key to supreme truths. The Scientific Revolution was born.

Objectivity became a critical component of the new scientific method. The investigator was an observer, rather than a participant in the enquiry process. A mechanistic view of the universe evolved.

We believed that we could understand the whole by performing an examination of the individual parts. Experimentation and deduction became the tools of the scholar. For two hundred years, the new paradigm slowly evolved to become part of the reality framework of society. The Age of Enlightenment had arrived.

Scientific research methodology was very successful at explaining natural phenomena. It provided a systematic way of knowing. Western philosophers embraced this new structure of enquiry. Eastern philosophy continued to stress the importance of the one seeking knowledge. By the beginning of the twentieth century, a complete schism had occurred. Western and Eastern philosophies were mutually exclusive and incompatible.

Then something remarkable happened. Einstein's proposed that the observer was not separate from the phenomena being studied. Indeed, his theory of relativity actually stressed the role of the observer. Quantum mechanics carried this a step further and stated that the performance of observation could change the thing being observed. The researcher was not simply an observer, but in fact, was an integral part of the process. In physics, Western and Eastern philosophies have met.

This idea has not been incorporated into the standard social science research model, and today's social science community see themselves as objective observers of the phenomena being studied. However, "it is an established principle of measurement that instruments react with the things they measure." The concept of instrument reactivity states that an instrument itself can disturb the thing being measured.

SCIENTIFIC RESEARCH

Generally, research is understood to follow a certain structural process. Though step order may vary depending on the subject matter and researcher, the following steps are usually part of most formal research, both basic and applied:

- Formation of the topic,
- Hypothesis,
- Conceptual definitions,
- Operational definitions,
- Gathering of data,
- Analysis of data,
- Test, revising of hypothesis,
- Conclusion, iteration if necessary.

A common misunderstanding is that by this method a hypothesis can be proven or tested. Generally a hypothesis is used to make predictions that can be tested by observing the outcome of an experiment. If the outcome is inconsistent with the hypothesis, then the hypothesis is rejected. However, if the outcome is consistent with the hypothesis, the experiment is said to support the hypothesis.

This careful language is used because researchers recognize that alternative hypotheses may also be consistent with the observations. In this sense, a hypothesis can never be proven, but rather only supported by surviving rounds of scientific testing and, eventually, becoming widely thought of as true (or better, predictive), but this is not the same as it having been proven. A useful hypothesis allows prediction and within the accuracy of observation of the time, the prediction will be verified. As the accuracy of observation improves with time, the hypothesis may no longer provide an accurate prediction. In this case a new hypothesis will arise to challenge the old, and to the extent that the new hypothesis makes more accurate predictions than the old, the new will supplant it.

Scientific method refers to techniques for investigating phenomena, acquiring new knowledge, or correcting and integrating previous knowledge. To be termed scientific, a method of enquiry must be based on gathering observable, empirical and measurable evidence subject to specific principles of reasoning. A scientific method consists of the collection of data through observation and experimentation, and the formulation and testing of hypotheses.

Although procedures vary from one field of enquiry to another, identifiable features distinguish scientific enquiry from other methodologies of knowledge. Scientific researchers propose hypotheses as explanations of phenomena, and design experimental studies to test these hypotheses. These steps must be repeatable in order to dependably predict any future results. Theories that encompass wider domains of enquiry may bind many hypotheses together in a coherent structure. This in turn may help form new hypotheses or place groups of hypotheses into context.

Among other facets shared by the various fields of enquiry is the conviction that the process be objective to reduce a biased interpretation of the results. Another basic expectation is to document, archive and share all data and methodology so they are available for careful scrutiny by other scientists, thereby allowing other researchers the opportunity to verify results by attempting to reproduce them. This practice, called *full disclosure*, also allows statistical measures of the reliability of these data to be established. Since Ibn al-Haytham (Alhazen, 965–1039), one of the key figures in developing scientific method, the emphasis has been on seeking truth:

"Truth is sought for its own sake. And those who are engaged upon the quest for anything for its own sake are not interested in other things. Finding the truth is difficult, and the road to it is rough."

"How does light travel through transparent bodies? Light travels through transparent bodies in straight lines only.... We have explained this exhaustively in our *Book of Optics*. But let us now mention something to prove this convincingly: the fact that light travels in straight lines is clearly observed in the lights which enter into dark rooms through holes.... [T]he entering light will be clearly observable in the dust which fills the air."

The conjecture that "light travels through transparent bodies in straight lines only" was corroborated by Alhazen only after years of effort. His demonstration of the conjecture was to place a straight stick or a taut thread next to the light beam, to prove that light travels in a straight line.

Scientific methodology has been practiced in some form for at least one thousand years. There are difficulties in a formulaic statement of method, however. As William Whewell (1794–1866) noted in his *History of Inductive Science* (1837) and in *Philosophy of Inductive Science* (1840), "invention, sagacity, genius" are required at every step in scientific method. It is not enough to base scientific method on experience alone; multiple steps are needed in scientific method, ranging from our experience to our imagination, back and forth.

In the twentieth century, a hypothetico-deductive model for scientific method was formulated:

- Use your experience: Consider the problem and try to make sense of it. Look for previous explanations. If this is a new problem to you, then move to step 2.
- Form a conjecture: When nothing else is yet known, try to state an explanation, to someone else, or to your notebook.
- Deduce a prediction from that explanation: If you assume 2 is true, what consequences follow?
- Test: Look for the opposite of each consequence in order to disprove *2*. It is a logical error to seek *3* directly as proof of *2*. This error is called *affirming the consequent*.

This model underlies the scientific revolution. One thousand years ago, Alhazen demonstrated the importance of steps 1 and 4. Galileo (1638) also showed the importance of step 4 (also called Experiment) in Two New Sciences.

One possible sequence in this model would be 1, 2, 3, 4. If the outcome of 4 holds, and 3 is not yet disproven, you may continue with 3, 4, 1, and so forth; but if the outcome of 4 shows 3 to be false, you will have go back to 2 and try to invent a new 2, deduce a new 3, look for 4, and so forth.

Note that this method can never absolutely verify (prove the truth of) 2. It can only falsify 2. (This is what Einstein meant when he said "No amount of experimentation can ever prove me right; a single experiment can prove me wrong.") In the twentieth century, Ludwik Fleck (1896–1961) and others found that we need to consider our experiences more carefully, because our experience may be biased, and that we need to be more exact when describing our experiences. These considerations are discussed below.

Truth and Belief

Belief can alter observations; those with a particular belief will often see things as reinforcing their belief, even if they do not. Needham's *Science and Civilization in China* uses the 'flying horse' image as an example of observation: in it, a horse's legs are depicted as splayed, when the stop-action picture by

Eadweard Muybridge shows otherwise. Note that at the moment that no hoof is touching the ground, the horse's legs are gathered together and are not splayed.

Earlier paintings depict the incorrect flying horse observation. This demonstrates Ludwik Fleck's caution that people observe what they expect to observe, until shown otherwise; our beliefs will affect our observations (and therefore our subsequent actions). The purpose of the scientific method is to test a hypothesis, a proposed explanation about how things are, via repeatable experimental observations which can contradict the hypothesis so as to fight this observer bias.

Elements of Scientific Method

There are many ways of outlining the basic method shared by all fields of scientific enquiry. The following examples are typical classifications of the most important components of the method on which there is wide agreement in the scientific community and among philosophers of science. There are, however, disagreements about some aspects.

The following set of methodological elements and organization of procedures tends to be more characteristic of natural sciences than social sciences. In the social sciences mathematical and statistical methods of verification and hypotheses testing may be less stringent. Nonetheless the cycle of hypothesis, verification and formulation of new hypotheses will resemble the cycle described below.

The essential elements of a scientific method are iterations, recursions, interleavings, and orderings of the following:

- Characterizations (observations, definitions, and measurements of the subject of enquiry).
- Hypotheses (theoretical, hypothetical explanations of observations and measurements of the subject).
- Predictions (reasoning including logical deduction from the hypothesis or theory).
- Experiments (tests of all of the above).

Each element of a scientific method is subject to peer review for possible mistakes. These activities do not describe all that scientists do but apply mostly to experimental sciences (*e.g.*, physics, chemistry). The elements above are often taught in the educational system.

Scientific method is not a recipe: it requires intelligence, imagination, and creativity. It is also an ongoing cycle, constantly developing more useful, accurate and comprehensive models and methods. For example, when Einstein developed the Special and General Theories of Relativity, he did not in any way refute or discount Newton's *Principia*. On the contrary, if the astronomically large, the vanishingly small, and the extremely fast are reduced out from

Einstein's theories — all phenomena that Newton could not have observed — Newton's equations remain. Einstein's theories are expansions and refinements of Newton's theories, and observations that increase our confidence in them also increase our confidence in Newton's approximations to them.

A linearized, pragmatic scheme of the four points above is sometimes offered as a guideline for proceeding:

- Define the question.
- Gather information and resources (observe).
- Form hypothesis.
- Perform experiment and collect data.
- Analyse data.
- Interpret data and draw conclusions that serve as a starting point for new hypothesis.
- Publish results.
- Retest (frequently done by other scientists).

The iterative cycle inherent in this step-by-step methodology goes from point 3 to 6 back to 3 again.

While this schema outlines a typical hypothesis/testing method, it should also be noted that a number of philosophers, historians and sociologists of science (perhaps most notably Paul Feyerabend) claim that such descriptions of scientific method have little relation to the ways science is actually practiced.

The "operational" paradigm combines the concepts of operational definition, instrumentalism, and utility: The essential elements of a scientific method are operations, observations, models, and a utility function for evaluating models.

- Operation - Some action done to the system being investigated.
- Observation - What happens when the operation is done to the system.
- Model - A fact, hypothesis, theory, or the phenomenon itself at a certain moment.
- Utility Function - A measure of the usefulness of the model to explain, predict, and control, and of the cost of use of it. One of the elements of any scientific utility function is the refutability of the model. Another is its simplicity, on the Principle of Parsimony also known as Occam's Razor.

The Keystones of Science project, sponsored by the journal *Science*, has selected a number of scientific articles from that journal and annotated them, illustrating how different parts of each article embody scientific method. Here is an annotated example of this scientific method example titled *Microbial Genes in the Human Genome: Lateral Transfer or Gene Loss?*

DNA example

Each element of scientific method is illustrated below by an example from the discovery of the structure of DNA:

- *DNA-characterizations*: in this case, although the significance of the gene had been established, the mechanism was unclear to anyone, as of 1950.
- *DNA-hypotheses*: Crick and Watson hypothesized that the gene had a physical basis - it was helical.
- *DNA-predictions*: from earlier work on tobacco mosaic virus, Watson was aware of the significance of Crick's formulation of the transform of a helix. Thus he was primed for the significance of the X-shape in photo 51.
- *DNA-experiments*: Watson sees photo 51.

The examples are continued in "Evaluations and iterations" with *DNA-iterations*.

Characterizations

Scientific method depends upon increasingly more sophisticated characterizations of the subjects of investigation. (The *subjects* can also be called *unsolved problems* or the *unknowns*.) For example, Benjamin Franklin correctly characterized St. Elmo's fire as electrical in nature, but it has taken a long series of experiments and theory to establish this. While seeking the pertinent properties of the subjects, this careful thought may also entail some definitions and observations; the observations often demand careful measurements and/or counting.

- "I am not accustomed to saying anything with certainty after only one or two observations."—Andreas Vesalius (1546).

The systematic, careful collection of measurements or counts of relevant quantities is often the critical difference between pseudo-sciences, such as alchemy, and a science, such as chemistry or biology. Scientific measurements taken are usually tabulated, graphed, or mapped, and statistical manipulations, such as correlation and regression, performed on them. The measurements might be made in a controlled setting, such as a laboratory, or made on more or less inaccessible or unmanipulatable objects such as stars or human populations.

The measurements often require specialized scientific instruments such as thermometers, spectroscopes, or voltmeters, and the progress of a scientific field is usually intimately tied to their invention and development.

Measurements in scientific work are also usually accompanied by estimates of their uncertainty. The uncertainty is often estimated by making repeated measurements of the desired quantity.

Uncertainties may also be calculated by consideration of the uncertainties of the individual underlying quantities that are used. Counts of things, such as the number of people in a nation at a particular time, may also have an uncertainty due to limitations of the method used. Counts may only represent a sample of desired quantities, with an uncertainty that depends upon the sampling method used and the number of samples taken.

Measurements demand the use of *operational definitions* of relevant quantities. That is, a scientific quantity is described or defined by how it is measured, as opposed to some more vague, inexact or "idealized" definition.

For example, electrical current, measured in amperes, may be operationally defined in terms of the mass of silver deposited in a certain time on an electrode in an electrochemical device that is described in some detail.

The operational definition of a thing often relies on comparisons with standards: the operational definition of "mass" ultimately relies on the use of an artifact, such as a certain kilogram of platinum-iridium kept in a laboratory in France.

The scientific definition of a term sometimes differs substantially from its natural language usage.

For example, mass and weight overlap in meaning in common discourse, but have distinct meanings in mechanics. Scientific quantities are often characterized by their units of measure which can later be described in terms of conventional physical units when communicating the work.

New theories sometimes arise upon realizing that certain terms had not previously been sufficiently clearly defined. For example, Albert Einstein's first paper on relativity begins by defining simultaneity and the means for determining length. These ideas were skipped over by Isaac Newton with, "*I do not define time, space, place and motion, as being well known to all.*" Einstein's paper then demonstrates that they (*viz.*, absolute time and length independent of motion) were approximations.

Francis Crick cautions us that when characterizing a subject, however, it can be premature to define something when it remains ill-understood. In Crick's study of consciousness, he actually found it easier to study awareness in the visual system, rather than to study free will, for example. His cautionary example was the gene; the gene was much more poorly understood before Watson and Crick's pioneering discovery of the structure of DNA; it would have been counterproductive to spend much time on the definition of the gene, before them.

Example of Characterizations

DNA-characterizations

The history of the discovery of the structure of DNA is a classic example of the elements of scientific method: in 1950 it was known that genetic inheritance had a mathematical description, starting with the studies of Gregor Mendel. But the mechanism of the gene was unclear. Researchers in Bragg's laboratory at Cambridge University made X-ray diffraction pictures of various molecules, starting with crystals of salt, and proceeding to more complicated substances. Using clues which were painstakingly assembled over the course of decades, beginning with its chemical composition, it was determined that it should be possible to characterize the physical structure of DNA, and the X-ray images would be the vehicle.

Precession of Mercury

The characterization element can require extended and extensive study, even centuries. It took thousands of years of measurements, from the Chaldean, Indian, Persian, Greek, Arabic and European astronomers, to record the motion of planet Earth.

Newton was able to condense these measurements into consequences of his laws of motion. But the perihelion of the planet Mercury's orbit exhibits a precession that is not fully explained by Newton's laws of motion. The observed difference for Mercury's precession between Newtonian theory and relativistic theory (approximately 43 arc-seconds per century), was one of the things that occurred to Einstein as a possible early test of his theory of General Relativity.

Hypothesis Development

A hypothesis is a suggested explanation of a phenomenon, or alternately a reasoned proposal suggesting a possible correlation between or among a set of phenomena.

Normally hypotheses have the form of a mathematical model. Sometimes, but not always, they can also be formulated as existential statements, stating that some particular instance of the phenomenon being studied has some characteristic and causal explanations, which have the general form of universal statements, stating that every instance of the phenomenon has a particular characteristic.

Scientists are free to use whatever resources they have — their own creativity, ideas from other fields, induction, Bayesian inference, and so on — to imagine possible explanations for a phenomenon under study. Charles Sanders Peirce, borrowing a page from Aristotle (*Prior Analytics*, 2.25) described the incipient stages of enquiry, instigated by the "irritation of doubt" to venture a plausible guess, as *abductive reasoning*. The history of science is filled with stories of scientists claiming a "flash of inspiration", or a hunch, which then motivated them to look for evidence to support or refute their idea.

Michael Polanyi made such creativity the centerpiece of his discussion of methodology. William Glen observes that: the success of a hypothesis, or its service to science, lies not simply in its perceived "truth", or power to displace, subsume or reduce a predecessor idea, but perhaps more in its ability to stimulate the research that will illuminate ... bald suppositions and areas of vagueness.

In general scientists tend to look for theories that are "elegant" or "beautiful". In contrast to the usual English use of these terms, they here refer to a theory in accordance with the known facts, which is nevertheless relatively simple and easy to handle. Occam's Razor serves as a rule of thumb for making these determinations.

DNA-hypotheses

Linus Pauling proposed that DNA was a triple helix. Francis Crick and James Watson learned of Pauling's hypothesis, understood from existing data that Pauling was wrong and realized that Pauling would soon realise his mistake. So, the race was on to figure out the correct structure — except that Pauling did not realise at the time that he was in a race!

Predictions from the Hypothesis

Any useful hypothesis will enable predictions, by reasoning including deductive reasoning. It might predict the outcome of an experiment in a laboratory setting or the observation of a phenomenon in nature. The prediction can also be statistical and only talk about probabilities.

It is essential that the outcome be currently unknown. Only in this case does the eventuation increase the probability that the hypothesis be true. If the outcome is already known, it's called a consequence and should have already been considered while formulating the hypothesis.

If the predictions are not accessible by observation or experience, the hypothesis is not yet useful for the method, and must wait for others who might come afterwards, and perhaps rekindle its line of reasoning. For example, a new technology or theory might make the necessary experiments feasible.

DNA-predictions

The hypothesis (by James Watson and Francis Crick among others) that DNA had a helical structure implied the prediction that it would produce an x shaped X-ray diffraction pattern. This followed from the work of Cochran, Crick and Vand (and independently by Stokes) who had provided a mathematical basis for the empirical observation that helical structures produce x shapes.

Also in their first paper, Watson and Crick predicted that the double helix structure provided a simple mechanism for DNA replication, writing "It has not escaped our notice that the specific pairing we have postulated immediately suggests a possible copying mechanism for the genetic material".

General Relativity

Einstein's theory of General Relativity makes several specific predictions about the observable structure of space-time, such as a prediction that light bends in a gravitational field and that the amount of bending depends in a precise way on the strength of that gravitational field. Arthur Eddington's observations made during a 1919 solar eclipse supported General Relativity rather than Newtonian gravitation.

Experiments

Once predictions are made, they can be tested by experiments. If test results contradict predictions, then the hypotheses are called into question and explanations may be sought. Sometimes experiments are conducted incorrectly and are at fault.

If the results confirm the predictions, then the hypotheses are considered likely to be correct but might still be wrong and are subject to further testing. The experimental control is a technique for dealing with observational error.

This technique uses the contrast between multiple samples (or observations) under differing conditions, to see what varies or what remains the same. We vary the conditions for each measurement, to help isolate what has changed. Mill's canons can then help us figure out what the important factor is. Factor analysis is one technique for discovering the important factor in an effect.

Depending on the predictions, the experiments can have different shapes. It could be a classical experiment in a laboratory setting, a double-blind study or an archaeological excavation. Even taking a plane from New York to Paris is an experiment which tests the aerodynamical hypotheses used for constructing the plane.

Scientists assume an attitude of openness and accountability on the part of those conducting an experiment.

Detailed record keeping is essential, to aid in recording and reporting on the experimental results, and providing evidence of the effectiveness and integrity of the procedure.

They will also assist in reproducing the experimental results. Traces of this tradition can be seen in the work of Hipparchus (190-120 BCE), when determining a value for the precession of the Earth, while controlled experiments can be seen in the works of Muslim scientists such as Geber (721-815 CE), al-Battani (853–929) and Alhacen (965-1039).

DNA-Experiments

Watson and Crick showed an initial (and incorrect) proposal for the structure of DNA to a team from Kings College - Rosalind Franklin, Maurice Wilkins, and Raymond Gosling. Franklin immediately spotted the flaws which concerned the water content.

Later Watson saw Franklin's detailed X-ray diffraction images which showed an X-shape and confirmed that the structure was helical. This rekindled Watson and Crick's model building and led to the correct structure.

Evaluation and Iteration

Testing and Improvement

The scientific process is iterative. At any stage it is possible that some consideration will lead the scientist to repeat an earlier part of the process. Failure to develop an interesting hypothesis may lead a scientist to re-define the subject they are considering.

Failure of a hypothesis to produce interesting and testable predictions may lead to reconsideration of the hypothesis or of the definition of the subject. Failure of the experiment to produce interesting results may lead the scientist to reconsidering the experimental method, the hypothesis or the definition of the subject.

Other scientists may start their own research and enter the process at any stage. They might adopt the characterization and formulate their own hypothesis, or they might adopt the hypothesis and deduce their own predictions.

Often the experiment is not done by the person who made the prediction and the characterization is based on experiments done by someone else. Published results of experiments can also serve as a hypothesis predicting their own reproducibility.

DNA-iterations

After considerable fruitless experimentation, being discouraged by their superior from continuing, and numerous false starts, Watson and Crick were able to infer the essential structure of DNA by concrete modeling of the physical shapes of the nucleotides which comprise it. They were guided by the bond lengths which had been deduced by Linus Pauling and by Rosalind Franklin's X-ray diffraction images...*DNA Example*

Confirmation

Science is a social enterprise, and scientific work tends to be accepted by the community when it has been confirmed. Crucially, experimental and theoretical results must be reproduced by others within the science community.

Researchers have given their lives for this vision; Georg Wilhelm Richmann was killed by ball lightning (1753) when attempting to replicate the 1752 kite-flying experiment of Benjamin Franklin.

To protect against bad science and fraudulent data, government research granting agencies like NSF and science journals like *Nature* and *Science* have a policy that researchers must archive their data and methods so other researchers can access it, test the data and methods and build on the research that has gone before. Scientific data archiving can be done at a number of national archives in the U.S. or in the World Data Centre.

Models of Scientific Enquiry

Classical Model

The classical model of scientific enquiry derives from Aristotle, who distinguished the forms of approximate and exact reasoning, set out the threefold scheme of abductive, deductive, and inductive inference, and also treated the compound forms such as reasoning by analogy.

Pragmatic Model

Charles Peirce (1839-1914) considered scientific enquiry to be a species of the genus *enquiry*, which he defined as any means of fixing belief, that is, any means of arriving at a settled opinion on a matter in question. He observed that enquiry in general begins with a state of uncertainty and moves towards a state of certainty, sufficient at least to terminate the enquiry for the time being.

Peirce held that, in practical matters, slow and stumbling ratiocination is not generally to be automatically preferred over instinct and tradition, and held that scientific method is best suited to theoretical enquiry. What recommends the specifically scientific method of enquiry above all others is the fact that it is deliberately designed to arrive, eventually, at the ultimately most secure beliefs, upon which the most successful actions can eventually be based. In 1877, he outlined four methods for the fixation of belief, the settlement of doubt, graded by their success in achieving a sound settlement of belief:

- The method of tenacity — persisting in that which one is inclined to think.
- The method of authority — conformity to a source of ready-made beliefs.
- The method of congruity or the a priori or the dilettante or "what is agreeable to reason" — leading to argumentation that gets finally nowhere.
- The scientific method.

Peirce characterized scientific method in terms of the uses of inference, and paid special attention to the generation of explanations. As a question of presuppositions of reasoning, he defined truth as the correspondence of a sign (in particular, a proposition) to its object and, pragmatically, not as any actual consensus of any finite community (*i.e.*, such that to enquire would be to go ask the experts for the answers), but instead as that ideal final opinion which all reasonable scientific intelligences would reach, sooner or later but still inevitably, if they pushed investigation far enough.

In tandem he defined the real as a true sign's object (be that object a possibility or quality, or an actuality or brute fact, or a necessity or norm or law), which is what it is independently of any finite community's opinion and, pragmatically, has dependence only on the ideal final opinion. That is an opinion as far or nears as the truth itself to you or me or any finite community of minds. Thus his theory of enquiry boils down to "do the science." He characterized the scientific method as follows:

- ***Abduction (or retroduction).*** Generation of explanatory hypothesis. From abduction, Peirce distinguishes induction as inferring, on the basis of tests, the proportion of truth in the hypothesis. Every enquiry, whether into ideas, brute facts, or norms and laws, arises as a result of surprising observations in the given realm or realms, and the pondering of the phenomenon in all its aspects in the attempt to resolve the wonder. All explanatory content of theories is reached by way of abduction, the most insecure among modes of inference. Induction as a process is far too slow for that job, so economy of research demands abduction, whose modicum of success depends on one's being somehow attuned to nature, by dispositions learned and, some of them, likely inborn. Abduction has general justification inductively in that it works often enough and that nothing else works, at least not quickly enough when science is already properly rather slow, the work of indefinitely many generations.

Peirce calls his pragmatism "the logic of abduction". His Pragmatic Maxim is: "Consider what effects that might conceivably have practical bearings you conceive the objects of your conception to have. Then, your conception of those effects is the whole of your conception of the object".

His pragmatism is a method of sorting out conceptual confusions by equating the meaning of any concept with the conceivable practical consequences of whatever it is which the concept portrays.

It is a method of experimentational mental reflection arriving at conceptions in terms of conceivable confirmatory and disconfirmatory circumstances — a method hospitable to the generation of explanatory hypotheses, and conducive to the employment and improvement of verification to test the truth of putative knowledge.

Given abduction's dependence on mental processes not necessarily conscious and deliberate but, in any case, attuned to nature, and given abduction's being driven by the need to economize the enquiry process, its explanatory hypotheses should be optimally simple in the sense of "natural" (for which Peirce cites Galileo and which Peirce distinguishes from "logically simple"). Given abduction's insecurity, it should have consequences with conceivable practical bearing leading at least to mental tests, and, in science, lending themselves to scientific testing.

- ***Deduction.*** Analysis of hypothesis and deduction of its consequences in order to test the hypothesis. Two stages:
  - ***Explication.*** Logical analysis of the hypothesis in order to render it as distinct as possible.

- ***Demonstration (or deductive argumentation).*** Deduction of hypothesis's consequence. Corollarial or, if needed, Theorematic.

- ***Induction.*** The long-run validity of the rule of induction is deducible from the principle (presuppositional to reasoning in general) that the real is only the object of the final opinion to which adequate investigation would lead In other words, if there were something to which an inductive process involving ongoing tests or observations would *never* lead, then that thing would not be real. Three stages:
  - ***Classification.*** Classing objects of experience under general ideas.
  - ***Probation (or direct Inductive Argumentation):*** Crude (the enumeration of instances) or Gradual (new estimate of proportion of truth in the hypothesis after each test). Gradual Induction is Qualitative or Quantitative; if Quantitative, then dependent on measurements, or on statistics, or on countings.
  - ***Sentential Induction.*** "...which, by Inductive reasonings, appraises the different Probations singly, then their combinations, then makes self-appraisal of these very appraisals themselves, and passes final judgement on the whole result".

Computational Approaches

Many subspecialties of applied logic and computer science, such as artificial intelligence, machine learning, computational learning theory, inferential statistics, and knowledge representation, are concerned with setting out computational, logical, and statistical frameworks for the various types of inference involved in scientific enquiry.

In particular, they contribute hypothesis formation, logical deduction, and empirical testing. Some of these applications draw on measures of complexity from algorithmic information theory to guide the making of predictions from prior distributions of experience, for example, see the complexity measure called the *speed prior* from which a computable strategy for optimal inductive reasoning can be derived.

Philosophy and Sociology of Science

Philosophy of science looks at the underpinning logic of the scientific method, at what separates science from non-science, and the ethic that is implicit in science. We find ourselves in a world that is not directly understandable. We find that we sometimes disagree with others as to the facts of the things we see in the world around us, and we find that there are things in the world that are at odds with our present understanding.

The scientific method attempts to provide a way in which we can reach agreement and understanding. A "perfect" scientific method might work in such a way that rational application of the method would always result in agreement and understanding; a perfect method would arguably be algorithmic, and so not leave any room for rational agents to disagree. As with all philosophical topics, the search has been neither straightforward nor simple.

Logical Positivist, empiricist, falsificationist, and other theories have claimed to give a definitive account of the logic of science, but each has in turn been criticized.

Thomas Samuel Kuhn examined the history of science in his *The Structure of Scientific Revolutions*, and found that the actual method used by scientists differed dramatically from the then-espoused method. His observations of science practice are essentially sociological and do not speak to how science is or can be practiced in other times and other cultures.

Imre Lakatos and Thomas Kuhn have done extensive work on the "theory laden" character of observation. Kuhn (1961) said the scientist generally has a theory in mind before designing and undertaking experiments so as to make empirical observations, and that the "route from theory to measurement can almost never be traveled backward". This implies that the way in which theory is tested is dictated by the nature of the theory itself, which led Kuhn (1961, p. 166) to argue that "once it has been adopted by a profession... no theory is recognized to be testable by any quantitative tests that it has not already passed".

Paul Feyerabend similarly examined the history of science, and was led to deny that science is genuinely a methodological process. In his book *Against Method* he argues that scientific progress is *not* the result of applying any particular method. In essence, he says that "anything goes", by which he meant that for any specific methodology or norm of science, successful science has been done in violation of it. Criticisms such as his led to the strong programme, a radical approach to the sociology of science.

In his 1958 book, *Personal Knowledge*, chemist and philosopher Michael Polanyi (1891-1976) criticized the common view that the scientific method is purely objective and generates objective knowledge. Polanyi cast this view as a misunderstanding of the scientific method and of the nature of scientific enquiry, generally.

He argued that scientists do and must follow personal passions in appraising facts and in determining which scientific questions to investigate. He concluded that a structure of liberty is essential for the advancement of science - that the freedom to pursue science for its own sake is a prerequisite for the production of knowledge through peer review and the scientific method.

The postmodernist critiques of science have themselves been the subject of intense controversy. This ongoing debate, known as the science wars, is the result of conflicting values and assumptions between the postmodernist and realist camps.

Whereas postmodernists assert that scientific knowledge is simply another discourse (note that this term has special meaning in this context) and not representative of any form of fundamental truth, realists in the scientific community maintain that scientific knowledge does reveal real and fundamental truths about reality.

Many books have been written by scientists which take on this problem and challenge the assertions of the postmodernists while defending science as a legitimate method of deriving truth.

Communication, Community, Culture

Frequently the scientific method is not employed by a single person, but by several people cooperating directly or indirectly. Such cooperation can be regarded as one of the defining elements of a scientific community.

Various techniques have been developed to ensure the integrity of the scientific method within such an environment.

Peer Review Evaluation

Scientific journals use a process of *peer review*, in which scientists' manuscripts are submitted by editors of scientific journals to (usually one to three) fellow (usually anonymous) scientists familiar with the field for evaluation. The referees may or may not recommend publication, publication with suggested modifications, or, sometimes, publication in another journal.

This serves to keep the scientific literature free of unscientific or crackpot work, helps to cut down on obvious errors, and generally otherwise improve the quality of the scientific literature.

Documentation and Replication

Sometimes experimenters may make systematic errors during their experiments, unconsciously veer from the scientific method (Pathological science) for various reasons, or, in rare cases, deliberately falsify their results.

Consequently, it is a common practice for other scientists to attempt to repeat the experiments in order to duplicate the results, thus further validating the hypothesis.

Archiving

As a result, researchers are expected to practice scientific data archiving in compliance with the policies of government funding agencies and scientific journals.

Detailed records of their experimental procedures, raw data, statistical analyses and source code are preserved in order to provide evidence of the effectiveness and integrity of the procedure and assist in reproduction.

These procedural records may also assist in the conception of new experiments to test the hypothesis, and may prove useful to engineers who might examine the potential practical applications of a discovery.

Data Sharing

When additional information is needed before a study can be reproduced, the author of the study is expected to provide it promptly - although a small charge may apply. If the author refuses to share data, appeals can be made to the journal editors who published the study or to the institution who funded the research.

Limitations

Note that it is not possible for a scientist to record *everything* that took place in an experiment. He must select the facts he believes to be relevant to the experiment and report them. This may lead, unavoidably, to problems later if some supposedly irrelevant feature is questioned. For example, Heinrich Hertz did not report the size of the room used to test Maxwell's equations, which later turned out to account for a small deviation in the results. The problem is that parts of the theory itself need to be assumed in order to select and report the experimental conditions. The observations are hence sometimes described as being 'theory-laden'.

Dimensions of Practice

The primary constraints on contemporary western science are:

- Publication, *i.e.* Peer review
- Resources (mostly funding)

It has not always been like this: in the old days of the "gentleman scientist" funding (and to a lesser extent publication) were far weaker constraints.

Both of these constraints indirectly bring in a scientific method — work that too obviously violates the constraints will be difficult to publish and difficult to get funded. Journals do not require submitted papers to conform to anything more specific than "good scientific practice" and this is mostly enforced by peer review. Originality, importance and interest are more important.

Criticisms of these restraints are that they are so nebulous in definition (*e.g.* "good scientific practice") and open to ideological, or even political, manipulation apart from a rigorous practice of a scientific method, that they often serve to censor rather than promote scientific discovery.

Apparent censorship through refusal to publish ideas unpopular with mainstream scientists (unpopular because of ideological reasons and/or because they seem to contradict long held scientific theories) has soured the popular perception of scientists as being neutral or seekers of truth and often denigrated popular perception of science as a whole.

The development of the scientific method is inseparable from the history of science itself. Ancient Egyptian documents, such as early papyri, describe methods of medical diagnosis. In ancient Greek culture, the method of empiricism was described. The first experimental scientific method was developed by Muslim scientists, who introduced the use of experimentation and quantification to distinguish between competing scientific theories set within a generally empirical orientation, which emerged with Alhazen's optical experiments in his *Book of Optics* (1021).

The modern scientific method crystallized no later than in the 17th and 18th centuries. In his work *Novum Organum* (1620) — a reference to Aristotle's *Organon* — Francis Bacon outlined a new system of logic to improve upon the old philosophical process of syllogism. Then, in 1637, René Descartes established the framework for a scientific method's guiding principles in his treatise, *Discourse on Method*. The writings of Alhazen, Bacon and Descartes are considered critical in the historical development of the modern scientific method. In the late 19th century, Charles Sanders Peirce proposed a schema that would turn out to have considerable influence in the development of current scientific method generally.

Peirce accelerated the progress on several fronts. Firstly, speaking in broader context in "How to Make Our Ideas Clear" (1878), Peirce outlined an objectively verifiable method to test the truth of putative knowledge on a way that goes beyond mere foundational alternatives, focusing upon both *deduction* and *induction*. He thus placed induction and deduction in a complementary rather than competitive context (the latter of which had been the primary trend at least since David Hume, who wrote in the mid-to-late 18th century).

Secondly, and of more direct importance to modern method, Peirce put forth the basic schema for hypothesis/testing that continues to prevail today. Extracting the theory of enquiry from its raw materials in classical logic, he refined it in parallel with the early development of symbolic logic to address the then-current problems in scientific reasoning. Peirce examined and articulated the three fundamental modes of reasoning that, as discussed above in this article, play a role in enquiry today, the processes that are currently known as abductive, deductive, and inductive inference.

Thirdly, he played a major role in the progress of symbolic logic itself — indeed this was his primary specialty. Karl Popper denied the existence of evidence and of scientific method. Popper holds that there is only one universal method, the negative method of trial and error. It covers not only all products of the human mind, including science, mathematics, philosophy, art and so on, but also the evolution of life.

Relationship with Mathematics

Science is the process of gathering, comparing, and evaluating proposed models against observables. A model can be a simulation, mathematical or chemical formula, or set of proposed steps. Science is like mathematics in that researchers in both disciplines can clearly distinguish what is *known* from what is *unknown* at each stage of discovery. Models, in both science and mathematics, need to be internally consistent and also ought to be *falsifiable* (capable of disproof).

In mathematics, a statement need not yet be proven; at such a stage, that statement would be called a conjecture. But when a statement has attained mathematical proof, that statement gains a kind of immortality which is highly prized by mathematicians, and for which some mathematicians devote their lives.

Mathematical work and scientific work can inspire each other. For example, the technical concept of time arose in science, and timelessness was a hallmark of a mathematical topic. But today, the Poincaré conjecture has been proven using time as a mathematical concept in which objects can flow.

Nevertheless, the connection between mathematics and reality (and so science to the extent it describes reality) remains obscure. Eugene Wigner's paper, *The Unreasonable Effectiveness of Mathematics in the Natural Sciences*, is a very well-known account of the issue from a Nobel Prize physicist.

In fact, some observers (including some well known mathematicians such as Gregory Chaitin, and others such as Lakoff and Nunez) have suggested that mathematics is the result of practitioner bias and human limitation (including cultural ones), somewhat like the post-modernist view of science. George Pólya's work on problem solving, the construction of mathematical proofs, and heuristic show that mathematical method and scientific method differ in detail, while nevertheless resembling each other in using iterative or recursive steps.

	Mathematical method	*Scientific method*
1	Understanding	Characterization from experience and observation
2	Analysis	Hypothesis: a proposed explanation
3	Synthesis	Deduction: prediction from the hypothesis
4	Review/Extend	Test and experiment

In Pólya's view, *understanding* involves restating unfamiliar definitions in your own words, resorting to geometrical figures, and questioning what we know and do not know already; *analysis*, which Pólya takes from Pappus, involves free and heuristic construction of plausible arguments, working backward from the goal, and devising a plan for constructing the proof; *synthesis* is the strict Euclidean exposition of step-by-step details of the proof; *review* involves reconsidering and re-examining the result and the path taken to it.

DEFINITION AND PROBLEM RECOGNITION

All research begins with a question. Intellectual curiosity is often the foundation for scholarly enquiry. Some questions are not testable. The classic philosophical example is to ask, "How many angels can dance on the head of a pin?" While the question might elicit profound and thoughtful revelations, it clearly cannot be tested with an empirical experiment. Prior to Descartes, this is precisely the kind of question that would engage the minds of learned men.

Their answers came from within. The modern scientific method precludes asking questions that cannot be empirically tested. If the angels cannot be observed or detected, the question is considered inappropriate for scholarly research. A paradigm is maintained as much by the process of formulating questions as it is by the answers to those questions.

By excluding certain types of questions, we limit the scope of our thinking. It is interesting to note, however, that modern physicists have began to ask the same kinds of questions posed by the Eastern philosophers.

"Does a tree falling in the forest make a sound if nobody is there to hear it?" This seemingly trivial question is at the heart of the observer/observed dichotomy. In fact, quantum mechanics predicts that this kind of question cannot be answered with complete certainty. It is the beginning of a new paradigm.

Defining the goals and objectives of a research project is one of the most important steps in the research process. Clearly stated goals keep a research project focused. The process of goal definition usually begins by writing down the broad and general goals of the study.

As the process continues, the goals become more clearly defined and the research issues are narrowed.

Exploratory research goes hand-in-hand with the goal clarification process. The literature review is especially important because it obviates the need to reinvent the wheel for every new research question. More importantly, it gives researchers the opportunity to build on each others work.

The research question itself can be stated as a hypothesis. A hypothesis is simply the investigator's belief about a problem. Typically, a researcher formulates an opinion during the literature review process. The process of reviewing other scholar's work often clarifies the theoretical issues associated with the research question. It also can help to elucidate the significance of the issues to the research community.

The hypothesis is converted into a null hypothesis in order to make it testable. "The only way to test a hypothesis is to eliminate alternatives of the hypothesis."

Statistical techniques will enable us to reject a null hypothesis, but they do not provide us with a way to accept a hypothesis. Therefore, all hypothesis testing is indirect.

PROCESS STRATEGIES

The world keeps changing. It always has and always will. This is the fundamental importance of strategic management, for the use of strategic planning is to make decisions now to guide an organization's future directions.

In terms of future directions, the basic problem of any company is survival. And to survive over the long term, as Lowell Steele of General Electric succinctly summarized, a company must have two strategic capabilities: the ability to prosper and the ability to change.

PROSPERITY

The failure to prosper imperils survival because when expenses exceed income over a long enough period a company fails in bankruptcy. Moveover, prosperity now requires not only profitability but long-term growth. Modern stock markets often value long-term asset growth over short-term dividends. In these days of corporate takeovers, continual corporate growth in earnings and sales is necessary for management to retain control. Together, this combination of continuing profitability and continual growth presents a tough strategic problem because all markets eventually mature and growth in a company's business is limited by the growth of its markets.

In the second half of the twentieth century, this need for continual corporate growth not only created both the driving force for corporate diversification but was also a major cause of the dissolution of large companies. Successful management of a portfolio of different businesses in the same company became a major top corporate leadership challenge. An illustration of this was the successful growth of General Electric in the last two decades of the twentieth century. The CEO who provided strategic management for GE during that time, Jack Welch, became well known in the business world growing GE in two decades from a market value of $12 billion to $500 billion—then a rare corporate feat. In his intended last year at GE,Welch bought more growth for GE by acquiring Honeywell:

- "It was vintage Jack Welch. At the Oct. 23 press conference announcing General Eletric Co.'s $45 billion acquisition of the aeospace and industrial conglomerate Honeywell International Inc, the GE chairman and CEO strutted around the stage, boasting of the promise of the deal... Welch spoke bullishly of the acquisition— 'It's exciting.... ' "

In the fall of the year before Welch's intended retirement, Welch had learned that the Honeywell was agreeing to be acquired by United Technologies, and Welsh rushed in with a higher offer to buy Honeywell. Honeywell would add 7 per cent growth to GE's earnings. GE had revenues of $131 billion with operating profits of $19 billion. Honeywell had $25 billion revenue and $4 billion profits. Growth was important to GE to maintain a high stock value— through continuing growth.

Then Welch's business fame was so extensive that he had earlier received a $ 7.1 million advance for his projected memoirs. It was one of the highest book advances in publishing history; and the publisher, Time Warner's Doubleday, would have to sell at least 1.6 million copies in North America to make a profit:

- Executives of Doubleday had prepared a complete book jacket and marketing plan to pitch to Mr. Welch. Sitting in his shirt sleeves at a conference table, Mr. Welch preferred discussing his ideas about

> management over marketing details... At one point, the conversation turned to Lee Iacocca, the legendary chairman of Chrysler Motors whose autobiography sold 2.6 million copies in hardcover and 3.5 million in document back in North America. Mr. Welch told them that he would consider a book like Mr. Iacocca's a failure, because it was about a personality rather than ideas. Mr.Welch said he preferred the 1964 book by Alfred P. Sloan, MyYears with General Motors...

Strategic management is about ideas. Worth magazine asked several successful CEOs about what they thought was important in the job of the CEO.

Two of them, Koichi Nishimura of Solectron and Eric Schmidt of Novell, responded:

- *Nishimuara*: Four things, I think, are important. First, communicate a vision of where the company is and what you are doing. The second is that when you communicate, you want to be able to motivate people. Third, you want feedback. And fourth, you want to take action.
- *Schmidt*: I think the job breaks down into three parts. First, setting a strategic vision that is implementable. That's number one. Second is recruiting and leading great human beings. The third is worrying about shareholder value. If you follow those three rules, then everything else sort of works.... I think the question from an investor should be, Does the CEO have a strategy that you believe can win?

Strategic vision, communicating vision, recruiting and motivating good people, obtaining feedback, and taking action that creates shareholder prosperity—these are essential elements in corporate leadership. Strategy is ideas about the longterm future.

Change

Attaining the kind of growth and prosperityWelch had achieved atGErequired him to make great changes within the company. On taking office back in 1981,Welch first sold off a hundred of GE's businesses and then consolidated the rest into 14 business groups.

This massive restructuring gaveWelch a tough reputation:

- Neutron Jack, as he is sometimes called, is widely regarded as one of the world's most ruthless managers. The truth is more complex. Some of his actions are indeed harsh, and he antagonized people inside the company and out by fixing something they didn't think was broke. What is becoming clear only now is how those moves fit into a larger plan to strengthen the enterprise and to make its remaining employees more secure.

Welch's success at GE was to strategically change GE from primarily manufacturing businesses into primarily financial service businesses. In 1980, manufacturing produced 70 per cent of GE's revenues, with services contributing 30 per cent. By 1999, manufacturing produced only 26 per cent of revenues, with services having grown to 74 per cent. Welch's strategy was to retain only a selective group of manufacturing businesses and grow financial services: "ChairmanWelch unloaded the consumer electronics division and built financial services into a powerhouse, while keeping GE dominant in turbines and jet engines." Periodic change in a large organization is necessary to help the firm adapt to new times, for new times keep on occurring.

One of Jack Welch's most widely quoted strategic precepts was:

- "Control your own destiny, or someone else will."

The failure to make appropriate changes at the right time, imperials survival because the company may become competitively obsolete in its products, services, and value to customers. Change requires an ability to anticipate the external dynamics of the environments in which a company operates—markets, competition, innovation, government regulation, economic conditions, globalization, and so on. Change also requires an ability to alter a company's directions.

Lowell Steele nicely summarized the emphasis of change as the focus of strategic thinking:

- Strategy is concerned overwhelmingly with questions of change. How much must the enterprise change in order to survive and to continue to prosper? How much change can it finance and manage? How fast can it change? These are profoundly difficult questions.

Strategic management is about the difficult questions of future business—whether it should go and how should it change—a particularly risky set of questions for a large business that is already successful. In many of the older books on strategy, it was presumed that the logic of strategy should begin with a "mission and vision" statement. A mission statement is a statement of what kind of business is the organization; and a vision statement is what kind of business the organization would like to become. However, this older kind of "strategic logic" is not really useful for an ongoing organization, unless the mission changes.

What is useful in vision for an organization is foresight on change to the mission.

The "vision thing" is: how should the mission change to take advantage of future market opportunities and meet future competitive threats? Strategic thinking is not about the mission of the business but changes to the mission.

Strategic Thinking

CEOs like Jack Welch become successful and famous because of their ability to think and act strategically. And because of the fundamental importance of strategy to long-term corporate survival, this ability to think strategically became recognized as an important leadership skill for executives.

For example, one can often see specifications for the ability to strategize in common recruitment advertisements for executive positions, such as the following ad, which appeared in The New York Times in May 2000:

- ... Corporation, a publicly traded manufacturer of products... has an excellent opportunity in its Engineered Products headquarters office.... The successful candidate will have hands-on experience in sourcing components. The position will report to Group VP and be responsible for purchasing in (5) divisions.... The individual must thrive on multitasking, have outstanding negotiating skills, be a good manager of people and projects, and be a strategic thinker. Highly competitive compensation package. For confidential consideration, forward resume and salary requirements to..

This is the fundamental management skill which we address in this book. What is a strategic thinker? How can hands-on experience improve a manager's ability to think strategically? Which practical techniques facilitate effective strategic planning in a large organization? What important strategic concepts used by successful leaders such as Sloan and Welch? Change in a company environment always forces strategic redirection. Changes in automobile technology provided the strategic ground for Sloan's successful management of General Motors, and changes in services and medical technologies provided some of the impetus for Welch's successful strategic management of General Electric.

Information Technology

By the end of the twentieth century, progress in information technology had become the strongest and most pervasive force for strategic change in businesses throughout the world.

One example of IT's impact was Thomas Middelhoff's strategic exhortation to his company in 2000:

- We have to reach every brain to explain that we have nothing less than an industrial revolution. That makes it necessary to change how we see and run our business. That means speed is king. That means we have to be decentralized on the one hand and also more corporate. We have without any question a generational change at Bertelsmann.

The growth of the Internet was a rapid phenomena. For example, in the United States, 14 per cent of the population used the Internet in 1996, jumping to 22 per cent in 1997, 31 per cent in 1998, 38 per cent in 1999, and 44 per cent in 2000. In 2000, the average monthly hours a user spent on line was 19 hours. U.S. consumer spending online had grown from a few million in 1996 to $3 billion dollars in 1997, $7 billion in 1998, $19 billion in 1999, and $36 billion in 2000. Of the $36 billion spent in 2000, $11.0 billion was for travel, $7.7 billion for PCs, $2.4 billion for clothes, $13.4 billion for books, and $13.4 billion for other merchandise. In October 2000, advertising revenues of the Internet in the U.S. totaled $600 million. In business history, the decade of the 1990s will likely be called the decade of the Internet. Its innovation and rapid impact on business made it an interesting and challenging time—that brought to everyone's immediate attention the great importance of progress in information technology upon all business strategy. The dramatic experience of that decade was nicely summarized by Joseph Nocera and Time Carvell:

- The Internet decade has seen the unscrupulous rewarded, the dimwitted suckered, the ill-qualified enriched at a pace greater than at any other time in history. The Internet has been a gift to charlatans, hypemeisters, and merchants of vapour... and despite all that, it still changes everything.

The Internet was an example of a larger class of phenomena in business history called pervasive innovations. William Abernathy and Kim Clark even introduced a new term to strategic management—transilience of innovation—to emphasize the importance of a pervasiveness of an innovation upon the operations of a firm. Transilience means the ability to pass through a system, and it emphasizes the range of business impacts that a transilient innovation may have upon the value-adding capabilities of a firm, passing through its activities to make changes in:

- The kinds of products and way the firm produces products.
- The kinds of customers and markets the business serves.

Abernathy and Clark classified the types of transilient innovation impacts upon a firm by the innovation's potential to alter either product/production or market/customer competencies:

- In product/production competency, innovations may alter
  - Product design
  - Production systems
  - Technical skills and knowledge base
  - Materials and capital equipment
- Under market/customer competency, innovations may alter
  - Customer bases
  - Customer applications
  - Channels of distribution and service
  - Customer knowledge and modes of communication

  For any of these factors the impact of innovation may range from strengthening existing competencies to making existing competencies obsolete. Accordingly, Abernathy and Clark also classified innovations:

  i. A technological innovation that conserved both existing production and market competencies was called a regular innovation.

ii. A technological innovation that conserved existing production competency but altered market competency was called a niche-creation innovation.

iii. A technological innovation that made an existing production competency obsolete but preserved existing market competency was called a revolutionary innovation.

iv. A technological innovation that obsoleted both existing production and market competencies was called an architectural innovation.

The innovation of the Internet was an architectural innovation. Historically, many firms have usually successfully exploited regular or niche creation innovations, for they sustain current operations. But many large firms have perished during revolutionary or architectural innovations. For example, Clayton Christensen examined reasons why large U.S. firms historically have often failed to profit from revolutionary or architectural innovations:

- Resource dependence in large firms, influenced by investors and current customers.
- The emergent markets of radical innovations are early-on perceived as too small for big firm growth needs.
- The ultimate use of radical innovations are often not known early.
- The performance and features of radical new innovations are often not attractive to current markets.

The architectural impact information technology made on business strategy was summarized by Bill Miller who spent a long career and argued that IT was:

- Altering the competitive dynamics of both products and services, leading to the new importance of dominant designs and platforms in product/service strategy.
- Flattening organizational hierarchy or even dissolving boundaries into networked forms, such as "virtual enterprises".
- Impacting management styles through introducing both a "transparency" of the business model to all levels of employees and making their jobs more complex, through the increased need for teaming and direct attention to the bottom-lines of business goals.

Information technologies could strategically impact businesses in different ways:

- A business can be in the information technology business, providing information technology goods and services.
- A business can use information technology as a core technology in its production of goods and delivery of services.
- A business can use information technology as a supporting technology in its design of products/services;

- A business can use information technology as a marketing tool to attract customers to its product/services.

As suggested, address this new challenge of IT to strategic management, using a strategy process in which information technology integrates with business strategy.

Strategic Management

Strategy, planning, budgeting, and knowledge are the four forward-looking activities of management, and it is important that they be clearly distinguished. Budgeting is the allocation of resources for the future operations of an organization. Budgeting is neither planning nor strategy. All organizations budget, but they do not necessarily plan nor strategize. Organizations annually budget in order to allocate the resources for continuing operations. Thus the managers of all organizations do formulate budgets; but not all managers plan or formulate strategy. Planning is thinking out of tactics for the continuing operations of an organization. Planning is not strategy but the implementation of strategy. Managers plan when the tactics of operations change from year to year. Organizations that need to annually plan are those with significant changes in tactics and operations from one year to the next.

Strategy is neither planning nor budgeting. Strategy is the perspective for long term change. Many organizations do not even begin to formulate strategy until an immediate emergency requires change; but by then, it may be too late to formulate effective strategy. Effective strategy requires looking out ahead, anticipating the need for change and preparing for it. A strategy is a change in the direction of the objectives of the operations over a course of years.

Few organizations do strategy when external conditions, markets, and competition all are stable. Strategy is needed when external conditions change—change in technology, change in markets, change in competitors. Knowledge is the basis for improving and controlling the future value-adding operations of a business enterprise. Progress in information technology provides new tools for managing the development of the knowledge assets of the business. Knowledge has been and continues to be the major force in strategic changes in business. Thus in a modern theory of strategy:

- Strategy is change in direction,
- Planning is future tactics,
- Budgeting is allocation of resources,
- Strategic knowledge is future innovation.

Case Study: Merger of AOL and Time Warner

The first historical case as suggested, examine happened just as the twenty-first century began. It is important in illustrating the rapid advance of new forms of business practice due to progress in information technology. One of the new companies in what then was called the "new economy" took over an older and larger business in the "old economy". The case shows how innovation that creates rapid market growth can be exceedingly highly valued by a stock market.

In this case, the market valued the new markets being created by AOL over the older markets then being served by Time Warner. The historical setting was when the then-new electronic commerce, or e-commerce, had spawned a whole new raft of companies and media industry. The booming U.S. stock market of that decade had priced most of these new companies exceedingly high. America Online was one of these, providing service access to the Internet to subscribers. In January, it used its very high market value to merge with an older media company, Time Warner. The business community took this merger as the first sign that e-commerce companies were beginning to mature.

For example, Richard Siklow and Catherine Yang of Business Week wrote:

- On the surface, it looked like just another awesome megadeal... America Online is the acquirer. The trading symbol for the new company, tellingly, is AOL. Given the realities of the New Economy, it could hardly be otherwise. By now, the pattern is clear: the digital will prevail over the analog, new media will grow faster than old, and the leaders of the Net economy will become the 21st century Establishment.

On December 10, 1999, the market capitalization of America Online was about $250 billion dollars, whereas the market capitalization of Time Warner was about $85 billion. The difference was in the stock markets multiplication of their relative price-to-earnings ratios. In the last 12 months, AOL had earnings of about $1 billion, so that its P/E ratio was 250/1. TimeWarner's earnings were about $1.3 billion, so that its P/E ratio was about 65 to 1. Thus AOL's P/E was being valued over TimeWarner's P/E at a multiple of 250/65.

This was the heart of the deal. AOL's vast P/E ratio gave it the leverage to take over Time Warner, and Time Warner was willing to be acquired, hoping the resulting company would have a PE ratio more like AOL's than Time Warner's. Time Warner had a major debt load, which AOL did not have. Moreover, AOL was in a rapidly growing new market, e-commerce, into which Time Warner had tried to enter but failed. Yet in terms of assets-valuable products and steady, proved earnings- Time Warner had a much larger asset base. For example, TimeWarner had 73 million consumer subscriptions compared to AOL's 24 million. Time Warner product brands included:

- Time, People, Sports showed, Fortune, Money magazines
- The cable companies of HBO, Cinemax, CNN, TNT,
- The movie and music production companies of Warner Bros.

In contrast, America Online had AOL, Netscape Navigator, and stakes in several companies. Time Warner brought to the merger a powerhouse of media contentproducing companies, whereas America Online principally brought success in the new electronic businesses of the time. Barry Schuler, then president of AOL Interactive Services, characterized AOL's strengths:"We are good at aggregating eyeballs and delivering services".

AOL purchased Time Warner for $183 billion, but with AOL having just one-fifth TimeWarner's revenue and only 15 per cent of its employees. TimeWarner, an upstart in the 1920s, had become a major media establishment company by the 1990s. The deal was to have AOL shareholders receive one share in the new company for current AOL shares, and for TimeWarner shareholders to receive 1.5 shares for each of theirs. AOL shareholders ended up with 55 per cent of the new company, and Time Warner shareholders with 45 per cent of the new company.

At the time, the Time Warner shareholders expected a market premium of 70 per cent for their shares. What were the strategies of the two CEOs of AOL and Time Warner in creating the merger? Steven Case, founder and then CEO of AOL, had two major strategies. The first was to transmute AOL's high trading multiple of the booming market stock market of 1999 into assets and revenue stream, which would survive any drop in the high-tech companies valuation of that time:

- TimeWarner stood out as the only company with the content, distribution, global reach and customers. Case wants it all: The branded content fromWarner Music, Turner cable networks, and Time Inc. Magazines that can be digitized and sold online. The cable pipes to speed delivery of AOL. A global promotional platform that will save AOL a fortune in ad spending. Relationships with about 73 million subscribers to Time Warner cable systems, HBO, and Time Inc. Magazines.... Time Warner's old-fashioned media properties deliver a stable stream of revenues, about $27.1 billion in 1999, and cash flow, about $6 billion... that are shielded from the vagaries of the Internet world.

From a bottom-up kind of strategic perspective, Case's strategic perspective on the cash-flows of Time-Warner's major publication and television empire would provide AOL a steady and major source of income over the long term. Also from a bottom-up strategic perspective, the acquisition of Time Warner's businesses would provide a step in the direction solving AOL's bandwidth problem. AOL had been providing Internet service of connection through existing copper telephone lines of customers—slow and technically limited to 54 Kbit modem connections. The market demand for Internet connections was broadband. Time Warner owned a major cable company that could provide a much faster broadband connection to its cable customers. Through the merger Time Warner gave AOL access to a market of 20 million cable customers. The CEO of TimeWarner before the merger was Gerald Levin.

His strategic perspective for Time Warner also involved kinds of top-down and bottom-up perspectives of strategy. From the top-down—looking out on the growing importance of the Internet and electronic commerce—Levin saw the need to continue moving TimeWarner into the digital world:

- Levin can empathize as a cable and tech guy stuck atop a content giant.... Before Ted Turner dreamed up CNN, Levin made his reputation by putting HBO onto a satellite in 1975. He's also been burned by technology, notably when Time Warner spent upwards of $100 million on a prototype interactive TV network in Orlando. But his biggest tech bet, on the potential of two-way cable lines, paid off handsomely... TimeWarner's stock a so-so performer for much of the 1990s, surged... during the period since Levin took over in 1993.

From the bottom-up perspective of Time Warner's recent business capabilities, Levin saw a strategic advantage for immediately merging Time Warner into one of the biggest successful players in electronic commerce.

Levin's ventures for Time Warner into the Internet world had not been strategically successful:

- But Levin's hard-won reputation as a tech-savvy executive has faded since then. He passed up the opportunity to buy a portal like Lycos or Excite, and Time Warner's own Internet hub, called Pathfinder, flopped.... So when Case called to offer him the chance to be CEO of AOL Time Warner—the biggest game in cyberspace and media!—why, how could Levin resist?

In July 2000, shareholders of both companies approved the merger, but its success was still not certain.

As Gretchen Morgenson, of The New York Times commented:

- For months, if not years, the virtual has trounced the real in the stock market valuations of Internet concerns vastly exceed the values that investors assigned to companies unlucky enough to own tangible assets... Last week... thetables turned... and investors are about to experience the Great Internet Shakeout... A big indication that the tectonic plates of the virtual world were shifting was the bid of the high flying America Online to acquire the landlocked TimeWarner... 'If calendar 1999 was one of discovery of the internet, 2000 is going to be characterized by much more rigorous scrutiny of the business models... ' "

Before the stock market bubble of dot.com burst, Case had transformed equity of AOL into more equity by acquiring Time Warner.

Case Analysis

In this case, we see two important theoretical ideas about strategy. The first is the importance of information strategy to business strategy. Both AOL and Timer Warner were in the businesses of information. AOL was in the business of being an information channel provider as an Internet service provider. TimeWarner was both in the business of providing information channels and creating information content in these channels. Progress in information technology was bringing both firms into similar business strategies— channels and content. The second idea about strategy is how strategy was formulated by both C¸ EOs, using two kinds of perspectives on their company's future—a top-down perspective from the big picture of the Internet innovation and from a bottom-up perspective of the little picture of the companies' businesses future operations.

Strategic thinking by both CEO's required two kinds of views on the future:

- A perspective on changes in the larger environment of the business and
- A perspective on future business operations about their current strengths and weaknesses to changes in operations for future strengths.

TOP-DOWN AND BOTTOM-UP PERSPECTIVE

Let us first examine the idea that there are two basic perspectives in strategic thinking—strategic views from the top of the organization and strategic views from the bottom.

As showed in Figure, these different perspectives create different views and even different kinds of logics in stratregic thinking:

- A big-picture view with a logic of proceeding from the general to the specific changes of the future.
- An operational-reality view with a logic of proceeding from the specific to the general changes of the future.

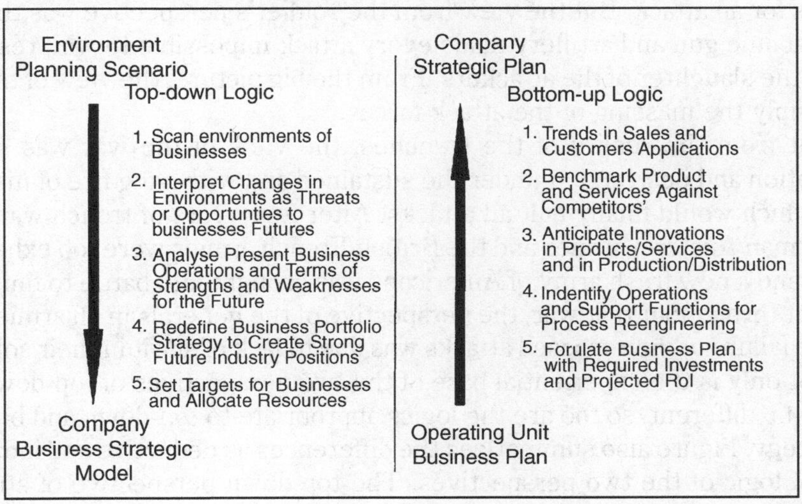

In the logic of strategic thinking, one can always look to the future by describing the big picture of everything and then deducing how changes there can impact upon the particular situation of one's own future action. For example, in this way one can see oneself as a member of a general economic class, cultural class, or generation and ask how one's particular life is impacted by trends and changes happening to these general categories of people and life.

This is the deductive approach to strategy—going from the general trends to the particular descriptions of future life. Also and conversely in the logic of strategic thinking, one can always look at changes in the particular situation of one's future and then generalize that similar changes are happening to others like oneself. For example, in this way one can generalize changes in one's own life as an exemplar of the kinds of general categories of other people and lives. This is the inductive approach to strategy—going from the particular examples to the general descriptions of future life. At the top of an organization, information to see the big picture is more readily available there than at the bottom of an organization. Conversely, at the bottom of an organization, information to see the reality of operations is more readily available there than at the top of the organization.

A famous and bitter example of these differences in information between the big-picture-of-the-world and the reality-of-operations was the difference in perspective between the generals and the soldiers in the First World War in Europe in the early twentieth century. From 1914 to 1918, the war stagnated into trench warfare, with the generals on both sides planning one more great battle to win the war. Each battle resulted in thousands of deaths with no substantial gain in territory or weakening of the ability of the other army to fight.

The view from the general's perspective was the massing of artillery and soldiers for an attack. But the view from the soldier's perspective was that the new machine gun and artillery made every attack impossible to win, resulting only in the slaughter of the attackers. From the big picture, the view of the war was simply the massing of the attack forces.

But from the reality of the trenches, the view of the war was simply devastation and destruction under the sustained and withering fire of machine guns, which would finally halt all attacks. After four years of trench war, both the German/Austrian armies and the British/French armies were too exhausted to win, and a new fresh army of Americans was brought into battle to finish the war. But throughout that war, the perspective of the generals in all armies was that the failure of their massed attacks was due to lack of spirit in their soldiers.

Not only is the experiential base of the two perspectives of top-down and bottom-up different, so too are the logics appropriate to top-down and bottom-up strategy. Figure also summarizes the differences as deductive and inductive kinds of logic of the two perspectives. The top-down perspective of strategy uses a deductive logic that begins with the great and goes down towards the small.

In formulating strategy, top leadership should look around at the environments of the firm and its businesses to:

- Scan the environments of a firm to identify major future trends and changes in government, the economy, territorial markets and competitors, and in the scientific and technological culture.
- Interpret the changes as threats and opportunities to the businesses of the firm.
- Analyse the present firm's activities in terms of strengths and weaknesses to face such threats or seize such opportunities.
- Redefine the missions of the firm's businesses to match the future operations to future threats and opportunities.
- Set goals and targets for businesses to meet in a proper time horizon.

In contrast, at the operating levels of businesses in a firm, managers should look to the strategic immediacy of the business's markets, competitors, operations, and knowledge:

- Examine the trends in sales in the markets of the businesses of the firm and identify innovations that can alter these markets.
- Benchmark a firm's products and processes against competitors' products and processes and identify changes needed to maintain or surpass any competitor's current advantages.
- Investigate progress in information technology and in the knowledge bases of the business's product and production processes.
- Reexamine current operations and control, and identify innovations in operations and control of operations needed to adapt to changes in market, competition, and new information and knowledge capabilities.
- Formulate a business plan, with targets for market-share and profits along with required investments and resources needed to achieve the plan.

These different perspectives of the big-picture and trench-reality are both vital to a good strategy process. Therefore, what is critical to good strategy formulation is the interaction of these perspectives. Now, although the top-down and bottomup perspectives in strategic thinking are important to formulating good strategy, coordinating them is extremely difficult to pull off in a large organization because of the hierarchy of authority. In large organizations, these perspectives become quite different because of the hierarchical nature of authority.

For example in a diversified firm, there are usually at least four levels of management hierarchy:

- *Firm level*: Board, CEO and firm executive team.
- *Business level*: President and business executive team.

- *Department level*: Department head and staff.
- *Office level*: Office manager and assistant.

The hierarchical levels of authority in a firm usually begin at the top of the firm level with a board of directors and a chief executive officer. The CEO and his or her executive team are responsible for the strategy of the whole firm. This strategy includes what businesses are and should be within the firm and the overall financial performance of the firm. The planning scenario needed at this level should include anticipation of change in all the industries of the firm's businesses.

The bottom-up input to the firm's strategy should be provided by the participation of the business's presidents to the CEO in the strategy process. At the next organizational level, below that of the firm, is the business unit, and its president is responsible for strategy for the business as a whole.

Part of the business's planning scenario is the industrial context of the firm as well as the territories and cultures in the markets to which the business sells. Another part of its planning scenario are goals and targets specified for it by the firm-level strategy, the strategic firm model.

The outcome of strategic planning for the business will be a strategic business model specifying changes for its future policies. The final two levels within a company, department and office, are levels in which managers should provide bottom-up information to the business level in formulating the strategic business model. Policies of this model then provide the guidance for planning and improving operations and activities of the departments and offices.

Since it is organizationally natural for the bottom of the organization to listen more closely to the top than for the top to listen to the bottom, two kinds of misunderstandings are common in strategic thinking in large organizations:

- The managers of operating units frequently do not think that the top executives understand the strategic problems and challenges in operations.
- The top executives frequently do not believe the operating units are trying hard enough to implement the strategic goals they formulate.

This is the first challenge of strategic thinking in large organizations, to encourage real and accurate communication of strategic perspectives between the top and the bottom. Therefore, in a good strategy process, one needs to formalize these two perspectives as two views of a firm's totalities, those of the environments of the firm and those of the operations of the firm. The top-to-down perspective looks at the big picture and formulates strategic policies for long-term direction. The bottomto- top perspective looks at the specific nuts and bolts of the company's operations to try to carry out the desirable long-term direction.

- The critical problem in the strategy process of any organization is to facilitate a positive, constructive, and creative interaction between the two perspectives in strategic thinking.

Moreover, this problem is exacerbated by the periodic and non-continuous requirements of strategic thinking. The actual process of formulating strategy is infrequent but recurrent, exploratory and interactive with the different experiential bases of the top management and of lower management levels.

While the results of strategic planning may look as if created by a linear process, the strategic process is non-linear and recursive and interactive with different experiential bases of the company top and bottom. For example, Arthur A.

Thompson and A. J. Strickland nicely summarized the recurrent nature of the strategy process:

- The march of external and internal events guarantees that a company's vision, objectives, strategy, and implementation approaches will have to be revisited, recon sidered, and eventually revised. This is why the task of evaluating performance and initiating corrective adjustments is both the end and the beginning of the strategic management cycle.

Since the strategic management process is interactive and cyclic, the information flow must be recurrently both bottom-up and top-down between the views of the environment and the business. The cyclic nature of strategic planning is also coupled into the budget cyclic of any business, going from yearly planning to yearly planning.

Furthermore, in a multibusiness firm, there are two kinds of the top-down and bottom-up perspectives:

- Firm-to-business perspectives.
- Businesses-to-business divisions perspectives.

This makes the top-down and bottom-up communications in a multibusiness firm even more challenging than in a single business firm. Using an interactive approach to the strategy process is important in the practice of strategic management because the principle cause of failure in the strategy of large organizations has often been due to a lack of proper internal interaction between the two strategic perspectives:

- Inadequate top-down perspective of innovative changes in environments.
- Inadequate bottom-up perspectives of the need for new business models for innovative change.
- Inadequate communication between executive levels and operational levels about needed strategic change.

How can leadership in a large organization avoid these common kinds of mistakes in strategy processes? Good interactions between the strategic perspectives from the top and from the bottom are necessary to create a potentially profitable vision of the future—a strategic vision of the challenges, opportunities, and direction of the future business and how operations need to change to succeed in that future.

The planning process in a large organization can use two kinds of strategic techniques to assist this:

- A strategic technique for effectively summarizing the changes in the environment's future is called a "planning scenario."
- A strategic technique for effectively summarizing the desirable changes in operations for such a future environment is called a "strategic business model."

PLANNING SCENARIOS AND STRATEGIC BUSINESS MODELS

It is always important to strategically think about the big picture of changes in the environments of business. It is equally important to strategically think about the smaller picture of how a particular business can exploit the business opportunities in that change. For strategic thinking in a large organization, we need to consider what kinds of techniques can formally assist groups of managers reach to consensus about what is important:

- About changes of the future and
- Their implications for future operations.

To help a group to strategically think about the big picture, the technique of the planning scenario is effective. To help a group strategically think about operational realities of the future, the technique of a strategic business model is effective. These two techniques can help a large organization describe the two key totalities of strategic thinking—future environments of the company and the future company itself.

Planning Scenario

Strategic thinking needs to grasp the big picture of changes in the environments of a company. For example two of the CEOsWorth interviewed in 2000, Raymond Gilmartin CEO of Merck and Koichi Nishimura CEO of Solectron, commented:

- *Gilmartin*: Part of leadership is saying in touch with what's going on outside your company.... You need to gather information to see the patterns, to tell if you're on the wrong track, to take risks and make decisions that go against the grain.
- *Nishimura*: Getting it right comes from pattern recognition.You integrate information and you go "humm."

Gathering information and constructing patterns of trends and changes in the environments of business is the purpose of scenario planning in the strategy process. To systematically gather information and create insightful "humm patterns," the strategy technique of scenario narrative is very useful. All strategy is based upon assumptions about the future and its business opportunities and challenges. A modern technique for exploring and expressing these pictures of the future is called a scenario, and when used for planning, a planning scenario. Scenario planning uses scenario narratives and societal models. Scenario narratives provide a method for describing and thinking about the possible impacts of the future upon a current business. Strategic stories envision adventures of the business in the future. The future will be an adventure that will challenge business. Experience is always of the present, with memories and stories of the past. The future consists of anticipations and/ or surprises and plans for the future conceived in the present.

All existence is always in the present:

- In the mind only exists intelligent perception of the past and imagination of the future.

As we saw in the case of Rakuten, the major changes in the environments of a business are changes in structures of the society in which the business operates. To build a planning scenario that captures this kind of complexity and completeness of possible future change, one needs to use a general classification of all the societal environments of a business. In all human societies, traditional or modern, there have been general classes of social patterns that create societal structures. These include categories of territory, culture, economy, government.

Planning scenarios should address issues of change in the large patterns of society, such as:

- Will there be changes in how the control of territory is decided in the future?
- Will there be changes in the culture of the nation?
- Will there be changes in the economy of the nation, world?
- Will there be changes in government of a nation?

Strategic Business Model

Strategic thinking also needs to think about what kind of business model can meet the challenges and exploit the future opportunities in the environments of the company. So the second strategic totality to be considered in the planning process is the future of the business of the corporation. The strategic technique effective for this is a model of how one's company now operates but should change in the future, a strategic business model. Strategic models of the business of a corporate summarize the future policies of the company which will prepare it to perform in the future.

The strategic importance of the concept of a 'business model' was nicely expressed by Geoffrey Colvin, commenting on the troubles Xerox was having in 2000:

- "The quote of the year for 2000 comes from Xerox CEO Paul Allaire... He gets the Distinguished Service Cross for extraordinary executive heroism because he told analysts in a conference call, 'We have an unsustainable business model.' In the past CEOs of big, established companies didn't say things like that. They didn't tell the people who rate their stock that the way they make money doesn't work anymore... The largest fact of life in business today is that virtually every company... has to change its business model to make it sustainable in the Internet worked, infotech-based world."

A business model is an abstraction of a business identifying how that business makes money. Business models are abstracted about how inputs to an organization are transformed to value-adding outputs. All models of organizations are models of kinds of open systems. One important version of this was the now famous value-added model of Michael Porter. As a value-adding open-system model, an organization is described as taking resources from its environment and transforming them to value-added outputs sold back into its market environment. The transformation of input resources into output products/services is performed by the processes and operations of the business. The Porter model is only one of several kinds of business models, one can use in strategic planning.

- A strategic business model abstracts the basic value-adding transformation that describes how a business makes its money.

Strategic thinking about how a business now makes money and how it must change to continue making money is the 'bottom-line' for strategic management. For example, in thinking about the future capabilities of an organization, Clayton Christensen and Michael Overdorf emphasized the need to consider resources, processes, and values in an existing organization compared to the challenge of needed change. The resources of a business consist of tangible resources and intangible resources. The processes of a business consist of the activities and procedures with which a business procures resources, adds value, and produces and sells products and services. Thus dealing with change also requires determining what changes in processes and procedures are necessary to produce new kinds of value and/or address the needs of new kinds of customers. The value dimension of an organization are the standards by which management and other employees set priorities and judge the importance of activities and results.

Values are standards about how resources are used and how processes are run, as Christensen and Overdorf comment:

- An organization's values the standards by which employees set priorities.... A company's values reflect its cost structure or its business model because they define the rules its employees must follow for the company to prosper.
- A strategic business model is a systematic list of the policies that will guide the future specification of inputs, outputs, processes and values of the complete operations of the business of the corporation.

The importance of conceiving of a good business model was emphasized by the experience of the many new companies begun in the Internet growth years of 1996–2000. Then hundreds of these dot.coms were begun with extensive venture capital funding, and many without having a viable business model. Next in the year 2000, over 125 of these companies folded as they ran out of capital and had not yet become profitable.

The often repeated moral then was that a good business model was necessary for profitability and survival. Strategic business models need to be constructed around strategic issues of change in markets and innovation, competition and structure, operations and control, information and knowledge, asking strategic questions such as:

- What are likely to be the changes in the markets that a business will serve and innovations that will impact these markets?
- What are likely to be changes in competition against which a business will compete and in the structure of the industrial sectors in which competition occurs?
- What is likely to be the progress in information technologies that a business can strategically exploit and how can this improve the knowledge assets of a business?
- What must be the changes in operations and control of business processes that the business needs to implement to be efficient and effective in its future value-adding processes?

STRATEGIC VISION

In a large organization, strategic vision needs to arise from strategic thinking exercises of constructing planning scenarios of the future environments of the company and a strategic business model of the company's business(es). The reason this is so important in a large organization is that the experiences of being at the top and at the bottom are so different that both top and bottom perspectives are severely limited.

From the top, it is really hard to see the real problems in the trenches; and from the experiences at the bottom, it is equally hard to see the pressures of control on the organization. A good strategic vision is essential in strategic planning because strategic change cannot occur without top leadership's having a vision of and a commitment to change.

The relationship of leadership to strategic vision and change is critical in the strategy process:

- Strategic vision is the fundamental responsibility of leadership since only top management has the authority to make major changes in operating organizations.
- Strategic change is only periodically necessary; but to be effective such change must be envisioned, anticipated, and planned.

- Sources for strategic vision are either external in the environments of the organization or internal as opportunities developed within the organization.

For example, Worth magazine interviews with some successful CEOs in 2000 also showed their concern with the importance of providing visionary leadership, such as in comments by Koici Nishimura of Solectron and Raymond Gilmartin of Merck and by Eric Schmidt of Novell:

- *Nishimura*: When you are leading a company, you have to figure out, conceptually, what you are trying to do. Once you have decide that, and you think it's okay, the second thing you have to figure out is: What tactics are you going to use... ?You continually have to ask: Are the assumptions I made still good? My job is to continually reassess the assumptions or the foundation that the company is built on.
- *Gimartin*: You need to have a vision that is the anchor point for what you're doing.... There needs to be some form of overarching statement that makes sense and on which the ECO stakes his or her job.
- *Schmidt*: Leadership is defined about perception, not just reality. So there's always this tension in leadership to overhype. And to make promises that you can't keep and articulate things that can't happen.... You want to do some level of overselling, but the problem is that the people you're communicating to are smart. If they think you're a snake-oil salesman, then your whole credibility goes to zero. So leadership is also defined by credibility.

Why leadership in large organizations often fails to envision and prepare for change arises from the nature of leadership in large organizations. In large organizations, leaders are usually selected as those who are committed to doing more of the same. Managers often rise to leadership because they embody a vision of the organization's past. The vision of the past represented a tested story of success. Past leadership built organizational structures and culture that evolved into a successful company.

Later when the business environment changes, the earlier structures and cultures and leadership became ineffectual in the new conditions. Yet despite the tendency for management not to make changes, still the need for long-term change is indigenous in organizations because organizations have little control over change in their environments—and thus they may be forced by competition to change or die. Many students of strategy and organization have argued that instability is a periodic experience for all organizations.

For example, Michael Tushman and Elaine Romanelli argued that organizations experience periods of relative stability interrupted by sharp strategic reorientations. They and others have seen organizational change as a kind of evolution, stimulated by responding to change in business and economic structures. Michael Tushman and Elaine Romanelli with Beverly Virany nicely summarized the connection between strategic vision, environmental change and organizational decline:

- At least part of the reason for substantial organization decline in the face of environmental change lies with the executive team. A set of executives who have been historically successful may become complacent with existing systems and/or be less vigilant to environmental changes. Or, even if an executive team registers external threat, they may not have the energy and/or competence to effectively deal with fundamentally different competitive conditions. The importance of an effective executive team is accentuated in industries where the rate of change in underlying technologies is substantial.

Also students of innovation have documented that a major source of changes in the business environment and within the economic structure consists of applied knowledge discontinuities, which Tushman called "technology discontinuities" and later Clayton Christensen called "disruptive change". Progress in information technology has created many disruptive changes.

As an example, Tushman and his colleagues looked at the mini computer industry, focusing on fifty-nine firms started between 1967 and 1971. They compared firm records of success and failure over a subsequent 14-year period. In their analysis of the reasons some firms survived and many failed, they argued that one must understand how the conduct of the firm in the context of the changing economic structure affected the performance of the firm. The conduct of firms consists of the strategic, tactical and organizational activities guided by the executive team. Conduct must alter as the context of the firm changes when alterations in the economic structure affect competition.

Changes can arise from:

- Technological changes,
- Market changes,
- Resource changes,
- Regulation changes,
- Competitive changes.

Successful leadership performance depends upon the executive team's ability to envision, anticipate a correct future and formulate a correct strategy and organization for the future operations of the business. Such vision, strategy and organization correctly anticipates technological opportunities for new products, market changes for new needs and applications, resource changes that affect the availability and cost of materials and energy, and changes in government regulations that affect safety, monopolies, taxes, and so on. When industries faced changes, Tushman et al. found that those firms whose executive teams lacked vision and made no changes in strategy and organization and product failed after the change occurred. Even those firms with correct visionbut whose executives constantly made changes in strategy, organization, and product failed.

The firms that survived and prospered through a competitive discontinuity, a disruptive change, were those whose executive teams:

- Envision and correctly anticipate the discontinuity and prepare for it with appropriate product strategy and reorganization.
- After making the appropriate strategic change, hold a steady course to produce proper products/services with quality and low costs.

It is particularly difficult for a company to formulate a new product strategy when it hits a competitive discontinuity generated by new applied knowledge.

The principal reasons in the difficulty of formulating a new product strategy in a competitive discontinuity are:

- The technical uncertainties of a new applied knowledge vision.
- The differing perspectives among the different product-group managers and the technical staff about that vision.

For a company to develop a new next-generation product-line strategy, the whole company must fight out different visions about the product plans in a new applied knowledge situation.

To formulate a next-generation product plan for an applied-knowledge competitive-discontinuity, it is necessary for a high-level executive to envision and force the strategic issue and to organize the effort necessary to formulate and implement a new strategy for the whole company.

Competitive discontinuities are a common problem for a firm initially successful in a radically new industry because applied knowledge in the industry continues to progress for a time.

The reason for the crisis is that competitive discontinuities due to rapid progress in applied knowledge force not only changes in product strategy but changes in business strategy to exploit the changing market. This is why competitive discontinuities are strategically challenging. And this is why strategic vision that foresees discontinuities and strategic planning that prepares for discontinuities are the key challenges of strategic thinking.

PLANNING

Strategic plans need to be formulated as guided by the direction in a strategic vision.Yet the actual implementation of a strategic plan will require that it be put into action through a sequence of operational plans.

Accordingly, we next need to review the differences between strategic and operational plans:

- Strategic planning is a concern for and laying out of the directions for the long-term future.
- Operational planing is a concern for and laying out of the directions for the short-term future.

The conceptual duality of controlling both long-term and short-term events makes strategic planning and operational planning complementary cognitive functions of management. In the case of HP, it had good operational planning capability but not good long-term strategic planning capability. The ink-jet product success was a result of good short-term product development and planning.

Stasis and Change in Operations

Operational planning is aimed at controlling the steadiness of organizational operations, or stasis. Stasis in management attention attends to the immediate efficiency of operations, for it is efficiency that in the short term determines profitability in a commercial organization. Efficient repetition of operations, as the production and sales of a large volume of products, creates economies of scale, and upon such economies rests profitability of operations. In the long-term performance, management practice additionally needs to focus upon making desirable changes for future operations, strategy. Strategy focuses on the long-term, mediate effectiveness of operations—not to the shortterm, immediate efficiency of operations.

- Efficiency of business operations produces profits in the short term, but effectiveness of business operations creates survivability in the long term.

It is the effectiveness of business strategy in the long term that creates the right kinds of products and services for market share and dominance. It is in market share and dominance that a business survives over time.

Thus both stasis of current operations and change in future operations are essential to strategic management thinking. Stasis produces the short-term, immediate benefits of organizations, whereas change produces the long-term, benefits mediated through intervening events.

Stasis and change are complementary. Few steady-state operations can go on forever without needing change because many aspects of an organization are not static—markets, technology, competition, politics, etc. Thus periodically—at the beginning of an organization, through the growth of an organization, and at subsequent critical periods of an organization—operations need to change for the organization's long-term effectiveness and survival.

Planning needs both to continually optimize stasis and periodically change stasis:

- Operational planning focuses upon optimization of stasis in operations in the immediate, short-time horizon.
- Strategic planning focuses upon change in future operations for survival in the mediate, long-term horizon.

Both operational planning and strategic planning become integrated in the annual budgeting activity of organizations. But conceptually they are different.

Thus in the planning and implementation procedures of strategic management, the procedures need to facilitate both short-term and long-term planning.

Implementing Operational and Strategic Plans

How is operational planning implemented? How is strategic planning implemented? To answer these questions, we need to remind ourselves of the levels of decision logic in the control of an organization's activities. Organizations conduct repetitive activities in their operations to add value— such as manufacturing and selling products or providing and delivering services. Thus the ground logical level of any organization is its repetitive activities that directly transform inputs of resources into value-added outputs of products/services.

The scheme, or order, of how repetitive activities are to be carried out in an organization is called its "operations." Operations are the patterns of order that govern, or control, activities. For example, in automobile manufacturing operations it is the order of the assembly line, where engines are first assembled in parallel with chassis and body assemblies and then engines are mounted onto chassis and then bodies are attached. In a large organization, precisely how these operations are to be conducted are specified as organizational "procedures." Procedures are the instructions on how to carry out an operation.

For example, in automobile manufacturing, there are designs which specify the tooling for production and standards for performing operations. Procedures as designs and standards control operations. The next decision-logic level in organizations is "policies," which specify the purpose of procedures. For example, in automobile manufacturing, policies determine the types of autos to be designed, the extent of annual model change, the markets to be targeted for the auto designs, the cost targets for production, and so on. Policies control procedures.

The highest decision-logic level in organizations is "strategies," which provide the directions of change for policies. For example, in automobile manufacturing, strategies determine the product lines to be produced, acquisition of new brands, extent of vertical integration of production, and so on. Strategies control changes in policies.

In summary, the hierarchy of decision logic in an organization consists of the following control levels:

- Activities that transform inputs to outputs,
- Operations that control activities,
- Procedures that control operations,
- Policies that control procedures,
- Strategies that control policies,

The relationship of operational and strategic planning can now be seen in how their implementation affects differently these levels of decision-control in organizations. Operational planning is implemented by changing the lower-two levels of operations and procedures, whereas strategic planning is implemented by changing the upper two levels of policies and strategy: 0perational planning specifies operations and procedures and strategic planning specifies policies and strategy:

- Operational plans are implemented through targets of operations and changes of procedures.
- Strategic plans are implemented through targets of strategy and changes in polices.

Furthermore, when we look in detail at these two kinds of planning as suggested, find that their logics and processes are really very different:

- Operations planning uses the logics of known action and specific directions to specify how to achieve specific goals of repetitive types of action.
- Strategic planning uses the logics of unknown action and preparation to launch exploration into action never previously experienced.

The logic of planning is the logic of operations—knowing how to get to someplace we have gone before. The logic of strategy is the logic of exploration— preparing to go someplace we have never gone before. In the logic of an operational plan, one can clearly state the ends and means of action—goals and tactics— since we have performed this operational action before, repetitively, and we understand what it takes to do it.

Thus operations plans can be summarized in bullet form, for everyone involved can fill in the story's details—been there, done that—know how to do it again. An operations plan just says how much we are going to do again. However, in the logic of a strategic plan, one is going exploring, rather that repeating an action previously performed. The logic of strategy consists—not of spelling out the means and ends of known action—but of refining perception, creating commitments, preparing for action. Together—perception, commitment, and preparation—constitute the real logic of strategic exploration.

Strategy is not planning:

- Strategy is change in long-term direction.
- Strategic planning lays out the sequence of steps to implement long-term change.
- Operational planning details the immediate steps of implementing long-term change and of continuing stasis.

STRATEGY PROCESS

Now we can put these ideas together and depict an effective modern strategy process. We recall that strategic thinking is a process, and a strategic plan is a result of the process.

The problem of a strategy process in a large organization is how to have planning procedures that:

- Focuses management thinking on long-term prosperity.
- Anticipates relevant change.
- Stimulates constructive interaction between top-down and bottom-up perspectives.
- Creates effective strategic vision.
- Transforms strategy into action.

Strategic Planning Teams

Look at the first step in Figure, which shows that the first two steps in creating a strategic thinking process in an organization is to establish a planning process that encourages the interaction of top-down and bottom-up perspectives by,

- Forming top-down and bottom-up strategic-planning teams.
- Scheduling interactions between teams.

The composition of a top-down strategy team needs to consist of a firm-level planning staff and executives of the businesses or divisions that compose the company. A bottom-up strategy team should consist of managers of the businesses in the firm.

Since there are hierarchical differences in the authority positions in these teams, it is important to formally schedule interactive presentations of their planning work to one another as the planning efforts proceed to stimulate appropriate interaction of perspectives.

PlanningScenario and Strategic Business Model

Look again at Figure, which shows that the next step is to focus the strategy teams upon creating formal descriptions of the environments and the businesses as outputs of the interactions.

A planning scenario anticipates from the top-down perspective the future environments of the company.

Formulating such a scenario requires anticipating changes in the structures of the societies in which a company operates. In industrialized societies, four general structures exist, economic structures, governmental structures, territorial structures, and cultural structures.

The technique of scenario planning provides a systematic way of examining trends and forecasts of possible and likely changes in the future in these structures. A strategic model of a business summarizes from the bottom-up perspective the intended future policies of the business.

- The kind of strategic business model one uses to depict future business policies depends upon which kind of corporate performance one wishes to optimize.

In formulating any strategic business model, important strategic issues are those of markets and innovation competition and structure, operations and control, and information and knowledge.

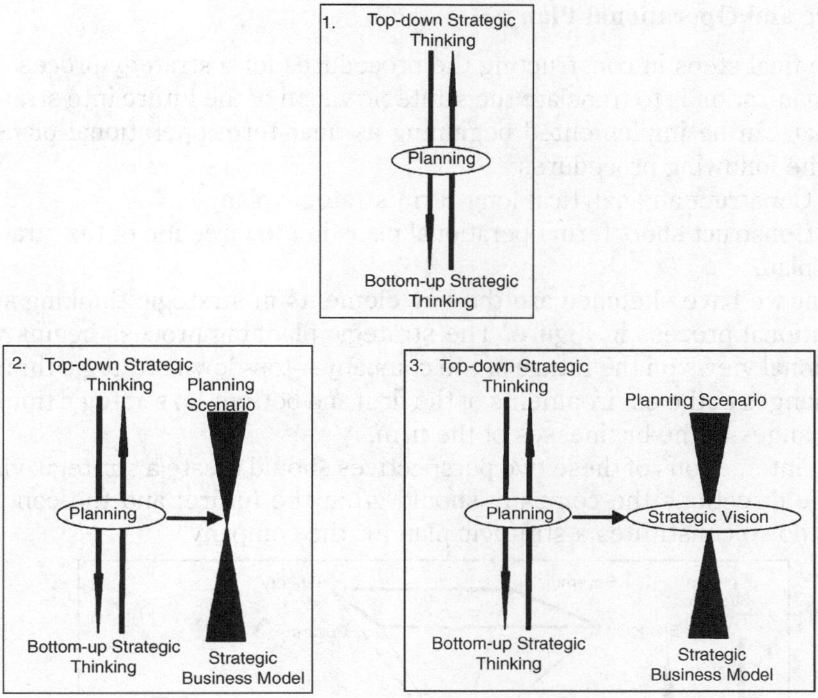

Strategic Vision

The procedures for creating a planning scenario and strategic business models facilitate the two perspectives on the future from the general to the particular and from the particular to the general; and from this interaction the third step to add in the planning process is an integrative picture of the future:

- Formulate an intuitive strategic vision.

A strategic vision is an intuitive view of the future. For example, in the merger of AOL and Time Warner, both CEOs, Case and Levin, developed a strategic vision of the future merged company, that is, altering boundaries of AOL and Time Warner to become a new firm with the boundaries of content creation and delivery.

For AOL, Case's vision was to vertically integrate AOL from media service delivery back into media content creation. Acquiring the media-content creation businesses of Time Warner would change AOL's future business capabilities.

For TimeWarner, Levins' vision was to merge TimeWarner into a major e-commerce business Vision results from the intuitive cognitive function of the mind—vision is a synthetic view of a totality—a gestalt. How to facilitate intuition in a group setting is a difficult problem.

For now, theimportant point is to emphasize that the procedures for strategic plan need to create a strategic vision arising from the team interactions of constructing a planning scenario and a strategic business model.

Strategic and Operational Plan

The final steps in constructing the procedures for a strategy process in a large organization is to translate the strategic vision of the future into strategic plans that can be implemented beginning as near-term operational plans by adding the following procedures:

- Construct an analytical long-term strategic plan.
- Construct short-term operational plans in the direction of the strategic plan.

What we have sketched are the key elements in strategic thinking as an organizational process in Figure. The strategic planning process begins with bidirectional views on the future of the company—top-down strategic thinking about changes in the environments of the firm and bottom-up strategic thinking about changes in the businesses of the firm.

The interactions of these two perspectives should create a strategic vision about the directions the company should go in the future; and the concrete steps to do so constitutes a strategic plan for the company.

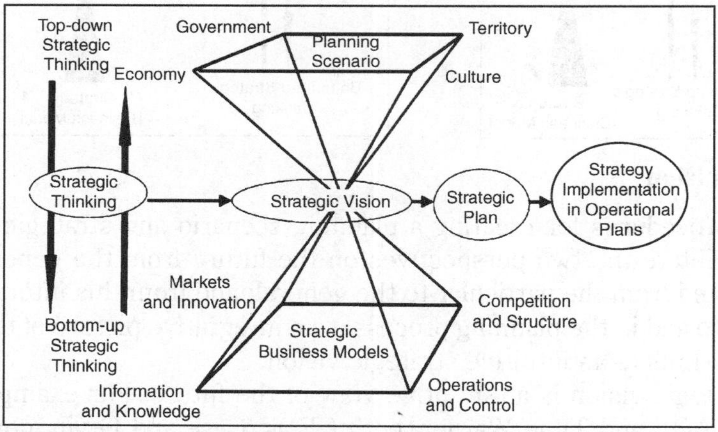

The top-down view arises from the construction of a planning scenario, which anticipates the kinds of changes in the environments that will be relevant to the businesses of the firm in the future. The bottom-up view arises from the construction of a strategic business model for each business of the firm.

This model anticipates the kinds of changes desired and needed to prepare the firm and its businesses for a competitive and successful future.

Multi-Business Firm Strategy

The strategy process depicted in Figure assumes a company is a singlebusiness firm, yet most large corporations are multi-business firms.

Strategy changes dramatically at the different levels of a multi-business corporation. For example, Lowell Steele emphasized the perspective differences in strategy between single and multiple business companies:

- One must distinguish between single-business companies and multi-business companies. Strategic planning at the corporate level for a multi-business enterprise cannot be the same for a company with a single line or closely related product lines."

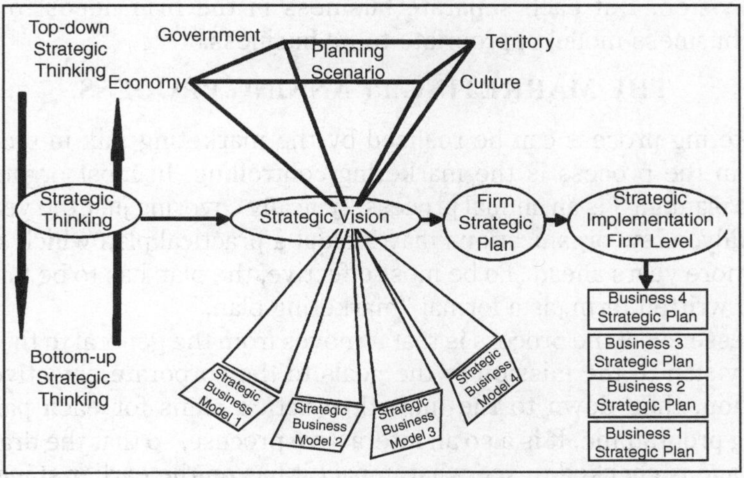

Fig. Strategy Process—Multibusiness Firm

The strategic differences arise from the kinds of competition each kind of company,—single-business or diversified-businesses—faces. The single business company finds its principle competition in the marketplace—face-to-face with customers and competitors also directly in contact with customers:

- Competition for a single-business entity is in the market place, offering superior value to customers. If it does that effectively, its performance will be satisfactory— provided that its markets permit an acceptable rate of return.

Accordingly, competitive strategy for the single business company must focus primarily upon its products and services—product, production, and marketing strategies. Strategy needs to be focused upon the variables that directly add value to customers, such as product attributes, quality, cost, safety, differentiation, distribution channels, advertising, and so on. In contrast, the multiple-business company is primarily a financial holder of businesses, so that it performance is not in the customer market but in the financial market:

- Competition for the multi-business enterprise is in the capital markets: Does its present portfolio of businesses and mode of management produce a competitive rate of return... ? Multi-business strategy focuses first and foremost on portfolio optimization— what mix of sources of revenue is desired and what allocation of resources will best bring about this preferred mix.

Multi-business company strategy must focus principally upon variables that directly impact the rate-of-return of capital, such as business portfolio, position of a business in its industry, business investments, business leadership, business acquisitions and divestitures, and so on. Accordingly, the strategy process for a multi-business firm needs to be modified as shown in Figure. Therein a common planning scenario is still appropriate for the entire firm and a common strategic vision. But each separate business in the firm needs to create a strategic business model appropriate to its business.

THE MARKETING PLANNING PROCESS

Marketing process can be realised by the marketing mix in step 4. The last step in the process is the marketing controlling. In most organizations, "strategic planning" is an annual process, typically covering just the year ahead. Occasionally, a few organizations may look at a practical plan which stretches three or more years ahead. To be most effective, the plan has to be formalized, usually in written form, as a formal "marketing plan."

The essence of the process is that it moves from the general to the specific, from the vision to the mission to the goals to the corporate objectives of the organization, then down to the individual action plans for each part of the marketing programme. It is also an interactive process, so that the draft output of each stage is checked to see what impact it has on the earlier stages, and is amended.

Marketing Planning Aims and Objectives

Behind the corporate objectives, which in themselves offer the main context for the marketing plan, will lie the "corporate mission," which in turn provides the context for these corporate objectives. In a sales-oriented organization, the marketing planning function designs incentive pay plans to not only motivate and reward frontline staff fairly but also to align marketing activities with corporate mission.

This "corporate mission" can be thought of as a definition of what the organization is, of what it does: "Our business is ...". This definition should not be too narrow, or it will constrict the development of the organization; a too rigorous concentration on the view that "We are in the business of making meat-scales," as IBM was during the early 1900s, might have limited its subsequent development into other areas.

On the other hand, it should not be too wide or it will become meaningless; "We want to make a profit" is not too helpful in developing specific plans. Abell suggested that the definition should cover three dimensions: "customer groups" to be served, "customer needs" to be served, and "technologies" to be used. Thus, the definition of IBM's "corporate mission" in the 1940s might well have been: "We are in the business of handling accounting information for the larger US organizations by means of punched cards." Perhaps the most important factor in successful marketing is the "corporate vision."

Surprisingly, it is largely neglected by marketing textbooks, although not by the popular exponents of corporate strategy - indeed, it was perhaps the main theme of the book by Peters and Waterman, in the form of their "Superordinate Goals." "In Search of Excellence" said: "Nothing drives progress like the imagination.

The idea precedes the deed." If the organization in general, and its chief executive in particular, has a strong vision of where its future lies, then there is a good chance that the organization will achieve a strong position in its markets. This will be not least because its strategies will be consistent and will be supported by its staff at all levels. In this context, all of IBM's marketing activities were underpinned by its philosophy of "customer service," a vision originally promoted by the charismatic Watson dynasty. The emphasis at this stage is on obtaining a complete and accurate picture.

A "traditional" - albeit product-based - format for a "brand reference book" was suggested by Godley more than three decades ago:

- *Financial data*: Facts for this part will come from management accounting, costing and finance parts.
- *Product data*: From production, research and development.
- *Sales and distribution data*: Sales, packaging, distribution parts.
- *Advertising, sales promotion, merchandising data*: Information from these departments.
- *Market data and miscellany*: From market research, who would in most cases act as a source for this information. His sources of data, however, assume the resources of a very large organization. In most organizations they would be obtained from a much smaller set of people.

It is apparent that a marketing audit can be a complex process, but the aim is simple: "it is only to identify those existing factors which will have a significant impact on the future plans of the company." It is clear that the basic material to be input to the marketing audit should be comprehensive.

The best approach is to accumulate this material continuously, as and when it becomes available; since this avoids the otherwise heavy workload involved in collecting it as part of the regular, typically annual, planning process itself - when time is usually at a premium.

Even so, the first task of this annual process should be to check that the material held in the current facts book or facts files actually is comprehensive and accurate, and can form a sound basis for the marketing audit itself. The structure of the facts book will be designed to match the specific needs of the organization, but one simple format - suggested by Malcolm McDonald - may be applicable in many cases. This splits the material into three groups:

- Review of the marketing environment. A study of the organization's markets, customers, competitors and the overall economic, political, cultural and technical environment; covering developing trends, as well as the current situation.

- Review of the detailed marketing activity. A study of the company's marketing mix; in terms of the 7 Ps
- Review of the marketing system. A study of the marketing organization, marketing research systems and the current marketing objectives and strategies. The last of these is too frequently ignored. The marketing system itself needs to be regularly questioned, because the validity of the whole marketing plan is reliant upon the accuracy of the input from this system, and 'garbage in, garbage out' applies with a vengeance.
  - *Portfolio planning*: In addition, the coordinated planning of the individual products and services can contribute towards the balanced portfolio.
  - 80:20 rule. To achieve the maximum impact, the marketing plan must be clear, concise and simple. It needs to concentrate on the 20 per cent of products or services, and on the 20 per cent of customers, that will account for 80 per cent of the volume and 80 per cent of the profit.
  - 7 Ps: Product, Place, Price and Promotion, Physical Environment, People, Process. The 7 Ps can sometimes divert attention from the customer, but the framework they offer can be very useful in building the action plans.

It is only at this stage that the active part of the marketing planning process begins. This next stage in marketing planning is indeed the key to the whole marketing process. The "marketing objectives" state just where the company intends to be at some specific time in the future. James Quinn succinctly defined objectives in general as: Goals state what is to be achieved and when results are to be accomplished, but they do not state "how" the results are to be achieved. They typically relate to what products will be where in what markets. They are essentially about the match between those "products" and "markets."

Objectives for pricing, distribution, advertising and so on are at a lower level, and should not be confused with marketing objectives. They are part of the marketing strategy needed to achieve marketing objectives. To be most effective, objectives should be capable of measurement and therefore "quantifiable." This measurement may be in terms of sales volume, money value, market share, percentage penetration of distribution outlets and so on. An example of such a measurable marketing objective might be "to enter the market with product Y and capture 10 per cent of the market by value within one year."

As it is quantified it can, within limits, be unequivocally monitored, and corrective action taken as necessary. The marketing objectives must usually be based on the organization's financial objectives; converting these financial measurements into the related marketing measurements.He went on to explain his view of the role of "policies," with which strategy is most often confused: "Policies are rules or guidelines that express the 'limits' within which action should occur."Simplifying somewhat, marketing strategies can be seen as the means, or "game plan," by which marketing objectives will be achieved and, in the framework that we have chosen to use, are generally concerned with the 8 P's. Examples are:

- *Price*: The amount of money needed to buy products.
- *Product*: The actual product.
- *Promotion*: Getting the product known.
- *Placement*: Where the product is located.
- *People*: Represent the business.
- *Physical environment*: The ambiance, mood, or tone of the environment.
- *Process*: How do people obtain your product.
- *Packaging*: How the product will be protected.

In principle, these strategies describe how the objectives will be achieved. The 7 Ps are a useful framework for deciding how the company's resources will be manipulated to achieve the objectives. However, they are not the only framework, and may divert attention from the real issues. The focus of the strategies must be the objectives to be achieved - not the process of planning itself. Only if it fits the needs of these objectives should you choose, as we have done, to use the framework of the 7 Ps. The strategy statement can take the form of a purely verbal description of the strategic options which have been chosen.

Alternatively, and perhaps more positively, it might include a structured list of the major options chosen. One aspect of strategy which is often overlooked is that of "timing." Exactly when it is the best time for each element of the strategy to be implemented is often critical. Taking the right action at the wrong time can sometimes be almost as bad as taking the wrong action at the right time.

Timing is, therefore, an essential part of any plan; and should normally appear as a schedule of planned activities.Having completed this crucial stage of the planning process, you will need to re-check the feasibility of your objectives and strategies in terms of the market share, sales, costs, profits and so on which these demand in practice. As in the rest of the marketing discipline, you will need to employ judgement, experience, market research or anything else which helps you to look at your conclusions from all possible angles.

Detailed Plans and Programmes

At this stage,you will need to develop your overall marketing strategies into detailed plans and programme. Although these detailed plans may cover each of the 7 Ps, the focus will vary, depending upon your organization's specific strategies. A product-oriented company will focus its plans for the 7 Ps around each of its products. A market or geographically oriented company will concentrate on each market or geographical area.

Each will base its plans upon the detailed needs of its customers, and on the strategies chosen to satisfy these needs. Brochures and Web sites are used effectively. Again, the most important element is, indeed, that of the detailed plans, which spell out exactly what programmes and individual activities will take place over the period of the plan. Without these specified - and preferably quantified - activities the plan cannot be monitored, even in terms of success in meeting its objectives.It is these programmes and activities which will then constitute the "marketing" of the organization over the period. As a result, these detailed marketing programmes are the most important, practical outcome of the whole planning process.

These plans must therefore be:

- *Clear*: They should be an unambiguous statement of 'exactly' what is to be done.
- *Quantified*: The predicted outcome of each activity should be, as far as possible, quantified, so that its performance can be monitored.
- *Focused*: The temptation to proliferate activities beyond the numbers which can be realistically controlled should be avoided. The 80:20 Rule applies in this context too.
- *Realistic*: They should be achievable.
- *Agreed*: Those who are to implement them should be committed to them, and agree that they are achievable. The resulting plans should become a working document which will guide the campaigns taking place throughout the organization over the period of the plan. If the marketing plan is to work, every exception to it must be questioned; and the lessons learnt, to be incorporated in the next year's.

Measurement of Progress

The final stage of any marketing planning process is to establish targets so that progress can be monitored. It is important to put both quantities and timescales into the marketing objectives and into the corresponding strategies. Changes in the environment mean that the forecasts often have to be changed. Along with these, the related plans may well also need to be changed. Continuous monitoring of performance, against predetermined targets, represents a most important aspect of this.

However, perhaps even more important is the enforced discipline of a regular formal review. Again, as with forecasts, in many cases the best planning cycle will revolve around a quarterly review. Best of all, at least in terms of the quantifiable aspects of the plans, if not the wealth of backing detail, is probably a quarterly rolling review - planning one full year ahead each new quarter. Of course, this does absorb more planning resource; but it also ensures that the plans embody the latest information, and - with attention focused on them so regularly - forces both the plans and their implementation to be realistic. Plans only have validity if they are actually used to control thé progress of a company: their success lies in their implementation, not in the writing'.

Performance Analysis

The most important elements of marketing performance, which are normally tracked, are:

Sales Analysis

Most organizations track their sales results; or, in non-profit organizations for example, the number of clients. The more sophisticated track them in terms of 'sales variance' - the deviation from the target figures - which allows a more immediate picture of deviations to become evident. `Micro-analysis', which is simply the normal management process of investigating detailed problems, then investigates the individual elements which are failing to meet targets.

Market Share Analysis

Few organizations track market share though it is often an important metric. Though absolute sales might grow in an expanding market, a firm's share of the market can decrease which bodes ill for future sales when the market starts to drop.

Where such market share is tracked, there may be a number of aspects which will be followed:

- Overall market share.
- Segment share - that in the specific, targeted segment.
- Relative share -in relation to the market leaders.
- Annual fluctuation rate of market share.
- also the specific market sharing of customers.

Expense Analysis

The key ratio to watch in this area is usually the 'marketing expense to sales ratio'; although this may be broken down into other elements.

Financial Analysis

The "bottom line" of marketing activities should at least in theory, be the net profit. There are a number of separate performance figures and key ratios which need to be tracked:

- Gross contribution<>net profit.
- Gross profit<>return on investment.
- Net contribution<>profit on sales.

There can be considerable benefit in comparing these figures with those achieved by other organizations; using, for instance, the figures which can be obtained from 'The Center for Interfirm Comparison'. The most sophisticated use of this approach, however, is typically by those making use of PIMS, initiated by the General Electric Company and then developed by Harvard Business School, but now run by the Strategic Planning Institute.

The performance analyses concentrate on the quantitative measures which are directly related to short-term performance. But there are a number of indirect measures, essentially tracking customer attitudes, which can also indicate the organization's performance in terms of its longer-term marketing strengths and may accordingly be even more important indicators.

Some useful measures are:

- *Market research*: Including customer panels lost business–the orders which were lost because, for example, the stock was not available or the product did not meet the customer's exact requirements.
- *Customer complaints*: How many customers complain about the products or services, or the organization itself, and about what?

Use of Marketing Plans

A formal, written marketing plan is essential; in that it provides an unambiguous reference point for activities throughout the planning period. However, perhaps the most important benefit of these plans is the planning process itself. This typically offers a unique opportunity, a forum, for information-rich and productively focused discussions between the various managers involved.

The plan, together with the associated discussions, then provides an agreed context for their subsequent management activities, even for those not described in the plan itself. Additionally, marketing plans are included in business plans, offering data showing investors how the company will grow and most importantly, how they will get a return on investment.

Budgets as Managerial Tools

The classic quantification of a marketing plan appears in the form of budgets. Because these are so rigorously quantified, they are particularly important. They should, thus, represent an unequivocal projection of actions and expected results. What is more, they should be capable of being monitored accurately; and, indeed, performance against budget is the main management review process.

The purpose of a marketing budget is, thus, to pull together all the revenues and costs involved in marketing into one comprehensive document. It is a managerial tool that balances what is needed to be spent against what can be afforded, and helps make choices about priorities. It is then used in monitoring performance in practice. The marketing budget is usually the most powerful tool by which you think through the relationship between desired results and available means. Its starting point should be the marketing strategies and plans, which have already been formulated in the marketing plan itself; although, in practice, the two will run in parallel and will interact. At the very least, the rigorous, highly quantified, budgets may cause a rethink of some of the more optimistic elements of the plans.

MARKETING PROBLEMS AND OPPORTUNITIES

The market research process begins with identifying and defining the problems and opportunities that exist for your business, such as:

- Launching a new product or service.
- Low awareness of your company and its products or services.
- Low utilization of your company's products or services. (The market is familiar with your company, but still is not doing business with you.)
- A poor company image and reputation.
- Problems with distribution, *i.e.*, your goods and services are not reaching the buying public in a timely manner.

SET OBJECTIVES, BUDGET AND TIMETABLES

Objective

With a marketing problem or opportunity defined, the next step is to set objectives for your market research operations. Your objective might be to explore the nature of a problem so you may further define it.

Or, perhaps it is to determine how many people will buy your product packaged in a certain way and offered at a certain price. Your objective might even be to test possible cause and effect relationships.

For example, if you lower your price by 10 per cent, what increased sales volume should you expect? What impact will this strategy have on your profit?

Budget

How much money are you willing to invest in your market research? How much can you afford? Your market research budget is a portion of your overall marketing budget. A method popular with small business owners to establish a marketing budget is to allocate a small percentage of gross sales for the most recent year. This usually amounts to about two per cent for an existing business. However, if you are planning on launching a new product or business, you may want to increase your budget figure, to as much as 10 per cent of your expected gross sales. Other methods used by small businesses include analyzing and estimating the competition's budget, and calculating your cost of marketing per sale.

Timetables

Prepare a detailed, realistic time frame to complete all steps of the market research process. If your business operates in cycles, establish target dates that will allow the best accessibility to your market. For example, a holiday greeting card business may want to conduct research before or around the holiday season buying period, when their customers are most likely to be thinking about their purchases.

MARKETING RESEARCH METHODS AND TECHNIQUES

There are two types of research: primary research or original information gathered for a specific purpose and secondary research or information that already exists somewhere.

Both types of research have a number of activities and methods of conducting associated with them.

Secondary research is usually faster and less expensive to obtain that primary research. Gathering secondary research may be as simple as making a trip to your local library or business information centre or browsing the Internet.

DESIGN RESEARCH INSTRUMENTS

The most common research instrument is the questionnaire. Poorly designed questionnaires do not uncover the information you are seeking. Pretest any question with a few people to see which questions are being misunderstood or are not effective in drawing out the type of response you are interested in.

Keep these tips in mind when designing your market research questionnaire:

- Keep it simple.
- Include instructions for answering all questions included on the survey.
- Begin the survey with general questions and move towards more specific questions.
- Keep each question brief.
- If the questionnaire is completed by the respondent and not by an interviewer or survey staff member, remember to design a questionnaire that is graphically pleasing and easy to read.
- Remember to pre-test the questionnaire. Before taking the survey to the printer, ask a few people-such as regular customers, colleagues, friends or employees-to complete the survey. Ask them for feedback on the survey's style, simplicity and their perception of its purpose.
- Mix the form of the questions. Use scales, rankings, open-ended questions and closed-ended questions for different sections of the questionnaire. The "form" or way a question is asked may influence the answer given.

Closed-ended Questions

Respondents choose from possible answers included on the questionnaire. Types of closed-end questions include:

- True/False questions which offer respondents the ability to answer yes or no.
- Multiple choice questions which offer respondents one or more choices from a list of several answers.
- Scales refer to questions that ask respondents to rank their answers or measure their answer at a particular point on a scale. For example, a respondent may have the choice to rank their feelings towards a particular statement. The scale have values such as Strongly Disagree, Disagree, Indifferent, Agree, and Strongly e.ree

Open-ended Questions

Respondents answer questions in their own words. Completely unstructured questions allow respondents to answer any way they choose. *Types of open-ended questions include*:

- Word association questions ask respondents to state the first word that comes to mind when a particular word is mentioned.
- Sentence, story or picture completion questions ask respondents to complete partial sentences, stories or pictures in their own words. For example, a question for commuters might read: "My daily commute between home and office is ______ miles and takes me an average of ______ minutes. I use the following mode of transportation: ________."

COLLECT DATA

To help you obtain clear, unbiased and reliable results, collect the data under the direction of experienced researchers. Before beginning the collection of data, it is important to train, educate and supervise your research staff. An untrained staff person conducting primary research will lead to interviewer bias.

Stick to the objectives and rules associated with the methods and techniques you have set in Step Two and Step Three. Try to be as scientific as possible in gathering your information.

Marketing research data collection (often called survey fielding) is the point at which the finalized questionnaire (survey instrument) is used in gathering information among the chosen sample segments. There are a variety of data collection methodologies to consider.

Selecting which is the most appropriate marketing research data collection methodology for a particular research project takes place during Steps 2 & 3 of the marketing research process. Marketing research data collection typically begins with field testing the final questionnaire with a small portion of the respondent sample to make sure it is gathering information correctly. Then data collection can be fairly automatic throughout the remainder of the marketing research data collection process. When quota groups and/or sample subgroups are being screened for, data collection will require more oversight, maintenance time and cost. Regardless of the data collection methodology chosen, the data collection process often takes from 25 per cent to 50 per cent of the total time needed to complete a research project.

ORGANIZE AND ANALYSE DATA

Once your data has been collected, it needs to be assembled into a format in which it can be analyzed easily. This involves editing, coding and tabulating the responses. Well-designed questionnaires can make a difference in how easy this step is.

Some helpful tips for organizing and analyzing your data are:

- Look for relevant data that focuses on your immediate market needs.
- Rely on subjective information only as support for more general findings of objective research.
- Look for consistency across different data sources. As an example, are the market demographics provided to you from the local media outlet consistent with your survey results?
- Quantify your results; look for common opinions that may be combined.
- Read between the lines. For instance, compare U.S. Census Bureau statistics on median income levels for a given location with the number of homeowners vs. renters in the area.

MARKETING RESEARCH FINDINGS

Once marketing information about your target market, competition and environment is collected and analyzed, present it in an organized manner to the decision makers of the business. For instance, you may want to report your findings in the market analysis section of your business plan. Also, you may want to familiarize your sales and marketing departments with the data or conduct a company-wide informational training seminar using the information.

The data gathered was created to help guide your business decisions, so it needs to be readily accessible and understandable to the decision makers.

IDENTIFYING PROBLEM

If you are considering conducting marketing research, chances are you have already identified a problem and an information need.

This step is always the first of the marketing research steps. At this point, the problem will have been recognized by at least one level of management, and internal discussions will have taken place. Sometimes, further definition of the issue or problem is needed, and for that there are several tools you can use.

Here at the outset of the marketing research steps, the most common tools are internal and external secondary research. Secondary research intelligence consists of information that was collected for another purpose, but can be useful for other purposes.

Examples of internal secondary research are sales revenues, sales forecasts, customer demographics, purchase patterns, and other information that has been collected about the customer. Often referred to as data mining, this information can be critical in diagnosing the problem for further exploration and should be leveraged when available and appropriate. The amount of internal secondary information that can be applied is typically limited.

External secondary research is typically far more available, especially since the Internet age. Most external secondary information is produced via research conducted for other purposes, financial performance data, expert opinions and analysis, corporate executive interviews, legal proceedings, competitive intelligence firms, etc..

6

Foreign Market Research

Understanding a market's key characteristics requires gathering a broad range of primary and secondary research, much of which you can source without cost from the internet.

Primary research, such as population figures, product compliance standards, statistics and other facts can be obtained without any cost from international organizations like United Nations and World Trade Organizations.

Analysis of export statistics over a period of several years helps an individual to determine whether the market for a particular product is growing or shrinking.

Secondary research, such as periodicals, studies, market reports and surveys, can be found through government web sites, international organisations, and commercial market intelligence firms.

FOREIGN MARKET SELECTION PROCESS

GATHER INFORMATION ON A BROAD RANGE OF MARKETS

Market selection process requires a broad range of informations depending upon the products or services to be exported, which includes:

- The demand for product/service.
- The size of the potential audience.
- Whether the target audience can affords product.
- What the regulatory issues are that impact on exports of product.
- Ease of access to this market – proximity/freight.
- Are there appropriate distribution channels for product/service.
- The environment for doing business – language, culture, politics etc.
- Is it financially viable to export to selected market.

You can gather much of the first step information yourself from a variety of sources at little or no cost. Sources of information include:

- Talking to colleagues and other exporters.
- Trade and Enterprise – web site, publications, call centre.
- The library.
- The Internet.

RESEARCH A SELECTION OF MARKETS IN-DEPTH

From the results of the first stage, narrow your selection down to three to five markets and undertake some in-depth research relating specifically to your product. While doing so, some of the questions that may arise at this stage are:

- What similar products are in the marketplace (including products that may not be similar but are used to achieve the same goal, *e.g.* the product in our sample matrix at the end of this document is a hair removal cream.
  As well as undertaking competitor research on other hair removal creams, we would also need to consider other products that are used for hair removal, *i.e.* razors, electrolysis, wax).
- What is your point of difference? What makes your product unique? What are the key selling points for your product?
- How do people obtain/use these products?
- Who provides them?
- Are they imported? If so from which countries?
- Is there a local manufacturer or provider?
- Who would your major competitors be? What are the key brands or trade names?
- What is the market's structure and shape?
- What is the market's size?
- Are there any niche markets, and if so how big are they?
- Who are the major importers/stockists/distributors/agencies or suppliers?
- What are the other ways to obtain sales/representation?
- What are the prices or fees in different parts of the market?
- What are the mark-ups at different distribution levels?
- What are the import regulations, duties or taxes, including compliance and professional registrations if these apply?
- How will you promote your product or service if there is a lot of competition?
- Are there any significant trade fairs, professional gathers or other events where you can promote your product or service?
- Packaging – do you need to change metric measures to imperial, do you need to list ingredients?
- Will you need to translate promotional material and packaging?
- Is your branding – colours, imagery etc., culturally acceptable?

FOREIGN MARKET SELECTION ENTRY

Having completed the market selection process and chosen your target market, the next step is to plan your entry strategy. There are a number of options for entering your chosen market. Most exporters initially choose to work through agents or distributors. In the longer term, however, you may consider other options, such as taking more direct control of your market, more direct selling or promotion, or seeking alliances or agreements.

INDIRECT AND DIRECT METHODS

The most common methods of exporting are indirect selling and direct selling. In indirect selling, an export intermediary such as an export management company or an export trading company normally assumes responsibility for finding overseas buyers, shipping products, and getting paid. In direct selling, the U.S. producer deals directly with a foreign buyer. The paramount consideration in determining whether to market indirectly or directly is the level of resources a company is willing to devote to its international marketing effort.

Other factors to consider when deciding whether to market indirectly or directly include:

- The size of your firm;
- The nature of your products;
- Previous export experience and expertise;
- Business conditions in the selected overseas markets.

APPROACHES TO EXPORTING

The way your company chooses to export its products can have a significant effect on its export plan and specific marketing strategies. The basic distinction among approaches to exporting relates to the company's level of involvement in the export process.

There are at least four approaches, which may be used alone or in combination:

- Passively filling orders from domestic buyers who then export the product. These sales are indistinguishable from other domestic sales as far as the original seller is concerned. Someone else has decided that the product in question meets foreign demand. That party takes all the risk and handles all of the exporting details, in some cases without even the awareness of the original seller.
- Seeking out domestic buyers who represent foreign end users or customers. Many U.S. and foreign corporations, general contractors, foreign trading companies, foreign government agencies, foreign distributors and retailers, and others in the United States purchase for export. These buyers are a large market for a wide variety of goods and services. In this case a company may know its product is

being exported, but it is still the buyer who assumes the risk and handles the details of exporting.

- *Exporting indirectly through intermediaries*: With this approach, a company engages the services of an intermediary firm capable of finding foreign markets and buyers for its products. EMCs, ETCs, international trade consultants, and other intermediaries can give the exporter access to well-established expertise and trade contacts. Yet, the exporter can still retain considerable control over the process and can realise some of the other benefits of exporting, such as learning more about foreign competitors, new technologies, and other market opportunities.
- *Exporting directly*: This approach is the most ambitious and difficult, since the exporter personally handles every aspect of the exporting process from market research and planning to foreign distribution and collections. Consequently, a significant commitment of management time and attention is required to achieve good results. However, this approach may also be the best way to achieve maximum profits and long-term growth. With appropriate help and guidance from the Department of Commerce, state trade offices, freight forwarders, international banks, and other service groups, even small or medium-sized firms can export directly if they are able to commit enough staff time to the effort. For those who cannot make that commitment, the services of an EMC, ETC, trade consultant, or other qualified intermediary are indispensable.

If the nature of the company's goals and resources makes an indirect method of exporting the best choice, little further planning may be needed. In such a case, the main task is to find a suitable intermediary firm that can then handle most export details. Firms that are new to exporting or are unable to commit staff and funds to more complex export activities may find indirect methods of exporting more appropriate. However, using an EMC or other intermediary does not exclude all possibility of direct exporting for your firm.

For example, your company may try exporting directly to such "easy" nearby markets as Canada, Mexico, or the Bahamas while letting an EMC handle more ambitious sales to Egypt or Japan. You may also choose to gradually increase the level of direct exporting later, after experience has been gained and sales volume appears to justify added investment. Consulting advisers before making these decisions can be helpful.

Distribution Considerations:

- Which channels of distribution should the firm use to market its products abroad?
- Where should the firm produce its products and how should it distribute them in the foreign market?

- What types of representatives, brokers, wholesalers, dealers, distributors, or end-use customers, and so forth should the firm use?
- What are the characteristics and capabilities of the available intermediaries?
- Should the assistance of an EMC or ETC be obtained?

INDIRECT EXPORTING

The principal advantage of indirect marketing for a smaller U.S. company is that it provides a way to penetrate foreign markets without the complexities and risks of direct exporting. Several kinds of intermediary firms provide a range of export services. Each type of firm offers distinct advantages for your company.

CONFIRMING HOUSES

Confirming houses or buying agents are finders for foreign firms that want to purchase U.S. products. They seek to obtain the desired items at the lowest possible price and are paid a commission by their foreign clients. In some cases, they may be foreign government agencies or quasi-governmental firms empowered to locate and purchase desired goods. An example is foreign government purchasing missions.

EXPORT MANAGEMENT COMPANIES

An EMC acts as the export department for one or several producers of goods or services. It solicits and transacts business in the names of the producers it represents or in its own name for a commission, salary, or retainer plus commission. Some EMCs provide immediate payment for the producer's products by either arranging financing or directly purchasing products for resale.

Typically, only larger EMCs can afford to purchase or finance exports. EMCs usually specialize either by product or by foreign market, or sometimes even both. Because of their specialization, the best EMCs know their products and the markets they serve very well and usually have well-established networks of foreign distributors already in place.

This immediate access to foreign markets is one of the principal reasons for using an EMC, since establishing a productive relationship with a foreign representative may be a costly and lengthy process.

One disadvantage of using an EMC is that a manufacturer may lose control over foreign sales. Most manufacturers are properly concerned that their product and company image be well maintained in foreign markets. An important way for a company to retain sufficient control in such an arrangement is to carefully select an EMC that can meet the company's needs and maintain close communication with it.

For example, a company may ask for regular reports on efforts to market its products and may require approval of certain types of efforts, such as advertising programmes or service arrangements. If a company wants to maintain this type of relationship with an EMC, it should negotiate points of concern before entering an agreement, since not all EMCs are willing to comply with the company's concerns.

EXPORT TRADING COMPANIES

An ETC facilitates the export of U.S. goods and services. Like an EMC, an ETC can either performance as the export department for producers or take title to the product and export for its own account. Therefore, the terms ETC and EMC are often used interchangeably. A special kind of ETC is a group organized and operated by producers. These ETCs can be organized along multiple or single-industry lines and can also represent producers of competing products.

EXPORT TRADING COMPANY ACT OF 1982 AND THE OFFICE OF EXPORT TRADING COMPANY AFFAIRS

The Export Trading Company Act of 1982 allows banks to make equity investments in commercial ventures that qualify as ETCs. In addition, the Export- Import Bank of the United States is allowed to make working capital guarantees to U.S. exporters. Through the Office of Export Trading Company Affairs within the International Trade Administration, the U.S. Department of Commerce promotes the formation and use of U.S. export intermediaries and issues export trade certificates of review providing limited immunity from U.S. antitrust laws.

OETCA informs the business community of the benefits of export intermediaries through conferences, presentations before trade associations and civic organizations, and publications. OETCA also maintains the Contact Facilitation Service database, a listing of U.S. producers of goods and services and of organizations that provide trade facilitation services.

Under a public-private sector arrangement, the CFS database is published annually in a directory entitled The Export Yellow Pages. The directory provides users with the names and addresses of banks, EMCs, ETCs, freight forwarders, manufacturers, and service organizations and names the export products or export-related services that these firms supply. By obtaining CFS registration forms from Commerce EACs, firms can register in the database free of charge and be listed in subsequent editions of The Export Yellow Pages.

The certificate of review programme provides exporters with an antitrust "insurance policy" intended to foster joint activities where economies of scale and risk diversification can be achieved. The performance also amends the Sherman Antitrust Act and the Federal Trade Commission Act to clarify the jurisdictional reach of these statutes to export trade. Both acts now apply to export trade only if there is a "direct substantial and reasonably foreseeable" effect on domestic or import commerce of the United States or the export commerce of a U.S. competitor.

Certificates of review are issued by the Secretary of Commerce with the concurrence of the U.S. Department of Justice. Any U.S. corporation or partnership, any resident individual, or any state or local entity may apply for a certificate of review. A certificate can be issued to an applicant if it is determined that the proposed "export trade activities and methods of operation" will not result in a substantial lessening of domestic competition or restraint of trade within the United States. For the conduct covered by the certificate, its holder and any other individuals or firms named as members are given immunity from government suits under U.S. federal and state antitrust laws.

In private party actions, liability is reduced from treble to single damages, greatly reducing the probability of nuisance suits. Moreover, in the event of private litigation involving conduct covered by the certificate of review, a prevailing certificate holder re-covers the costs of defending the suit, including reasonable attorney's fees.

EXPORT AGENTS, MERCHANTS, OR REMARKETERS

Export agents, merchants, or remarketers purchase products directly from the manufacturer, packing and marking the products according to their own specifications. They then sell these products overseas through their contacts in their own names and assume all risks for accounts.

In transactions with export agents, merchants, or remarketers, a U.S. firm relinquishes control over the marketing and promotion of its product. This situation could have an adverse effect on future sales efforts abroad if the product is underpriced or incorrectly positioned in the market, or if after-sales services are neglected. On the other hand, the effort required by the manufacturer to market the product overseas is very small and may lead to sales that otherwise would take a great deal of effort to obtain.

PIGGYBACK MARKETING

Piggyback marketing is an arrangement in which one manufacturer or service firm distributes a second firm's product or service. The most common piggy-backing situation is when a U.S. company has a contract with an overseas buyer to provide a wide range of products or services.

Often, this first company does not produce all of the products it is under contract to provide, and it turns to other U.S. companies to provide the remaining products. The second U.S. company thus piggybacks its products to the international market, generally without incurring the marketing and distribution costs associated with exporting. Successful arrangements usually require that the product lines be complementary and appeal to the same customers.

DIRECT EXPORTING

The advantages of direct exporting for a U.S. company include more control over the export process, potentially higher profits, and a closer relationship to the overseas buyer and marketplace. However, these advantages do not come easily since the U.S. company needs to devote more time, personnel, and corporate resources than indirect exporting requires. When a company chooses to export directly to foreign markets, it usually makes internal organizational changes to support more complex functions. A direct exporter normally selects the markets it wishes to penetrate, chooses the best channels of distribution for each market, and then makes specific foreign business connections in order to sell its product.

ORGANIZING FOR EXPORTING

A company new to exporting generally treats its export sales no differently than its domestic sales, using existing personnel and organizational structures. As international sales and enquiries increase, the company may separate the management of its exports from that of its domestic sales. The advantages of separating international from domestic business include the centralization of specialized skills needed to deal with international markets and the benefits of a focused marketing effort that is more likely to increase export sales.

A possible disadvantage is that segmentation might be a less efficient use of corporate resources. When a company separates international from domestic business, it may do so at different levels in the organization. For example, when a company first begins to export, it may create an export department with a full or part-time manager who reports to the head of domestic sales and marketing. At later stages, a company may choose to increase the autonomy of the export department to the point of creating an international division that reports directly to the president.

Larger companies at advanced stages of exporting may choose to retain the international division or to organize along product or geographic lines. A company with distinct product lines may create an international department in each product division. A company with products that have common end users may organize geographically.

For example, it may form a division for Europe and another for the Pacific Rim. A small company's initial needs may be satisfied by a single export manager who has responsibility for the full range of international activities. Regardless of how a company organizes its exporting efforts, the key is to facilitate the marketer's job.

Good marketing skills can help the firm operate in an unfamiliar market. Experience has shown that a company's success in foreign markets depends less on the unique attributes of its products than on its marketing methods. Once your company is organized to handle exporting, a proper channel of distribution needs to be carefully chosen for each market. These channels include sales representatives, agents, distributors, retailers, and end users.

SALES REPRESENTATIVES

Overseas, a sales representative is the equivalent of a manufacturer's representative in the United States. The representative uses the company's product literature and samples to present the product to potential buyers. A representative usually handles many complementary lines that do not conflict. The sales representative usually works on a commission basis, assumes no risk or responsibility, and is under contract for a definite period of time. The contract defines territory, terms of sale, method of compensation, reasons and procedures for terminating the agreement, and other details. The sales representative may operate on either an exclusive or a non-exclusive basis.

AGENTS

The widely misunderstood term "agent" means a representative who normally has authority, perhaps even a power of attorney, to make commitments on behalf of the firm he or she represents. Firms in the United States and other developed countries have stopped using the term and instead rely on the term "representative," since agent can imply more than intended. It is important that any contract state whether the representative or agent does or does not have legal authority to obligate the firm.

DISTRIBUTORS

The foreign distributor is a merchant who purchases goods from a U.S. exporter and resells it for a profit. The foreign distributor generally provides support and service for the product, thus relieving the U.S. company of these responsibilities. The distributor usually carries an inventory of products and a sufficient supply of spare parts and also maintains adequate facilities and personnel for normal servicing operations.

Distributors typically handle a range of non-conflicting but complementary products. End users do not usually buy from a distributor; they buy from retailers or dealers. The terms and length of association between the U.S. company and the foreign distributor are established by contract. Some U.S. companies prefer to begin with a relatively short trial period and then extend the contract if the relationship proves satisfactory to both parties.

FOREIGN RETAILERS

A company may also sell directly to foreign retailers, although in such transactions, products are generally limited to consumer lines. The growth of major retail chains in markets such as Canada and Japan has created new opportunities for this type of direct sale. This method relies mainly on traveling sales representatives who directly contact foreign retailers, although results might also be achieved by mailing catalogues, brochures, or other literature. The direct mail approach has the benefits of eliminating commissions, reducing traveling expenses, and reaching a broader audience. For optimal results, a firm that uses direct mail to reach foreign retailers should support it with other marketing activities. American manufacturers with ties to major domestic retailers may also be able to use them to sell abroad. Many large American retailers maintain overseas buying offices and use these offices to sell abroad when practical.

DIRECT SALES TO END USERS

A U.S. business may sell its products or services directly to end users in foreign countries. These buyers can be foreign governments; institutions such as hospitals, banks, and schools; or businesses. Buyers can be identified at trade shows, through international publications, or through Commerce's Export Contact List Service. The U.S. company should be aware that if a product is sold in such a direct fashion, the company is responsible for shipping, payment collection, and product servicing unless other arrangements are made. Unless the cost of providing these services is built into the export price, a company could have a narrower profit than originally intended.

LOCATING FOREIGN REPRESENTATIVES AND BUYERS

A company that chooses to use foreign representatives may meet them during overseas business trips or at domestic or international trade shows. There are other effective methods that can be employed without leaving the United States. Ultimately, the exporter may need to travel abroad to identify, evaluate, and sign overseas representatives; however, a company can save time by first conducting background research in the United States. The Commercial Service contact programmes, banks and service organizations, and publications are available to help in this manner..

CONTACTING AND EVALUATING FOREIGN REPRESENTATIVES

Once your company has identified a number of potential representatives or distributors in the selected market, it should write and/or fax directly to each. Just as the U.S. firm is seeking information on the foreign representative, the representative is interested in corporate and product information on the U.S. firm. The prospective representative may want more information than the company normally provides to a casual buyer. Therefore, the firm should provide full information on its history, resources, personnel, product line, previous export activity, and all other pertinent matters. The firm may wish to include a photograph or two of plant facilities and products, and even product samples when practical.

You may also want to consider inviting the foreign representative to visit its operations. Whenever the danger of piracy is significant, the exporter should guard against sending product samples that could be easily copied. A U.S. firm should investigate potential representatives or distributors carefully before entering into an agreement. The U.S. firm also needs to know the following points about the representative or distributor's firm:

- Current status and history, including background on principal officers;
- Methods of introducing new products into the sales territory;
- Trade and bank references;
- Data on whether the U.S. firm's special requirements can be met; and
- A view of the in-country market potential for the U.S. firm's products. This information is not only useful in gauging how much the representative knows about the exporter's industry, it is valuable market research in its own right.

A U.S. company may obtain much of this information from business associates who currently work with foreign representatives. However, U.S. exporters should not hesitate to ask potential representatives or distributors detailed and specific questions.

Suppliers have the right to explore the qualifications of those who propose to represent them overseas. Well-qualified representatives will gladly answer questions that help distinguish them from less-qualified competitors. Your company should also consider other private-sector sources for credit checks of potential business partners.

In addition, the U.S. company may wish to obtain at least two supporting business and credit reports to ensure that the distributor or representative is reputable. By using a second credit report from a different source, the U.S. firm may gain new or more complete information. Reports from a number of companies are available from commercial firms and from the Department of Commerce's International Company Profiles. Commercial firms and banks are also sources of credit information on overseas representatives. They can provide information directly or from their correspondent banks or branches overseas. Directories of international companies may also provide credit information on foreign firms.

If the U.S. company has the necessary information, it may wish to contact a few of the foreign firm's existing U.S. clients to obtain an evaluation of the representative's character, reliability, efficiency, and past performance. To protect itself against possible conflicts of interest, it is also important for the U.S. firm to learn about other product lines that the foreign firm represents.

Once the company has prequalified some foreign representatives, it may wish to travel to the foreign country to observe the size, condition, and location of offices and warehouses. In addition, the U.S. company should meet the sales force and try to assess its strength in the marketplace. If traveling to each distributor or representative is difficult, the company may decide to each of them at U.S. or at worldwide trade shows.

NEGOTIATING AN AGREEMENT WITH A FOREIGN REPRESENTATIVE

When the U.S. company has found a prospective representative that meets its requirements, the next step is to negotiate a foreign sales agreement. EACs can provide counseling to firms planning to negotiate foreign sales agreements with representatives and distributors. The International Chamber of Commerce also provides useful guidelines and can be reached at 212-206-1150.

Most representatives are interested in the company's pricing structure and profit potential. Representatives are also concerned with the terms of payment, product regulation, competitors and their market shares, the amount of support provided by the U.S. firm, training for sales and service staff, and the company's ability to deliver on schedule.

The agreement may contain provisions that the foreign representative:

- Not have business dealings with competing firms;
- Not reveal any confidential information in a way that would prove injurious, detrimental, or competitive to the U.S. firm;
- Not enter into agreements binding to the U.S. firm; and,
- Refer all enquiries received from outside the designated sales territory to the U.S. firm for action.

To ensure a conscientious sales effort from the foreign representative, the agreement should include a requirement that it apply the utmost skill and ability to the sale of the product for the compensation named in the contract. It may be appropriate to include performance requirements such as a minimum sales volume and an expected rate of increase. In the drafting of the agreement, special attention must be paid to safeguarding the supplier's interests in cases where the representative proves less than satisfactory.

It is vital to include an escape clause in the agreement, allowing the supplier to end the relationship safely and cleanly if the representative does not fulfil the firm's expectations. Some contracts specify that either party may terminate the agreement with written notice 30, 60, or 90 days in advance. The contract may also spell out exactly what constitutes just cause for ending the agreement. Other contracts specify a certain term for the agreement but arrange for automatic annual renewal unless either party gives written notice of its intention not to renew.

In all cases, escape clauses and other provisions to safeguard the supplier may be limited by the laws of the country in which the representative is located. For this reason, the supplier should learn as much as it can about the legal requirements of the representative's country and obtain qualified legal counsel in preparing the contract. These are some of the legal questions to consider:

- How far in advance must the representative be notified of the supplier's intention to terminate the agreement? Three months satisfy the requirements of many countries, but a verifiable means of conveyance may be needed to establish when the notice was served.
- What is just cause for terminating a representative? Specifying causes for termination in the written contract usually strengthens the supplier's position.
- Which country's laws govern a contract dispute? Laws in the representative's country may forbid the representative from waiving its nation's legal jurisdiction.
- What compensation is due to the representative on dismissal? Depending on the length of the relationship, the added value of the market the representative created for the supplier, and whether termination is for just cause as defined by the foreign country, the supplier may be required to compensate the representative for losses.
- What must the representative give up if dismissed? The contract should specify the return of property such as: patents, trademarks, name registrations, and customer records.
- Should the representative be referred to as an agent? In some countries, the word agent implies power of attorney. The contract needs to specify if the representative is or is not a legal agent with power of attorney.
- In what language should the contract be drafted? In most cases, the contract should be in both English and the official language(s) of the foreign country.

The supplier should also be aware of U.S. laws that govern such contracts. For instance, the supplier should seek to avoid provisions that could be contrary to U.S. anti-trust laws. The Export Trading Company Act of 1982 provides a means to obtain anti-trust protection when two or more companies combine for exporting. In any case, the supplier should obtain legal advice when preparing and entering into any foreign agreement.

Foreign representatives often request exclusivity for marketing in a country or region. It is recommended that suppliers not grant exclusivity until the foreign representative has proven his or her capabilities or that it be granted for a limited, defined period of time, such as one year, with renewal possible. The territory covered by exclusivity may also need to be defined, though some countries' laws may prohibit that type of limitation.

7

Role of Marketing Research in Business Decision Making

When research is used for decision-making, it means we are using the methods of science to the art of management. Every organization operates under some degree of uncertainty. This uncertainty cannot be eliminated completely, although its can be minimized with the help of research methodology. Research in particularly important in the decision making process of various business organizations.

To choose the best line of action (in the light of growing competition and increasing uncertainty). Research in common context refers to a search for knowledge. It can also be defined as a scientific and systematic search for gaining information and knowledge on a specific topic or phenomena. In management research is extensively used in various areas. For example, We all know that, Marketing is the process of Planning and Executing the concepts, pricing, promotion and distribution of ideas, goods, and services to create exchange that satisfy individual and organizational objectives.

Thus, we can say that, the Marketing Concept requires Customer Satisfaction rather than Profit Maximization to be the goal of an organization. The organization should be Consumer oriented and should try to understand consumer's requirements and satisfy them quickly and efficiently, in ways that are beneficial to both the consumer and the organization. This means that any organization should try to obtain information on consumer needs and gather market intelligence to help satisfy these needs efficiently. This can only be done only only by research. In this lecture as suggested, be discussing the role of research in management and its key ingredients. But first let us understand the meaning of research. It will be clear after going through some important definitions of research.

DEFINITION

Some of the definitions of Research are:

- Redman and Mory define research as a "systematized effort to gain new knowledge".

- Some people consider research as a movement, a movement from known to unknown. It is actually a voyage to discovery.
- Clifford Woody.

"Research comprises of defining and redefining problems, formulating hypothesis or suggested solutions; making deductions and reaching ceases; and at last carefully testing the ceases to determine whether they fit the formulating hypothesis".

On evaluating these definitions we can conclude that Research refers to the systematic method consisting of:

- Enunciating the problem,
- Formulating a hypothesis,
- Collecting the fact or data,
- Analyzing the facts and
- Reaching certain ceases either in the form of solutions towards the concerned problem or in certain generals for some theoretical formulation.

Market Research has become an important part in management decision-making. Marketing research is a critical part of such a Market intelligence system; it helps to improve management decision making by providing relevant, accurate, and timely information. Every decision poses unique needs for information gathered through marketing research.

Thus, we can say that marketing research is the function that links the:

- Consumer,
- Customer,
- The public to the marketer through information.

Information used to identify and define marketing opportunities and problems:

- Generate,
- Refine, and evaluate marketing actions;
- Monitor marketing performance; and
- Improve understanding of marketing as a process.

In the nut-shell we see that Marketing research specifies:

- The information required to address these issues,
- Designs the method for collecting information,
- Manages and implements the data collection process, analyses,
- communicates the findings and their implications

INTELLIGENT USE OF RESEARCH TOOLS IS THE KEY TO BUSINESS ACHIEVEMENT

I hope the meaning of research is clear. Research provides a base for your business sound decision - making. There are three parts involved in any of your systematic finding:

- Implicit question posed.
- Explicit answer proposed.
- Collection, analysis, and interpretation of the information leading from the question to answer Illustration.

Consider the Statement: "We recommend that Model X-240 of music system be priced at ₹.10, 000/-" Marketing Research Manager forwarded this recommendation to Marketing Vice-President. Implicit Question What should be the selling price of model X-240? *Explicit Answer*: The explicit answer is ₹.15000/–.

The third part deals with the collection, analysis, and interpretation of the information leading from the question to the answer of ₹.15000/. Research is a systematic approach to gather information required for sound management decisions. Research is not synonymous to common sense. The difference lies in the methods and procedures adopted to reach a cease.

ROLE OF RESEARCH IN IMPORTANT AREAS

Through research, an executive can quickly get a synopsis of the current scenario, which improves his information base for making sound decisions affecting future operations of the enterprise. The following are the major areas in which research plays a key role in making effective decisions.

MARKETING

Marketing research is undertaken to assist the marketing function. Marketing research stimulates the flow of marketing data from the consumer and his environment to marketing information system of the enterprise.

Market research involves the process of:

- Systematic collection,
- Compilation,
- Analysis,
- Interpretation of relevant data for marketing decisions.

This information goes to the executive in the form of data. On the basis of this data the executive develop plans and programmers. Advertising research, packaging research, performance evaluation research, sales analysis, distribution channel, etc., may also be considered in management research.

Research tools are applied effectively for studies involving:

- Demand forecasting,
- Consumer buying behaviour,
- Measuring advertising effectiveness,
- Media selection for advertising,
- Test marketing,
- Product positioning,
- Product potential.

CHARACTERISTICS OF RESEARCH

- *Systematic Approach*: Each step must of your investigation be so planned that it leads to the next step. Planning and organization are part of this approach. A planned and organized research saves your time and money.
- *Objectivity*: It implies that True Research should attempt to find an unbiased answer to the decision-making problem.
- *Reproducibl*: A reproducible research procedure is one, which an equally competent researcher could duplicate, and from it deduces approximately the same results. Precise information regarding samples-methods, collection etc., should be specified.
- *Relevancy:* It furnishes three important tasks:
  - It avoids collection of irrelevant information and saves time and money
  - It compares the information to be collected with researcher's criteria for action
  - It enables to see whether the research is proceeding in the right direction
- *Control*: Research is not only affected by the factors, which one is investigating but some other extraneous factors also. It is impossible to control all the factors. All the factors that we think may affect the study have to be controlled and accounted for. For Example Suppose we are studying the relationship between incomes and shopping behaviour, without controlling for education and age, it will be a height of folly, since our findings may reflect the effect of education and age rather than income.

CONTROL MUST CONSIDER

- All the factors, which are under control, must be varied as per the study demands.
- All those variables beyond the control should be recorded Structure of Research.

Most research projects share the same general structure. You might think of this structure as following the shape of an hourglass. The research process usually starts with a broad area of interest, the initial problem that the researcher wishes to study. For instance, the researcher could be interested in how to use computers to improve the performance of students in mathematics.

But this initial interest is far too broad to study in any single research project (it might not even be addressable in a lifetime of research). The researcher has to narrow the question down to one that can reasonably be studied in a research project. This might involve formulating a hypothesis or a focus question. For instance, the researcher might hypothesize that a particular method of computer instruction in math will improve the ability of elementary school students in a specific district. At the narrowest point of the research hourglass, the researcher is engaged in direct measurement or observation of the question of interest. Once the basic data is collected, the researcher begins to try to understand it, usually by analyzing it in a variety of ways. Even for a single hypothesis there are a number of analyses a researcher might typically conduct.

At this point, the researcher begins to formulate some initial ceases about what happened as a result of the computerized math programmme. Finally, the researcher often will attempt to address the original broad question of interest by generalizing from the results of this specific study to other related situations. For instance, on the basis of strong results indicating that the math programmme had a positive effect on student performance, the researcher might conclude that other school districts similar to the one in the study might expect similar results.

MARKETING RESEARCH

- *Product Research*: Assessment of suitability of goods with respect to design and price.
- *Market Characteristics Research (Qualitative)*: Who uses the product? Relationship between buyer and user, buying motive, how a product is used, analysis of consumption rates, units in which product is purchased, customs and habits affecting the use of a product, consumer attitudes, shopping habits of consumers, brand loyalty, research of special consumer groups, survey of local markets, basic economic analysis of the consumer market, etc.
- *Size of Market (Quantitative)*: Market potential, total sales quota, territorial sales quota, quota for individuals, concentration of sales and advertising efforts; appraisal of efficiency, etc.
- Competitive position and Trends Research
- *Sales Research*: Analysis of sales records.
- *Distribution Research*: Channels of distribution, distribution costs.
- *Advertising and Promotion Research*: Testing and evaluating, advertising and promotion
- New product launching and Product Positioning.

PRODUCTION

Research helps you in an enterprise to decide in the field of production on:

- What to produce?
- How much to produce?
- When to produce?
- For whom to produce?

Some of the areas you can apply research are:

- Product development,
- Cost reduction,

- Work simplification,
- Profitability improvement,
- Inventory control.

Materials: *The materials department uses research to frame suitable policies regarding*:

- Where to buy?
- How much to buy?
- When to buy?
- At what prices to buy?

Human Resource Development You must be Aware that The Human Resource Development department uses research to study wage rates, incentive plans, cost of living, employee turnover rates, employment trends, and performance appraisal. It also uses research effectively for its most important activity namely manpower planning.

SOLVING VARIOUS OPERATIONAL AND PLANNING PROBLEMS OF

Business and Industry Various types of researches, *e.g.*, market research, operations research and motivational research, when combined together, help in solving various complex problems of business and industry in a number of ways. These techniques help in replacing intuitive businessdecisions by more logical and scientific decisions

GOVERNMENT AND ECONOMIC SYSTEM

Research helps a decision maker in a number of ways, *e.g.*, it can help in examining the consequences of each alternative and help in bringing out the effect on economic conditions. Various examples can be quoted such as' problems of big and small industries due tò various factors–up gradation of technology and its impact on lab our and supervisory deployment, effect of government's liberal policy, WTO and its new guidances, ISO 9000/14000 standards and their impact on our exports allocation of national resources on national priority basis, etc.

Research lays the foundation for all Government Policies in our economic system. We all are aware of the fact that research is applied for brining out union finance budget and railway budget every year. Government also uses research for economic planning and optimum utilization of resources for the development of the country. For systematic collection of information on the economic and social structure of the country you need Research. Such types of information indicate what is happening to the national economy and what changes are taking place.

SOCIAL RELATIONSHIPS

Research in social sciences is concerned with both-knowledge for self and knowledge for helping in solving immediate problems of human relations. It is a sort of formal training, which helps a individual in a better way, *e.g.*

- It helps professionals to earn their livelihood.
- It helps students to know how to write and report various findings.
- It helps philosophers and thinkers in their new thin kings and ideas.
- It helps in developing new styles for creative work.
- It may help researchers, in general, to generalize new theories.

TYPES OF RESEARCH

On the basis of the fundamental objectives of the research, we can classify research into two types:

EXPLORATORY RESEARCH

Many times a decision maker is grappling with broad and poorly defined problems. If you attempt to secure better definitions by analytic thinking, it may be the wrong approach and may even be counter productive counter productive in the sense that this approach may lead to a definitive answer to the wrong question. Exploratory research uses a less formal approach. It pursues several, possibilities simultaneously and in a sense it is not quite sure of its objective. Exploratory research is designed to provide a background, to familiarize and, as the word implies, just "explore", the general subject. A part of exploratory research is the investigation of relationships among variables without knowing why they are studied. It borders on an, idle curiosity approach, differing from it only in that the investigator thinks there may be a payoff in the application some where in the forest of questions.

Three typical approaches in exploratory research are:

- The literature survey,
- The experience survey, and
- The analysis of "insight-stimulating" examples

The literature search is fast, economical way to develop a better understanding of a problem area in which you are investigating and have limited experience and knowledge. It also familiarizes you with past research results, data sources, and the type of data available. The experience survey concentrates on persons who are particularly knowledgeable in the particular area. In this representative samples are not desired. A covering of widely divergent views is better. Researchers are not looking for ceases; they are looking for ideas. The analysis of specific examples is a sort of case study approach, but again, researchers are looking for some fresh possible divergent views.

CONCLUSIVE RESEARCH

Exploratory research gives rise to several hypotheses, which you will have to tested for drawing definite ceases. These ceases when tested for validity lay the structure for your decision-making. Conclusive research is used for this purpose of testing the hypotheses generated by exploratory research. Conclusive research can further be classified as:

- Descriptive
- Experimental.

DESCRIPTIVE RESEARCH

Descriptive research as the name suggests is designed to describe something- for example, the characteristics of users of a given product; the degree to which product use varies with income, age, sex or other characteristics; or the number who saw a specific television commercial. To be of maximum benefit, a descriptive study must only collect, data for a definite purpose. Your objective and understanding should be clear and specific. Descriptive studies vary in the degree to which a specific hypothesis is the guide. It allows both implicit and explicit hypotheses to be tested depending on the research problem. For Example: A cereal company may find its sales declining. On the basis of market feedback the company may hypothesise that teenage children do not eat its cereal for breakfast. A descriptive study can then be designed to test this hypothesis.

EXPERIMENTAL RESEARCH

Experimentation will refer to that process of research in which one or more variables are manipulated under conditions, which permit the collection of data, which show the effects.

Experiments will create situation so that you as a researcher can obtain the particular data needed and can measure the data accurately. Experiments are artificial in the sense that the situations are usually created for testing purposes. This artificiality is the essence of the experimental method, since it gives you more control over the factors you are studying.

If you can control the factors, which are present in a given situation, you can obtain more conclusive evidence of cause and effect relationships between any two of them. Thus, the ability to set up a situation for the express purpose of observing and recording accurately the effect on one factor when another is deliberately changed permits you to accept or reject hypothesis beyond reasonable doubt If the objective is to validate in a resounding manner the cause and effect relationship among variables, then undoubtedly experiments are much more effective than descriptive technique Thus, we can conclude that:

- Research methodology minimizes the degree of uncertainty involved in management decisions. Research lays the structure for decision-making.
- Research is not synonymous with common sense.
- Research is characterized by - systematic, objective, reproducible, relevance, and control.
- The role of research in the important areas of management has been briefly covered. The areas include marketing, production, banking, materials, human resource development, and government.

- Research process involves the five important steps-problem definition, research design, data collection, data analysis, and interpretation of results. All these steps have been explained in detail with their key elements.
- We have dichotomized the types of research into - exploratory, and conclusive.
- While exploratory research enables the researcher to generate hypotheses, they are tested for validity by the conclusive research.
- Conclusive research could be further divided into-descriptive, and experimental.
- While the descriptive procedures merely test the hypotheses, the experimental research establishes in a more effective manner the cause and effect relationships among variables.

IMPORTANCE OF RESEARCH IN MANAGEMENT DECISION

The role of research has greatly increased in the field of business and economy as a whole. The study of research methods provides you with the knowledge and skills you need to solve the problems and meet the challenges of today's modern pace of development.

Three factors stimulate the interest in a scientific research to decision making:

- The manager's increased need for more and better information.
- The availability of improved techniques and tools to meet this need.
- The resulting information overload.

The usefulness and contribution of research in assisting marketing decisions is so crucial that it has given rise to the opening of a new field altogether called 'marketing research'. Market research is basically the systematic gathering, recording and analyzing of the facts about business problems with a view to investigate the structure and development of a market for the purpose of formulating efficient policies for purchasing, production and sales. Research with regard to demand and market factors has great utility in business. Market analysis has become an integral tool of business policy.

Once sales forecasting is done, the Master Production Schedule (MPS) and Material Requirement Planning (MRP) can be efficiently done within the limits of the projected capacity based on the MPS Budgetary control can be made more efficient, thus replacing subjective business decisions with more logical and scientific decisions. Modern industry with its large-scale operations tends to create a gulf between the customer and the manufacturer.

Particularly when business is too big and operations are too far-flung, one cannot depend upon casual contacts and personal impressions. Research methodology has been developed as the tool by which business executives keep in touch with their customers. If an entrepreneur has to make sound decisions, he must know who has customers are and what they want. To a certain extent he relies on his salesmen and his dealers to supply him with market information but in recent years, more and more firms/executives have turned to research methodology as a medium of communication between the customer and the company.

Marketing research is the link between the manufacturer and the consumer and the means of providing consumer-orientation in all aspects of the marketing function. It is the instrument of obtaining the knowledge about the market and consumer through objective methods, which guard against the manufacturer's subjective bias. Many Researchers define marketing research as gathering, recording and analyzing of all facts about problems relating to the transfer and sale of goods and services from producer to consumer. Research methodology is an essential prerequisite for consumeroriented marketing.

It is necessary for developing the marketing strategy where in factors under the control of the organization, *viz.*, product distribution system, advertising, promotion and price can be utilized so as to obtain maximum results in the context of the factors outside the control of the organization *viz.*, economic environment, competitor and laws of land. Application of Marketing Research Following are a number of examples on the applications of marketing research. They clearly bring out how marketing research has been helpful in resolving marketing problems or in identifying opportunities or the development of new products.

- A pharmaceutical company3 carried out a study on the prescription behaviour for a major brand on account of its declining sales. The study brought out interesting and even startling findings on a number of aspects such as the relationship between the sales and the age of the brand, its regular promotion, its core therapeutic emphasis and the role of retailers in servicing prescriptions. Prior to the study, all these aspects had been only a matter of conjecture all the while. On the basis of findings of the study, the company changed its marketing strategy. This enabled it to regain the lost market share of its brand.
- Malayala Manorama, which is Kerala's largest publication group, has recently launched a monthly women's magazine in Hindi, Vanita. While launching this magazine, the management observed that it was convinced through market research that there was a huge vacuum in the Hindi magazine segment. This new magazine Vanita has been positioned as a partner and friend that the modern woman can identify with. The first print run of Vanita was one lakh copies. Indications are that within a short time it may become one of the popular Hindi magazines.
- Cadbury India Limited launched Picnic from its international portfolio in February 1998. It is wrapped in vibrant colours of red, blue and

yellow in conformity with its international packaging. Earlier, Cadbury India Limited commissioned a consumer research study in Mumbai. The results of this study were encouraging and showed that the Indian youth is always interested in experimenting with new food options.

- Procter and Gamble (P&G) launched Menthol, an international vibrant of Head and Shoulders. This joins the extra-conditioning anti-dandruff shampoo of the same brand. The company conducted a market research study prior to its launch. The findings of the study indicated a distinct need for a menthol-based shampoo. The study showed that in hot and humid conditions as in India, consumers prefer a shampoo which not only removes dandruff but also provides a cool and tingling sensation to the scalp.
- Another example4 from PandG shows how marketing research is used to identify new opportunities in the marketplace. The company was getting a lot of data on Vicks- Vapourub. The analysis of such data revealed that the most common symptom of cold was a headache and that majority of adults typically take a pill to cure it. This disclosed an opportunity for a product that can treat the headache as well as the other symptoms. The company thus launched Action 500. It not only treated headache but also gave relief from blocked nose. Marketing research can therefore lead to the development of a new product.
- Pepsi Foods5 has assigned great importance-to marketing research. Through research it gets systematic information about its markets and its customers.

All its research is done by the IMRB. Broadly, research studies done for Pepsi Foods fall in the following three areas:

- Studies undertaken on a continuous basis like marketing tracking studies and retail audits.
- Studies that are commissioned for specific marketing problems faced by the company.
- Studies done from time to time as per the requirement of the company such as a study to ascertain the effectiveness of an ad campaign. All these three types of research studies have tremendously helped Pepsi Foods to strengthen its position in the market. It feels the pulse of the market and is always in touch with the latest developments in the market.

- Another multinational company Whirlpool Asia lays considerable emphasis on marketing research. In this company, every activity, strategy and decision is based on data collected through the research process. It believes in planning research in advance though it is rather difficult. It strives to have a meaningful dialogue with the consumer in order to know his real opinion about its products, what difficulties he experiences and what suggestions he has to offer. Information thus received proves to be quite useful to the company in modifying its products or in evolving new ones. Whirlpool has gained an insight into the various segments in the market. In India, it has segmented the market on the basis of the different stages of the product life cycle. We hope you have the clear picture of the functions of the manager in an organization and the role of research in decision-making.

- *On the basis of the functions we can state some of the general objectives of Managerial Research*:
  - Decision-making objectives
  - Economic and business objectives
  - Policy objectives
  - Product development
  - Profit objectives
  - Human Resource Development objectives
  - Market objectives
    i. Innovation objectives
    ii. Customer satisfaction objectives
  - Promotional objectives
  - Corporate change objectives

BUSINESS BUYING BEHAVIOUR

The business market is comprised of organizations that, in some form, are involved in the manufacturer, distribution or support of products or services sold or otherwise provided to other organizations.

The amount of purchasing undertaken in the business market easily dwarfs the total spending by consumers. Because the business market is so large it draws the interest of millions of companies worldwide that market exclusively to business customers.

For these marketers understanding how businesses make purchase decisions is critical to their organizations' marketing efforts.

In some ways understanding the business market is not as complicated as understanding the consumer market. For example, in certain business markets purchase decisions hinge on the outcome of a bidding process between competitors offering similar products and services.

In these cases the decision to buy is often whittled down to one concern – who has the lowest price.

Thus, unlike consumer markets, where building a recognizable brand is very important, for many purchase situations in the business market this is not the case.

However, in many other ways business buying is much more complicated. For instance, the demand by businesses for products and services is affected by consumer purchases (called derived demand) and because so many organizations may have a part in creating consumer purchases, a small swing in consumer demand can create big changes in business purchasing. Automobile purchases are a good example.

If consumer demand for cars increases many companies connected with the automobile industry will also see demand for their products and services increase (we will later refer to these companies as supply chain members). Under these conditions companies will ratchet up their operations to ensure demand is met, which invariably will lead to new purchases by a large number of companies. In fact, it is conceivable that an increase of just one or two per cent for consumer demand can increase business demand for products and services by five or more per cent. Unfortunately, the opposite is true if demand declines. Trying to predict these swings requires businesses to not only understand their immediate customers but also the end user, which as we will discuss, may be well down the supply chain from where the business operates.

WHO MAKES UP THE BUSINESS MARKET

There are millions of organizations worldwide selling their products and services to other businesses. They operate in many industries and range in size from huge multinational companies with thousands of employees to one-person small businesses. With such a large number of organizations and industries contained within the business market, a marketer can obtain a better picture of who is involved by looking at popular business classification systems set up by international governments, such as the North American Industrial Classification System (NAICS), which covers Canada, Mexico and the United States and the International Standard Industrial Classification (ISIC), which is widely used in Europe.

These reports provide descriptions of hundreds of industry classifications. For instance, the table below shows how US operators of "Golf Pro Shops" are listed in the NAICS coding system. Note the numeric sequence that occurs as one "drills down" in order to locate individual industry groups.

Once industry codes are known these can be used within various government and industry research reports to locate specific industry information such as number of firms operating in the industry, total industry sales, number of employees and more.

For the purposes of this tutorial, however, we will use a broader approach to categorizing businesses choosing to categorize based on the general business function an organization performs rather then by industry. We break the business market down into two broad categories - Supply Chain Members and Business User Markets.

SUPPLY CHAIN MEMBERS

Supply Chain Member	What They Do	Example
Raw Material Suppliers	These companies are generally considered the first stage in the supply chain and provide basic products through mining, harvesting, fishing, etc., that are key ingredients in the production of higher-order products.	Copper is mined and extracted from copper ore. Copper is then refined to remove impurities.
Processed Materials or Basic Component Manufacturers	Firms at this level use raw materials to produce more advanced materials or products contained within more advanced components.	Copper is purchased by electrical wire manufacturers.
Advanced Component Manufacturers	These companies use basic components to produce products that offer a significant function needed within a larger product.	Electrical wire is purchased by a manufacturer of electrical power supplies.
Product Manufacturers	This market consists of companies that purchase both basic and advanced components and then assemble these components into a final product designated for a user. These products may or may not be sold as stand-alone products. Some may be included within larger products.	Power supplies are purchased by manufacturers of desktop computers.
Support Service Firms	These companies offer services at almost any point in the supply chain and also to the business user market. Some services are directly related to the product while others focus on areas of the business not directly related to production.	Distribution companies, such as truck firms and storage facilities, assist in moving products from one supply chain member to another. However, in most cases they do not take ownership of products that pass through the supply chain.

The supply chain consists of mostly for-profit companies engaged in activities involving product creation and delivery. Essentially the chain represents major steps needed to manufacture a product that will eventually be sold as a final product. Each member of the supply chain purchases products and services enabling them to carry out its business objectives.

When making purchase decisions supply chain members may be motivated by such factors as: product cost, return on investment (*i.e.*, benefits obtained exceed price paid), assurance of consistent supply (*i.e.*, product is available and delivery is on-time), reciprocity with supplying firm (*i.e.*, we buy from you and you buy from us), and much more. Examples of purchasing occurring in the supply chain include: manufacturing and plant equipment, information technology, office supplies, professional business services, etc.

In the table below we arbitrarily identify five main categories of supply chain members primarily based on the stage at which they contribute to the manufacturing process. However, it is conceivable that these categories can be further divided in order to flush out more specific activities.

BUSINESS USER MARKETS

Market	What They Do	Considerations When Buying	What They Buy
Government	Made up of Federal, State, Local and International governments. They use purchases to assist with the functioning of the government that may include redistributing to others.	Mostly require suppliers to be approved, meet specifications and to bid for purchases.	Defense equipment, heavy equipment for public works projects, office supplies, pharmaceuticals, etc.
Not-For-Profit	Organizations whose tax structure precludes earning profits from operations and whose missions tend to be oriented to assisting others.	Look for purchases that will fit within tight budgetary restrictions and also within the mission of the organization.	Office equipment and supplies, office rental, professional services, etc.
Reseller	Also called distributors, these companies operate in both the consumer and the business markets. Their function involves purchasing large volumes of products from manufacturers (and sometimes from other resellers) and selling these products in smaller quantities. Includes wholesalers, retailers and industrial distributors.	Seek products that are of interest to the reseller's customers. Other issues include how delivery is handled and whether the supplier offers incentives to help the reseller promote the product.	Consumer and industrial products to be redistributed to other businesses and consumers.

Besides selling final products and services to supply chain companies, several additional user markets also make purchases either for their own consumption or they buy with the intention of redistributing to others. In these purchase situations the buyer generally does not radically change the product from its form when it was purchased from a Product Manufacturer. While technically these markets are also part of the supply chain, members of the business user market do not, in most cases, engage or directly assist in production activities.

HOW BUSINESS MARKETS COMPARE TO CONSUMER MARKETS

For marketers, the selling environment of business markets present uniquely different circumstances when compared to selling to consumers. At the beginning of this tutorial we saw two ways in which consumer and business markets differ: 1) business markets are more likely to be price driven than brand driven, and 2) demand in business markets tends to be more volatile than consumer markets. However, the two markets are dissimilar in other ways requiring marketers to take a different approach when selling to business customers than to consumers. These differences include:

- How Decisions Are Made?
- Existence of Experienced Purchasers,
- Time Needed to Make Buying Decision,
- Size of Purchases,
- Number of Buyers,
- Type of Promotional Effort Needed to Reach Buyer,

How Decisions Are Made

In the consumer market a very large percentage of purchase decisions are made by a single person. There are situations in which multiple people may be involved in a consumer purchase decision, such as a child influencing a parent to choose a certain brand of cereal or a husband and wife deciding together to buy a house, but most of the time purchases are individual decisions.

The business market is significantly different. While single person purchasing is not unusual, especially within a small company, a significant percentage of business buying, especially within larger organizations, requires the input of many.

In the marketing literature those associated with the purchase decision are known to be part of a Buying Centre, which consists of individuals within an organization that perform one or more of the following roles:

- *Buyer*: Responsible for dealing with suppliers and placing orders (*e.g.*, purchasing agent).
- *Decider*: Has the power to make the final purchase decision (*e.g.*, CEO).
- *Influencer*: Has the ability to affect what is ordered such as setting order specifications (*e.g.*, engineers, researchers, product managers).
- *User*: Those who will actually use the product when it is received (*e.g.*, office staff).
- *Initiator*: Any Buying Centre member who is the first to determine that a need exists.

- *Gatekeeper*: Anyone who controls access to other Buying Centre members (*e.g.*, administrative assistant).

For marketers confronting a Buying Centre it is important to first identify who plays what role. Once identified the marketer must address the needs of each member, which may differ significantly. For instance, the Decider, who may be the company president wants to make sure the purchase will not negatively affect the company's bottom line while the Buyer wants to be assured the product will be delivered on time. Thus, the way each Buying Centre member is approached and marketed to requires careful planning in order to address the unique needs of each member.

Experienced Purchasers

As noted in the discussion of the Buying Centre, organizations often employ purchasing agents or professional buyers whose job is to negotiate the best deals for their company. Unlike consumers, who often lack information when making purchase decisions, professional buyers are generally as knowledgeable about the product and the industry as the marketer who is selling to them.

Decision Making Time

Depending on the product, business purchase decisions can drag on for an extensive period. Unlike consumer markets where impulse purchasing is rampant, the number of people involved in business purchase decisions results in decisions taking weeks, months or even years.

Larger Purchases

For products that are regularly used and frequently purchased, businesses will often buy a larger volume at one time compared to consumer purchases. Because of this business purchasers often demand price breaks (*e.g.*, discounts) for higher order levels.

Number of Buyers

While there are several million companies worldwide that operate in the overall business market, within a particular market the number is much smaller. For example, while in the United States there are over 95 million households who may shop at a grocery store, there are only a few thousand grocery stores with many of these centrally controlled as part of a chain of stores. Additionally, within some industries buyers are highly concentrated in certain geographic areas. Consequently, compared to consumer products, marketing efforts are confined to a smaller targeted group.

Promotional Focus

Companies who primarily target consumers often use mass advertising methods to reach an often widely dispersed market. For business-to-business marketers the size of individual orders, along with a smaller number of buyers, makes person-to-person contact by sales representatives a more effective means of promotion.

TYPES OF BUSINESS PURCHASE DECISIONS

While it would appear business customers face the same four purchase situations faced by consumers (Minor New Purchase, Minor Re-Purchase, Major New Purchase, Major Re-Purchase), the nature of the business market noted above has led many marketing academics to group business purchase situations into only three categories. The reason is that the idea of a minor order may not hold as well in the business market, where buyers tend to place larger orders and where suppliers' marketing efforts are directed towards the most profitable buyers.

- *Straight Re-Purchase*: These purchase situations involve routine ordering. In most cases buyers simply reorder the same products or services that were previously purchased. In fact, many larger companies have programmed re-purchases into an automated ordering system that initiates electronic orders when inventory falls below a certain pre-determined level. For the supplier benefiting from the re-purchase this situation is ideal since the purchaser is not looking to evaluate other products. For competitors who are not getting the order it may require extensive marketing efforts to persuade the buyer to consider other product or service options.
- *Modified Re-Purchase*: These purchases occur when products or services previously considered a straight re-purchase are for some reason now under a re-evaluation process. There are many reasons why a product is moved to the status of a modified re-purchase. Some of these reasons include: end of purchase contract period, change in who is involved in making the purchase, supplier is removed from an approved suppliers list, mandate from top level of organization to re-evaluate all purchasing, or strong marketing effort by competitors. In this circumstance the incumbent supplier faces the same challenges they may have faced when they initially convinced the buyer to make the purchase. For competitors the door is now open and they must work hard to make sure their message is heard by those in charge of the purchase decision.
- *New Task Purchase*: As the name suggests, these purchases are ones the buyer has never or rarely made before. In some ways new task purchases can be considered as either minor or major depending on the total cost or overall importance of the purchase. In either case the buyer will spend considerably more time evaluating alternatives. For example, if faced with a major new task purchase, which often

involves complex items, such as computer systems, buildings, robotic assembly lines, etc., the purchase cycle from first recognizing the need to placement of the order may be months or even years. The business market we now look at how purchasing decisions are made. Business purchasing follows the same five-step buying process faced by consumers:

- Need Recognition
- Search:
- Evaluate Options
- Purchase
- After-Purchase Evaluation.

While the steps are the same as consumer purchasing, the activities occurring within each step are quite different as we discuss below.

NEED RECOGNITION

In a business environment needs arise from just about anywhere within the organization. The Buying Centre concept shows that Initiators are the first organizational members to recognize a need. In most situations the Initiator is also the User or Buyer. Users are inclined to identify the need for new solutions (*i.e.*, new products) while Buyers are more likely to identify the need to re-purchase products.

But marketers should also understand that more companies are replacing human involvement in re-purchase decisions with automated methods, thus making it more challenging for competitors to replace currently purchased products. In straight re-purchase situations, whether there is human intervention or not, the purchasing process often jumps from Need Recognition to Purchase and little search activity is performed. As part of this step, a specifications document may be generated that lays out the requirements of the product or service to be purchased. Several members of the Buying Centre may be involved in creation of the specifications. For the marketer, establishing close contact with those who draw up the specifications may help position the marketer's product for inclusion in the search phase.

SEARCH

The search for alternatives to consider as potential solutions to recognized needs is one of the most significant differences between consumer and business purchasing. Much of this has to do with an organization's motive to reduce costs. While a consumer will probably not search hard to save two cents a gallon on gas, a company that has a large fleet of cars or trucks certainly will. In fact, this step in the purchase process is where professional buyers make their mark.

The primary intention of their search efforts is to identify multiple suppliers who meet product specifications and then, through a screening process, offer a selected group the opportunity to present their products to members of the Buying Centre. Although in some industries, such as chemicals, online marketplaces and auction sites offer buyers another option for selecting suppliers that may not include supplier presentations.

For suppliers, the key to this step of the purchase process is to make sure they are included within the search activities of the Buyer or others in the Buying Centre. In some instances this may require that a supplier work to be included within an approved suppliers list. In the case of online marketplaces and auction sites, suppliers should work to be included within relevant sites.

EVALUATE OPTION

Once the search has produced options, members of the Buying Centre may then choose among the alternatives. In more advanced purchase situations, members of the Buying Centre may evaluate each option using a checklist of features and benefits sought by the buyer.

Each feature/benefit is assigned a weight that corresponds to its importance to the purchase decision. In many cases, especially when dealing with Government and Not-For-Profit markets, suppliers must submit bids with the lowest bidder often being awarded the order, assuming products or services meet specifications.

PURCHASE

To actually place the order may require the completion of paperwork (or electronic documents) such as a purchase order. Acquiring the necessary approvals can delay the order for an extended period of time. And for very large purchases, such as buildings or large equipment, financing options may need to be explored.

AFTER-PURCHASE EVALUATION

After the order is received the purchasing company may spend time reviewing the results of the purchase. This may involve the Buyer discussing product performance issues with Users. If the product is well received it may end up moving to a straight re-purchase status thus eliminating much of the evaluation process on future purchases.

DISTRIBUTION DECISIONS MAKING

Our discussions in the tutorials Product Decisions and Managing Products indicate product decisions may be the most important of all marketing decisions since these lead directly to the reasons (*i.e.*, offer benefits that satisfy needs) why customers decide to make a purchase. But having a strong product does little good if customers are not able to easily and conveniently obtain it. With this in mind we turn to the second major marketing decision area – distribution.

Distribution decisions focus on establishing a system that, at its basic level, allows customers to gain access and purchase a marketer's product. However, marketers may find that getting to the point at which a customer can acquire a product is complicated, time consuming, and expensive. The bottom line is a marketer's distribution system must be both effective (*i.e.*, delivers a good or service to the right place, in the right amount, in the right condition) and efficient (*i.e.*, delivers at the right time and for the right cost). Yet, as we will see, achieving these goals takes considerable effort.

Distribution decisions are relevant for nearly all types of products. While it is easy to see how distribution decisions impact physical goods, such as laundry detergent or truck parts, distribution is equally important for digital goods (*e.g.*, television programming, downloadable music) and services (*e.g.*, income tax services).

In fact, while the Internet is playing a major role in changing product distribution and is perceived to offer more opportunities for reaching customers, online marketers still face the same distribution issues and obstacles as those faced by offline marketers.

In order to facilitate an effective and efficient distribution system many decisions must be made including (but certainly not limited to):

- Assessing the best distribution channels for getting products to customers.
- Determining whether a reseller network is needed to assist in the distribution process.
- Arranging a reliable ordering system that allows customers to place orders.
- Creating a delivery system for transporting the product to the customer.
- For tangible and digital goods, establishing facilities for product storage.

CHANNELS OF DISTRIBUTION

We describe a supply chain as consisting of all parties and their supplied activities that help a marketer create and deliver products to the final customer. For marketers, the distribution decision is primarily concerned with the supply chain's front-end or channels of distribution that are designed to move the product (goods or services) from the hands of the company to the hands of the customer.

Obviously when we talk about intangible services the use of the word "hands" is a figurative way to describe the exchange that takes place. But the idea is the same as with tangible goods.

All activities and organizations helping with the exchange are part of the marketer's channels of distribution. Activities involved in the channel are wide and varied though the basic activities revolve around these general tasks:

- Ordering,
- Handling and shipping,
- Storage,
- Display,
- Promotion,
- Selling,
- Information feedback.

TYPE OF CHANNEL MEMBERS

Channel activities may be carried out by the marketer or the marketer may seek specialist organizations to assist with certain functions. We can classify specialist organizations into two broad categories: resellers and specialty service firms.

Resellers

These organizations, also known within some industries as intermediaries, distributors or dealers, generally purchase or take ownership of products from the marketing company with the intention of selling to others. If a marketer utilizes multiple resellers within its distribution channel strategy the collection of resellers is termed a Reseller Network. These organizations can be classified into several sub-categories including:

- *Retailers:* Organizations that sell products directly to final consumers.
- *Wholesalers:* Organizations that purchase products from suppliers, such as manufacturers or other wholesalers, and in turn sell these to other resellers, such as retailers or other wholesalers.
- *Industrial Distributors:* Firms that work mainly in the business-to-business market selling products obtained from industrial suppliers.

Specialty Service Firms

These are organizations that provide additional services to help with the exchange of products but generally do not purchase the product (*i.e.*, do not take ownership of the product):

- *Agents and Brokers*: Organizations that mainly work to bring suppliers and buyers together in exchange for a fee.
- *Distribution Service Firms:* Offer services aiding in the movement of products such as assistance with transportation, storage, and order processing.
- *Others:* This category includes firms that provide additional services to aid in the distribution process such as insurance companies and firms offering transportation routing assistance.

IMPORTANCE OF DISTRIBUTION CHANNELS

As noted, distribution channels often require the assistance of others in order for the marketer to reach its target market. But why exactly does a company need others to help with the distribution of their product? Wouldn't a company that handles its own distribution functions be in a better position to exercise control over product sales and potentially earn higher profits? Also, doesn't the Internet make it much easier to distribute products thus lessening the need for others to be involved in selling a company's product?

While on the surface it may seem to make sense for a company to operate its own distribution channel (*i.e.*, handling all aspects of distribution) there are many factors preventing companies from doing so. While companies can do without the assistance of certain channel members, for many marketers some level of channel partnership is needed. For example, marketers who are successful without utilizing resellers to sell their product (*e.g.*, Dell Computers sells mostly through the Internet and not in retail stores) may still need assistance with certain parts of the distribution process (*e.g.*, Dell uses parcel post shippers such as FedEx and UPS). In Dell's case creating their own transportation system makes little sense given how large such a system would need to be in order to service Dell's customer base. Thus, by using shipping companies Dell is taking advantage of the benefits these services offer to Dell and to Dell's customers.

When choosing a distribution strategy a marketer must determine what value a channel member adds to the firm's products. Customers assess a product's value by looking at many factors including those that surround the product (*i.e.*, augmented product). Several surrounding features can be directly influenced by channel members, such as customer service, delivery, and availability. Consequently, for the marketer selecting a channel partner involves a value analysis in the same way customers make purchase decisions. That is, the marketer must assess the benefits received from utilizing a channel partner versus the cost incurred for using the services.

Benefits Offered by Channel Members

- *Cost Savings in Specialization:* Members of the distribution channel are specialists in what they do and can often perform tasks better and at lower cost than companies who do not have distribution experience. Marketers attempting to handle too many aspects of distribution may end up exhausting company resources as they learn how to distribute, resulting in the company being "a jack of all trades but master of none."
- *Reduce Exchange Time:* Not only are channel members able to reduce distribution costs by being experienced at what they do, they often perform their job more rapidly resulting in faster product delivery. For instance, consider what would happen if a grocery store received direct shipment from EVERY manufacturer that sells products in the store. This delivery system would be chaotic as hundreds of trucks

line up each day to make deliveries, many of which would consist of only a few boxes. On a busy day a truck may sit for hours waiting for space so they can unload their products. Instead, a better distribution scheme may have the grocery store purchasing its supplies from a grocery wholesaler that has its own warehouse for handling simultaneous shipments from a large number of suppliers. The wholesaler will distributes to the store in the quantities the store needs, on a schedule that works for the store, and often in a single truck, all of which speeds up the time it takes to get the product on the store's shelves.

- *Customers Want to Conveniently Shop for Variety:* Marketers have to understand what customers want in their shopping experience. Referring back to our grocery store example, consider a world without grocery stores and instead each marketer of grocery products sells through their own stores. As it is now, shopping is time consuming, but consider what would happen if customers had to visit multiple retailers each week to satisfy their grocery needs. Hence, resellers within the channel of distribution serve two very important needs: 1) they give customers the products they want by purchasing from many suppliers (termed accumulating and assortment services), and 2) they make it convenient to purchase by making products available in single location.
- *Resellers Sell Smaller Quantities:* Not only do resellers allow customers to purchase products from a variety of suppliers, they also allow customers to purchase in quantities that work for them. Suppliers though like to ship products they produce in large quantities since this is more cost effective than shipping smaller amounts. For instance, consider what it costs to drive a truck a long distance. In terms of operational expenses for the truck (*e.g.*, fuel, truck driver's cost) let's assume it costs (US) $1,000 to go from point A to point B. Yet in most cases, with the exception of a little decrease in fuel efficiency, it does not cost that much more to drive the truck whether it is filled with 1000 boxes containing the product or whether it only has 100 boxes. But when transportation costs are considered on a per product basis ($1 per box vs. $10 per box) the cost is much less for a full truck. The ability of intermediaries to purchase large quantities but to resell them in smaller quantities (referred to as bulk breaking) not only makes these products available to those wanting smaller quantities but the reseller is able to pass along to their customers a significant portion of the cost savings gained by purchasing in large volume.
- Create Sales – Resellers are at the front line when it comes to creating demand for the marketer's product. In some cases resellers

perform an active selling role using persuasive techniques to encourage customers to purchase a marketer's product. In other cases they encourage sales of the product through their own advertising efforts and using other promotional means such as special product displays.

- *Offer Financial Support:* Resellers often provide programmes that enable customers to more easily purchase products by offering financial programmes that ease payment requirements. These programmes include allowing customers to: purchase on credit; purchase using a payment plan; delay the start of payments; and allowing trade-in or exchange options.
- *Provide Information:* Companies utilizing resellers for selling their products depend on distributors to provide information that can help improve the product. High-level intermediaries may offer their suppliers real-time access to sales data including information showing how products are selling by such characteristics as geographic location, type of customer, and product location (*e.g.*, where located within a store, where found on a web site). If high-level information is not available, marketers can often count on resellers to provide feedback as to how customers are responding to products. This feedback can occur either through surveys or interviews with reseller's employees or by requesting the reseller allow the marketer to survey customers.

Costs of Utilizing Channel Members

- Loss of Revenue – Resellers are not likely to offer services to a marketer unless they see financial gain in doing so. They obtain payment for their services as either direct payment (*e.g.*, marketer pays for shipping costs) or, in the case of resellers, by charging their customers more than what they paid the marketer for acquiring the product (termed markup). For the latter, marketers have a good idea of what the final customer will pay for their product which means the marketer must charge less when selling the product to resellers. In these situations marketers are not reaping the full sale price by using resellers, which they may be able to do if they sold directly to the customer.
- *Loss of Communication Control:* Marketers not only give up revenue when using resellers, they may also give up control of the message being conveyed to customers. If the reseller engages in communication activities, such as personal selling in order to get customers to purchase the product, the marketer is no longer controlling what is being said about the product. This can lead to

miscommunication problems with customers, especially if the reseller embellishes the benefits the product provides to the customer. While marketers can influence what is being said by training reseller's salespeople, they lack ultimate control of the message.

- *Loss of Product Importance:* Once a product is out of the marketer's hands the importance of that product is left up to channel members. If there are pressing issues in the channel, such as transportation problems, or if a competitor is using promotional incentives in an effort to push their product through resellers, the marketer's product may not get the attention the marketer feels it should receive.

CHANNEL ARRANGEMENTS

The distribution channel consists of many parties each seeking to meet their own business objectives. Clearly for the channel to work well, relationships between channel members must be strong with each member understanding and trusting others on whom they depend for product distribution to flow smoothly. For instance, a small sporting goods retailer that purchases products from a wholesaler trusts the wholesaler to deliver required items on-time in order to meet customer demand, while the wholesaler counts on the retailer to place regular orders and to make on-time payments.

Relationships in a channel are in large part a function of the arrangement that occurs between the members. These arrangements can be divided in two main categories: independent and dependent.

Independent Channel Arrangement

Under this arrangement a channel member negotiates deals with others that do not result in binding relationships. In other words, a channel member is free to make whatever arrangements they feel is in their best interest. This so-called "conventional" distribution arrangement often leads to significant conflict as individual members decide what is best for them and not necessarily for the entire channel. On the other hand, an independent channel arrangement is less restrictive than dependent arrangements and makes it easier for a channel members to move away from relationships they feel are not working to their benefit.

Dependent Channel Arrangement

Under this arrangement a channel member feels tied to one or more members of the distribution channel. Sometimes referred to as "vertical marketing systems" this approach makes it more difficult for an individual member to make changes to how products are distributed. However, the dependent approach provides much more stability and consistency since members are united in their goals. The dependent channel arrangement can be broken down into three types:

- *Corporate:* Under this arrangement a supplier operates its own distribution system in a manor that produces an integrated channel. This occurs most frequently in the retail industry where a supplier operates a chain of retail stores. Starbucks is a company that does this. They import and process coffee and then sell it under their own brand name in their own stores. It should be mentioned that Starbucks also distributes their products in other ways, such as through grocery stores and mail order. As we will see in more detail later, Starbucks is using a multi-channel structure to market their products.
- *Contractual:* Under this arrangement a legal document obligates members to agree on how a product is distributed. Often times the agreement specifically spells out which activities each member is permitted to perform or not perform. This type of arrangement can occur in several formats including:
  - *Wholesaler-sponsored*: Where a wholesaler brings together and manages many independent retailers including having the retailers use the same name
  - *Retailer-sponsored*: This format also brings together retailers but the retailers are responsible for managing the relationship
  - *Franchised:* Where a central organization controls nearly all activities of other members
- *Administrative*: In certain channel arrangements a single member may dominate the decisions that occur within the channel. These situations occur when one channel member has achieved a significant power position. This most likely occurs if a manufacturer has significant power due to brands in strong demand by target markets (*e.g.*, Procter &Gamble) or if a retailer has significant power due to size and market coverage (*e.g.*, Wal-Mart). In most cases the arrangement is understood to occur and is not bound by legal or financial arrangements.

FACTORS IN CREATING DISTRIBUTION CHANNELS

Like most marketing decisions, a great deal of research and thought must go into determining how to carry out distribution activities in a way that meets a marketer's objectives. The marketer must consider many factors when establishing a distribution system. Some factors are directly related to marketing decisions while others are affected by relationships that exist with members of the channel.

Next we examine the key factors to consider when designing a distribution strategy. We group these into two main categories: marketing decision issues and channel relationship issues. In turn, each of these categories contains several topics of concern to marketers. Distribution strategy can be shaped by how decisions are made in other marketing areas.

Product Issues

The nature of the product often dictates the distribution options available especially if the product requires special handling. For instance, companies selling delicate or fragile products, such as flowers, look for shipping arrangements that are different than those sought for companies selling extremely tough or durable products, such as steel beams.

Promotion Issues

Besides issues related to physical handling of products, distribution decisions are affected by the type of promotional activities needed to sell the product to customers. For products needing extensive salesperson-to-customer contact (*e.g.*, automobile purchases) the distribution options are different than for products where customers typically require no sales assistance (*i.e.*, bread purchases).

Pricing Issues

The desired price at which a marketer seeks to sell their product can impact how they choose to distribute. As previously mentioned, the inclusion of resellers in a marketer's distribution strategy may affect a product's pricing since each member of the channel seeks to make a profit for their contribution to the sale of the product. If too many channel members are involved the eventual selling price may be too high to meet sales targets in which case the marketer may explore other distribution options.

Target Market Issues

A distribution system is only effective if customers can obtain the product. Consequently, a key decision in setting up a channel arrangement is for the marketer to choose the approach that reaches customers in the most effective way possible. The most important decision with regard to reaching the target market is to determine the level of distribution coverage needed to effectively meet customer's needs. Distribution coverage is measured in terms of the intensity by which the product is made available. For the most part, distribution coverage decisions are of most concern to consumer products companies, though there are many industrial products that also must decide how much coverage to give their products. As we will see the marketer must take into consideration many factors when choosing the right level of distribution coverage. However, all marketers should understand that distribution creates costs to the organization. Some of these expenses can be passed along to customers (*e.g.*, shipping costs) but others cannot (*e.g.*, need for additional salespeople to handle more distributors). Thus, the process for determining the right level of distribution coverage often comes down to an analysis of the benefits (*e.g.*, more sales) versus the cost associated with gain the benefits.

There are three main levels of distribution coverage - mass coverage, selective and exclusive.

- *Mass Coverage*: The mass coverage (also known as intensive distribution) strategy attempts to distribute products widely in nearly all locations in which that type of product is sold. This level of distribution is only feasible for relatively low priced products that appeal to very large target markets (*e.g.*, see consumer convenience products). A product such as Coca-Cola is a classic example since it is available in a wide variety of locations including grocery stores, convenience stores, vending machines, hotels and many, many more. With such a large number of locations selling the product the cost of distribution is extremely high and must be offset with very high sales volume.
- *Selective Coverage:* Under selective coverage the marketer deliberately seeks to limit the locations in which this type of product is sold. To the non-marketer it may seem strange for a marketer to not want to distribute their product in every possible location. However, the logic of this strategy is tied to the size and nature of the product's target market. Products with selective coverage appeal to smaller, more focused target markets (*e.g.*, see consumer shopping products) compared to the size of target markets for mass marketed products. Consequently, because the market size is smaller, the number of locations needed to support the distribution of the product is fewer.
- *Exclusive Coverage:* Some high-end products target very narrow markets that have a relatively small number of customers. These customers are often characterized as "discriminating" in their taste for products and seek to satisfy some of their needs with high-quality, though expensive products. Additionally, many buyers of high-end products require a high level of customer service from the channel member from whom they purchase. These characteristics of the target market may lead the marketer to sell their products through a very select or exclusive group of resellers. Another type of exclusive distribution may not involve high-end products but rather products only available in selected locations such as company-owned stores. While these products may or may not be higher priced compared to competitive products, the fact these are only available in company outlets give exclusivity to the distribution.

We conclude this section by noting that while the three distribution coverage options just discussed serve as a useful guide for envisioning how distribution intensity works, the advent of the Internet has brought into question the effectiveness of these schemes. For all intents and purposes all products available for purchase over the Internet are distributed in the same way - mass coverage. So a better way to look at the three levels is to consider these as options for distribution coverage of products that are physically purchased by a customer (*i.e.*, walk-in to purchase).

Channel Relationship Issues

A good distribution strategy takes into account not only marketing decisions, but also considers how relationships within the channel of distribution can impact the marketer's product. In this section we examine three such issues:

CHANNEL POWER

A channel can be made up of many parties each adding value to the product purchased by customers. However, some parties within the channel may carry greater weight than others. In marketing terms this is called channel power, which refers to the influence one party within a channel has over other channel members.

When power is exerted by a channel member they are often in the position to make demands of others. For instance, they may demand better financial terms (*e.g.*, will only buy if prices are lowered, will only sell if price is higher) or demand other members perform certain tasks (*e.g.*, do more marketing to customers, perform more product services). Channel power can be seen in several ways:

- Backend or Product Power – Occurs when a product manufacturer or service provider markets a brand that has a high level of customer demand. The marketer of the brand is often in a power position since other channel members have little choice but to carry the brand or risk losing customers.
- Middle or Wholesale Power – Occurs when an intermediary, such as a wholesaler, services a large number of smaller retailers with products obtained from a large number of manufacturers. In this situation the wholesaler can exert power since the small retailers are often not in the position to purchase products cost-effectively and in as much variety as what is offered by the wholesaler.
- Front or Retailer Power – As the name suggests, the power in this situation rests with the retailer who can command major concessions from their suppliers. This type of power is most prevalent when the retailer commands a significant percentage of sales in the market they serve and others in the channel are dependent on the sales generated by the retailer.

CHANNEL CONFLICT

In an effort to increase product sales, marketers are often attracted by the notion that sales can grow if the marketer expands distribution by adding additional resellers. Such decisions must be handled carefully, however, so that existing dealers do not feel threatened by the new distributors who they may feel are encroaching on their customers and siphoning potential business. For marketers, channel strategy designed to expand product distribution may in fact do the opposite if existing members feel there is a conflict in the decisions made by the marketer. If existing members sense a conflict and feel the marketer is not sensitive to their needs they may choose to stop handling the marketer's products.

NEED FOR LONG-TERM COMMITMENTS

Channel decisions have long-term consequences for marketers since efforts to establish new relationships can take an extensive period of time while ending existing relationships can prove difficult.

For instance, Company A, a marketer of kitchen cabinets that wants to change distribution strategy, may decide to stop selling their product line through industrial supply companies that distribute cabinets to building contractors and instead sell through large retail home centers. If in the future Company

A decides to once again enter the industrial supply market they may run into resistance since supply companies may have replaced Company A's product line with other products and, given what happened to the previous relationship, may be reluctant to deal with Company A.

As another example of problems with long-term commitments, building contractors may be comfortable purchasing kitchen cabinets from industrial suppliers.

If Company A decides to change their reseller network they may find it difficult to regain the building contractor customer base, who may continue to purchase from the industrial suppliers but are now purchasing products from Company A's competitors.

In this case, Company A may have to give serious thought to whether breaking their long-term relationship with industrial suppliers is in the company's best interest.

OVERALL DISTRIBUTION DESIGN

Mindful of the factors affecting distribution decisions (*i.e.*, marketing decision issues and relationship issues), the marketer has several options to choose from when settling on a design for their distribution network. We stress the word "may" since while in theory an option would appear to be available, marketing decision factors (*e.g.*, product, promotion, pricing, target markets) or the nature of distribution channel relationships may not permit the marketer to pursue a particular option. For example, selling through a desired retailer may not be feasible if the retailer refuses to handle a product.

For marketers the choice of distribution design comes down to selecting between direct or indirect methods, or in some case choosing both.

Direct Distribution System

With a direct distribution system the marketer reaches the intended final user of their product by distributing the product directly to the customer. That is, there are no other parties involved in the distribution process that take ownership of the product. The direct system can be further divided by the method of communication that takes place when a sale occurs. These methods are:

- *Direct Marketing Systems:* With this system the customer places the order either through information gained from non-personal contact with the marketer, such as by visiting the marketer's web site or ordering from the marketer's catalog, or through personal communication with a customer representative who is not a salesperson, such as through toll-free telephone ordering.
- *Direct Retail Systems:* This type of system exists when a product marketer also operates their own retail outlets. As previously discussed, Starbucks would fall into this category.
- *Personal Selling Systems:* The key to this direct distribution system is that a person whose main responsibility involves creating and managing sales (*e.g.*, salesperson) is involved in the distribution process, generally by persuading the buyer to place an order. While the order itself may not be handled by the salesperson (*e.g.*, buyer physically places the order online or by phone) the salesperson plays a role in generating the sales.
- *Assisted Marketing Systems:* Under the assisted marketing system, the marketer relies on others to help communicate the marketer's products but handles distribution directly to the customer. The classic example of assisted marketing systems is eBay which helps bring buyers and sellers together for a fee. Other agents and brokers would also fall into this category.

Indirect Distribution System

With an indirect distribution system the marketer reaches the intended final user with the help of others. These resellers generally take ownership of the product, though in some cases they may sell products on a consignment basis (*i.e.*, only pay the supplying company if the product is sold). Under this system intermediaries may be expected to assume many responsibilities to help sell the product.

Indirect methods include:

- *Single-Party Selling System:* Under this system the marketer engages another party who then sells and distributes directly to the final customer. This is most likely to occur when the product is sold through large store-based retail chains or through online retailers, in which case it is often referred to as a trade selling system.

- *Multiple-Party Selling System:* This indirect distribution system has the product passing through two or more distributors before reaching the final customer. The most likely scenario is when a wholesaler purchases from the manufacturer and sells the product to retailers.

Multi-channel or Hybrid System

In cases where a marketer utilizes more than one distribution design the marketer is following a multi-channel or hybrid distribution system. As we discussed, Starbucks follows this approach as their distribution design includes using a direct retail system by selling in company-owned stores, a direct marketing system by selling via direct mail, and a single-party selling system by selling through grocery stores (they also use other distribution systems).

The multi-channel approach expands distribution and allows the marketer to reach a wider market, however, as we discussed under Channel Relationships, the marketer must be careful with this approach due to the potential for channel conflict.

ESTABLISHING CHANNEL RELATIONSHIPS

Since channel members must be convinced to handle a marketer's product it makes sense to consider channel partner's needs in the same way the marketer considers the final user's needs. However, the needs of channel members are much different than those of the final customer. As we noted, resellers seek products of interest to the reseller's customers but are also concerned with many other issues such as:

- *Delivery*: Resellers want the product delivered on-time and in good condition in order to meet customer demand and avoid inventory out-of-stocks.
- *Profit Margin:* Resellers are in business to make money so a key factor in their decision to handle a product is how much money they will make on each product sold. They expect that the difference (*i.e.*, margin) between their cost for acquiring the product from a supplier and the price they charge to sell the product to their customers will be sufficient to meet their profit objectives.
- *Other Incentives:* Besides profit margin, resellers may want other incentives to entice them especially if they are required to give extra effort selling the product. These incentives may be in the form of additional free products or even bonuses (*e.g.*, bonus, free trips) for achieving sales goals.
- *Packaging:* Resellers want to handle products as easily as possible and want their suppliers to ship and sell products in packages that fit within their system. For example, products may need to be a certain size or design in order to fit on a store's shelf, or the shipping package

must fit within the reseller's warehouse or receiving dock space. Also, many resellers are now requiring marketers to consider adding identification tags to products (*e.g.*, RFID tags) to allow for easier inventory tracking when the product is received and also when it is sold.

- *Training*: Some products require the reseller to have strong knowledge of the product including demonstrating the product to customers. Marketers must consider offering training to resellers to insure the reseller has the knowledge to present the product accurately.
- *Promotional Help:* Resellers often seek additional help from the product supplier to promote the product to customers. Such help may come in the form of funding for advertisements, point-of-purchase product materials, or in-store demonstrations.

We will continue our discussion of distribution decision in the next tutorial as we discuss in greater detail the reseller network – retailers and wholesalers - and the processes involved in physically handling product flow through the channel.

8

Development of Marketing Research and Measurement

LEVELS OF MEASUREMENT

Most texts on marketing research explain the four levels of measurement: nominal, ordinal, interval and ratio and so the treatment given to them here will be brief. However, it is an important topic since the type of scale used in taking measurements directly impinges on the statistical techniques which can legitimately be used in the analysis.

NOMINAL SCALES

This, the crudest of measurement scales, classifies individuals, companies, products, brands or other entities into categories where no order is implied. Indeed it is often referred to as a categorical scale. It is a system of classification and does not place the entity along a continuum. It involves a simply count of the frequency of the cases assigned to the various categories, and if desired numbers can be nominally assigned to label each category as in the example below:

Which of the following food items do you tend to buy at least once per month? (Please tick).

Okra	Palm Oil	Milled Rice
Peppers	Prawns	Pasteurised milk

The numbers have no arithmetic properties and act only as labels. The only measure of average which can be used is the mode because this is simply a set of frequency counts. Hypothesis tests can be carried out on data collected in the nominal form.

The most likely would be the Chi-square test. However, it should be noted that the Chi-square is a test to determine whether two or more variables are associated and the strength of that relationship. It can tell nothing about the form of that relationship, where it exists, *i.e.* it is not capable of establishing cause and effect.

Ordinal Scales

Ordinal scales involve the ranking of individuals, attitudes or items along the continuum of the characteristic being scaled. For example, if a researcher asked farmers to rank 5 brands of pesticide in order of preference he/she might obtain responses like those in table below.

Order of preference	Brand
1	Rambo
2	R.I.P.
3	Killalot
4	D.O.A.
5	Bugdeath

From such a table the researcher knows the order of preference but nothing about how much more one brand is preferred to another, that is there is no information about the interval between any two brands. All of the information a nominal scale would have given is available from an ordinal scale. In addition, positional statistics such as the median, quartile and percentile can be determined.

It is possible to test for order correlation with ranked data. The two main methods are Spearman's Ranked Correlation Coefficient and Kendall's Coefficient of Concordance. Using either procedure one can, for example, ascertain the degree to which two or more survey respondents agree in their ranking of a set of items.

Consider again the ranking of pesticides example in figure. The researcher might wish to measure similarities and differences in the rankings of pesticide brands according to whether the respondents' farm enterprises were classified as "arable" or "mixed" (a combination of crops and livestock). The resultant coefficient takes a value in the range 0 to 1. A zero would mean that there was no agreement between the two groups, and 1 would indicate total agreement. It is more likely that an answer somewhere between these two extremes would be found.

The only other permissible hypothesis testing procedures are the runs test and sign test. The runs test (also known as the Wald-Wolfowitz). Test is used to determine whether a sequence of binomial data - meaning it can take only one of two possible values *e.g.* African/non-African, yes/no, male/female - is random or contains systematic 'runs' of one or other value.

Sign tests are employed when the objective is to determine whether there is a significant difference between matched pairs of data.

The sign test tells the analyst if the number of positive differences in ranking is approximately equal to the number of negative rankings, in which case the distribution of rankings is random, *i.e.* apparent differences are not significant. The test takes into account only the direction of differences and ignores their magnitude and hence it is compatible with ordinal data.

Interval Scales

It is only with an interval scaled data that researchers can justify the use of the arithmetic mean as the measure of average.

The interval or cardinal scale has equal units of measurement, thus making it possible to interpret not only the order of scale scores but also the distance between them. However, it must be recognised that the zero point on an interval scale is arbitrary and is not a true zero.

This of course has implications for the type of data manipulation and analysis we can carry out on data collected in this form.

It is possible to add or subtract a constant to all of the scale values without affecting the form of the scale but one cannot multiply or divide the values. It can be said that two respondents with scale positions 1 and 2 are as far apart as two respondents with scale positions 4 and 5, but not that a person with score 10 feels twice as strongly as one with score 5. Temperature is interval scaled, being measured either in Centigrade or Fahrenheit.

DIFFICULTY OF MEASUREMENT

PELVIC MEASUREMENTS

Although researchers agree that birth weight is the most important measurable trait affecting calving difficulty, there is evidence that the size and shape of the pelvis also affect a heifer's ability to calve.

CALVING DIFFICULTY

Calving difficulty results in major economic loss to the beef cattle industry. Estimated losses resulting from dystocia (calving difficulty) equal or exceed $750,000,000 annually.

Calving difficulty influences the economics of a cow/calf enterprise through increased calf death loss, increased labour and veterinary costs, reduced subsequent reproductive performance of the cow, potential loss of the cow, and reduced milk production.

Calf mortality may be four to eight times greater in dystocia cases than in normal births. The majority of calf deaths occur within the first 24 hours following calving (58 per cent), with 75 per cent of the total occurring within the first week of life. Studies indicate that calf death loss due to dystocia accounts for the single largest perinatal and postnatal death loss category through the first 96 hours after birth. A number of factors affect calving difficulty, including:

- Birth weight of the calf,
- Pelvic area of the cow,
- Gestation length,
- Sex of calf,
- Inadequacies in heifer development,
- Body condition of the cow at calving,

- Abnormalities in hormone profiles at the time of birth,
- Abnormal presentation of the calf at birth,

We also know that the single major cause of dystocia is a disproportion between size of the calf at birth (birth weight) and the cow's birth canal (pelvic area). Differences in pelvic area are generally due to pelvic height, with discrepancies between the dam and fetus more likely to occur for pelvic height and depth of calf chest than for width measures.

Pelvic size, independent of cow weight, affects calving difficulty. Heifers of increased skeletal size usually have larger pelvic openings, but also tend to have heavier calves at birth. Hence, selection for cow size alone is ineffective.

Heifer weight and age generally have a positive relationship to pelvic area, but weight is not always a good indicator.

External dimensions such as width of hooks and length of rump are not good indicators of pelvic area or calving difficulty. For these reasons pelvic measurements can be a useful management tool to eliminate heifers with a higher potential for calving difficulty.

Table. Pelvic Area Per calf Birth Weight Ratios for Various Heifer Weights and Ages to Estimate Deliverable Calf Birth Weight.

	Heifer weightAge at time of measurement			
	8 to 9 months	**12 to 13 months**	**18 to 19 months**	**22 to 23 months**
500 pounds	1.7	2.0	–	–
600 pounds	1.8	2.1	–	–
700 pounds	1.9	2.2	2.6	–
800 pounds	–	2.3	2.73.1	
900 pounds	–	2.4	2.8	3.2
1,000 pounds	–	2.5	2.9	3.3
1,100 pounds	–	–	–	3.4

Structural traits in cattle tend to be highly heritable and pelvic area is no exception. This means there is a large genetic influence on pelvic area, which results in rapid response to selection. However, pelvic area is genetically correlated with many other traits, so selection for increased pelvic area alone can result in other traits changing for the worse. For example, selecting for increased pelvic area can result in increased birth weight and mature weight.

Pelvic measurements can be taken prior to the first breeding season and combined with a reproductive tract examination. Pelvic measurements should be used in addition to, not in place of, selection for size, weight, and above all, fertility. Producers should be aware that selection for pelvic area is likely to result in increased size of the entire skeleton and animal. Increased skeletal size of the dam will be reflected in higher birth weight and dimensions of the calf.

Pelvic measurements, on the other hand, can be used to successfully identify abnormally small or abnormally shaped pelvises. These situations, if left unidentified, are often associated with extreme dystocia, resulting in Cesarean delivery and even death of the calf or cow.

The vertical measurement is the vertical diameter between the symphysis pubis on the floor of the pelvis and the sacral vertebrae. The horizontal measurement is obtained by determining the horizontal diameter at its widest point between the left and right ileal shafts. These measurements are read in centimeters and multiplied together to obtain the total pelvic area in square centimeters.

Measurements may be obtained by a veterinarian or an experienced producer. It is important that the person doing the measuring have a thorough understanding of the birth canal, pelvic structure, and reproductive tract. Practice and experience are necessary before accurate measurements can be obtained.

Calving ease will continue to be an important consideration as the industry produces fast-growing muscular progeny by terminal sires. These sires should be selected on measures of direct calving ease by using EPD (expected progeny difference) values for calving ease and birth weight.

To accommodate fairly heavy birth weights, scientists at Colorado State University recommend that you develop a cow herd that excels in maternal calving ease. Sires of replacement females should be selected to maintain cow size and milk production at levels compatible with available resources. In addition, cows should be selected for total maternal calving ease along with gestation length.

Research indicates that bigger is not necessarily better when one considers actual pelvic measurements. In other words, heifers with large pelvic measurements fail to calve more easily than average-sized heifers. However, heifers with abnormally small pelvises or abnormally shaped pelvises generally experience a higher than normal incidence of calving difficulty and should be identified and culled from the herd.

MANUFACTURING'S NEXT FRONTIERS

The decade of the 1980s yielded many improvement initiatives that were focused on the manufacturing and materials management functions. Some initiatives were largely focused on improving management processes and empowering employees. JIT, Kanban, and Quality Circles are examples of "process-focused" initiatives. Other initiatives were primarily focused on technologies that supported or automated business or manufacturing processes. MRP, Bar Coding, CIM, and SPC are examples of "technology-focused" initiatives popular in the 1980s. Numerous manufacturers experienced significant measurable benefits from implementing these techniques. Cycle times in manufacturing were drastically reduced, inventories were managed-down to record low levels, and product quality was clearly improved in many segments of industry. Towards the end of the decade it was clear that a good deal of the "bang for the buck" was already "in pocket."

Some of the most positive indicators of improvement have been some of the most painful to appreciate. Highly trained manufacturing and materials managers and technicians are now on the street looking for jobs. Mergers, acquisitions, and bankruptcies of companies that supplied technologies to these areas are an everyday occurrence.

Well known companies like Prime Computer, Cullinet, Computer Partners, Automatix, and a host of others bit the dust or experienced significant corporate restructuring or downsizing. The "Big 8 Accounting" firms became the "Big 6" and the names of many of the internal consulting practices in these firms were changed. In many of these service firms, "system development" business services were re-focused to become "system integration" services. In almost every segment of industries that dealt with the manufacturing sector, significant changes were evident.

Most experts now agree that the vast majority of improvement opportunities that are "controllable and implementable" from within the manufacturing and materials functions have been achieved or are in process at this time. The exact figures being offered range from 60 per cent to 90 per cent penetration.

The major opportunities for future improvements in operations functions originate in functions that are not controllable by manufacturing. Again, macro industry trends are reflecting this reality.

Usher in Business Process Reengineering, TQM, and Self-Empowered Teams for management process improvements. Usher in Cross-Functional Systems and Product Data Management as examples of next-step technologies. Usher in Concurrent Engineering and Design For Manufacturing as examples of improvement initiatives that span both the process and technology environments.

A LESSON LEARNED

One of the major problems with initiatives in the 1980s, which in the author's opinion is on the verge of being repeated in the 1990s, is that the scope and duration of the attempted improvements is too big. Grand visions of "complete overhauls" that will pay benefits still abound.

GM's project Saturn is a great example. Huge sums of money and resources were invested to create a completely automated automobile production facility. The knowledge and goodwill that is resulting from this programme is benefiting many companies including GM, but it will be many years still before the investment pays for itself.

TQM is another fine example. TQM is still in its first decade as a prominent management goal and already public literature is questioning its effectiveness. The scope of TQM is not bounded. It includes every structure, process, technology, and communication within an organization. Further, this scope extends to all customers and suppliers.

Managing a "TQM Programme" is a multi-year undertaking which addresses every aspect of company operations. Simply said, TQM is impossible to define and then manage. It has no bounds.

Third, and the final example, is Business Process Reengineering-BPR. BPR is the hottest topic in corporate America in the early 1990s. Like TQM, the goal of BPR is admirable and tangible at a conceptual level. Like TQM, BPR also has no limitations on its scope.

The author's prediction is that BPR and TQM will end up in the same category once the approaches are tested over time. The post-mortem will read something like this. "We learned and we improved, but we spent huge sums of money and resources over a multi-year period that would have had much more impact if they had been more focused. In hind sight, we would limit and change our approach."

FOCUSED REENGINEERING

One of the primary arguments for "total reengineering" and TQM is that it is impossible to optimize the whole by optimizing the parts. From one view, this logic is quite sound and fundamental. From another view, it falls apart. If the scope of a project is so large that the risk measurably increases and the potential benefits are pushed into the distant future, then "where's the beef."

The Saturn project, as contrasted with the manufacturing industry in general, provides a reasonable illustration of this viewpoint. Manufacturing professionals spent a good part of the 1980s "linking islands of automation." First the work centres were optimized, then they were linked together. Changes to localized improvements had to be undone to optimize the flow of the whole operation, but benefits were being realized one cell at a time.

In contrast, GM had to wait many years for an entirely new "reengineered factory" to be built. The scope of the project was barely manageable and there were delays. The investment period was so extensive that it will take many years to recover it.

Companies should learn from their experiences. The author has a saying that summarizes these lessons learned. "Anything that is everything has a high probability of being nothing at all, or at the very least being disappointing." The goals of BPR and TQM are noble and tangible at a conceptual level, and are virtually not implementable. Improvement initiatives and projects should not be undertaken if the scope exceeds some of the practical realities that exist in the business world.

- Goals are not clearly definable and finite.
- Number of dependencies indeterminable.
- Market change cycle shorter than programme.
- Programme time exceeds employee durations.
- CEO uninvolved in unbounded projects.

While the "islands of automation" approach was not completely efficient, it was at least definable and manageable. And, it yielded benefits in a phased manner.

MARKET MEASUREMENT AND FORECASTING

Determining the potential of a market segment is indispensable for analysing the opportunities within a segment, and for deciding if it can possibly be chosen as a target market. It is not only the present market potential that is important and gives an indication of opportunities, but the firm must also be interested in market forecasts. The firm wants to survive in the long term and achieve its primary goal being to maximise profitability. Consequently market forecasting is also a very important aid for decision making by marketing management.

Measuring and forecasting requires an analysis of the market with an aim of expressing it in quantitative quantities both present and in the future. The quantitative measurement and forecasting of the market, together with its qualitative characteristics, are used as a basis for decision making by marketing management. Market measurement and forecasting can be seen as a subdivision of market research. This is a very superficial description of the important role market measurement and forecasting play.

THE IMPORTANCE OF MARKET MEASUREMENT AND FORECASTING

The main goal of market measurement and forecasting is to serve as an aid in the decisions that marketing management has to make. As has already been emphasised, the quality of decisions cannot be better than the information they are based on. Information gathered enables marketing management to make their decisions in a more objective and scientific manner and to lessen the risk and uncertainty that accompany subjective decisions and guesswork.

Naturally marketing management often make decisions which are not very important and/or do not hold a great risk. It would be ridiculous to arrange for the gathering of information by means of measurement and forecasting for all such small decisions of this nature.

Thus it must be emphasised that just as with market research, the importance and risk of the decision must be weighed up against the cost and time involved in the gathering and processing of information. Luckily there are various secondary sources which contain information regarding market measurement and forecasting. These sources include various published research reports which can be bought at a fraction of the price of a new market research project, and other sources which, for example, are available on computer and can be processed for clients' needs.

KEY CONCEPTS IN PERSPECTIVE

You have probably often heard of the concept"market potential". In marketing terms this means the maximum potential demand for a certain product in a specific market as a whole. Market potential is relevant to a specific geographical area, a specific period of time, specific types of products, a specific market segment, and is expressed in terms of all of these.

Another concept that is relatively seldom used in colloquial language is"sales potential", which pertains to the maximum demand for a firm's product. Sales potential, in the same way as market potential, pertains to a specific geographical area, period, and market segment.

Sales potential, however, does not pertain to the types of products a firm deals with, but to a specific product of the firm. Potential market share is the difference between market potential and sales potential and actually gives an indication of which part of the potential market the firm expects to gain.

Market potential, sales potential and potential market share can pertain either to the present and/or the future. A firm strives to enjoy its sales potential to the full. Market measurement and forecasting, however, are not only relevant to potential demand, but also to actual present and future sales.

The actual sales of a type of product in a specific area, period and market segment can also be called the effective demand. The market share of one of a firm's products is calculated by the ratio of the actual sales of the product concerned to the actual sales in terms of that type of product.

This ratio is expressed as a percentage. You have now learned the meaning of a few elementary concepts in terms of market measurement and forecasting. The marketer can compare these measurements to each other to gain insight into an important indicator of the success of the market offering in relation to other firms, the total market and the market potential.

MANAGEMENT OF MARKET MEASUREMENT AND FORECASTING

When you hear the management of market measurement and forecasting being expressed, by this stage you will already realise that it pertains to the planning, implementation and control of the market measurement and forecasting activities. Just as with any other scientific research, measurement and forecasting must be approached in a systematic and planned fashion to obtain the best value.

Problem and Information Needs

Seeing that it is very expensive to gather information, this step must be very carefully planned. The problem about which information should be gathered must be very clearly defined. Definition of the problem will determine which information must be clearly acquired so that only relevant data is gathered.

Gathering Relevant Information

Gathering information serves a dual purpose. Firstly, it provides sufficient data for the information need that is required to solve a problem, and secondly, it serves as a basis for the choice of particular methods of measurement and/or forecasting that are to be used.

Selecting the Methods of Market Measurement and Forecasting

The choice of measurement and forecasting methods begins with the evaluation of the data that has been gathered. There must be sufficient data of the right quality to provide a satisfactory answer to the problem by means of existing methods of analysis. Thereafter a suitable method can be selected by comparing the information needed and the abilities of the methods to meet the needs. The method is selected by taking the following factors into account:

- The nature and availability of data. Is there sufficient data of the right nature that can be processed with the help of the specific method? What pattern does the data follow? Certain methods of forecasting can only handle some data patterns effectively. The following patterns can appear in the data: tendencies, seasonal fluctuations and conjuncture patterns.
- The accuracy that is required for decision making is influenced by the choice of methods, as some methods supply a much more accurate answer than others.
- Costs play a role here, in the same way as they do in most business activities. Just as in the case of marketing research, the costs involved in the chosen method must be weighed up against the accuracy and importance of the required information. Some methods are able to deliver very reliable information, but at extra cost and time.
- *Time*: Careful consideration is necessary in deciding whether the period of time needed for measurement or forecasting will provide the desired result. Furthermore, the application of certain methods takes much more time than others.
- *Application*: The results must be useful to the people who have to base their decisions thereon. This means that the results must be of a nature that will enable these people to interpret and understand it effectively.

There are several methods that can be selected for measuring and forecasting the market.

Execution and Evaluation

Once suitable methods have been selected, processing of the information can begin. The results of measuring and forecasting must be evaluated for their accuracy so that corrections can be made in the future. Market forecasting pertains to the long term and unpredictable changes are likely to necessitate an adaptation of the results.

VALUE CHAIN

To analyse the specific activities through which firms can create a competitive advantage, it is useful to model the firm as a chain of value-creating activities. Michael Porter identified a set of interrelated generic activities common to a wide range of firms. The resulting model is known as the value chain and is depicted here: Primary Value Chain Activities:

Inbound Logistics > Operations > Outbound Logistics >

Marketing and Sales > Service

The goal of these activities is to create value that exceeds the cost of providing the product or service, thus generating a profit margin.

- Inbound logistics include the receiving, warehousing, and inventory control of input materials.
- Operations are the value-creating activities that transform the inputs into the final product.
- Outbound logistics are the activities required to get the finished product to the customer, including warehousing, order fulfillment, etc.
- Marketing and Sales are those activities associated with getting buyers to purchase the product, including channel selection, advertising, pricing, etc.
- Service activities are those that maintain and enhance the product's value including customer support, repair services, etc.

Any or all of these primary activities may be vital in developing a competitive advantage.

For example, logistics activities are critical for a provider of distribution services, and service activities may be the key focus for a firm offering on-site maintenance contracts for office equipment.

These five categories are generic and portrayed here in a general manner. Each generic activity includes specific activities that vary by industry.

SUPPORT ACTIVITIES

The primary value chain activities are facilitated by support activities. Porter identified four generic categories of support activities:

- *Procurement*: The function of purchasing the raw materials and other inputs used in the value-creating activities.
- *Technology Development*: Includes research and development, process automation, and other technology development used to support the value-chain activities.
- *Human Resource Management*: The activities associated with recruiting, development, and compensation of employees.
- *Firm Infrastructure*: Includes activities such as finance, legal, quality management, etc.

Support activities often are viewed as "overhead", but some firms successfully have used them to develop a competitive advantage, for example, to develop a cost advantage through innovative management of information systems.

VALUE CHAIN ANALYSIS

In order to better understand the activities leading to a competitive advantage, one can begin with the generic value chain and then identify the relevant firm-specific activities. Process flows can be mapped, and these flows used to isolate the individual value-creating activities. Once the discrete activities are defined, linkages between activities should be identified. A linkage exists if the performance or cost of one activity affects that of another. Competitive advantage may be obtained by optimizing and coordinating linked activities.

The value chain also is useful in outsourcing decisions. Understanding the linkages between activities can lead to more optimal make-or-buy decisions that can result in either a cost advantage or a differentiation advantage.

VALUE SYSTEM

The firm's value chain links to the value chains of upstream suppliers and downstream buyers. The result is a larger stream of activities known as the *value system*. The development of a competitive advantage depends not only on the firm-specific value chain, but also on the value system of which the firm is a part.

Bibliography

A. Pandu: *Global Marketing Management*, Global Research Publications, Delhi, 2009.

A. Parasuraman, Dhruv Grewal, R. Krishnan.: *Marketing Research*, Dreamtech Press, Delhi, 2009.

A.C. Mittal and B.S. Sharma.: *The Frontiers of Project Management Research*, Vista International, Delhi, 2010.

A.S. Rao: *Marketing Research*, Rajat Publications, Delhi, 2012.

Anil Kumar, Dinesh Chawla.: *Marketing Research*, Knowledge Book, Delhi, 2008.

Carl Mcdaniel, Jr., Roger Gates.: *Marketing Research*, Wiley Publications, Delhi, 2011.

Chandra Sekhar Gotlagunta: *Marketing Information Systems*, Kalpaz Publication, Delhi, 2012.

David A. Aaker, V. Kumar, George S. Day: *Marketing Research*, Wiley India, 2009.

Debashis Pati.: *Marketing Research*, Universities Press, 2002.

Dibyojyoti Bhattacharjee, Kishore K. Das.: *Statistics For Business And Marketing Research*, PHI Learning Publications, Delhi, 2010.

Dinesh Tomar.: *Marketing Research*, Vista International, Delhi, 2008.

G.S. Monga, Shalini Anand: *Marketing Management*, Deep and Deep Publications, Delhi, 2003.

K. Karunakaran: *Marketing Management*, Himalaya Publishing House, Hyderabad, 2011.

Kaushal Kumar.: *International Marketing Research Management*, Book Enclave, Jaipur, 2008.

Kiefer Lee, Steve Carter: *Global Marketing Management*, Oxford University Press, Jaipur, 2009.

M A Shewan: *Marketing Management*, Sonali Publications, Delhi, 2008.

M.L. Bhasin: *Cases in Marketing Management*, Vanity Books, Delhi, 2001.

N Tirupati Reddy.: *Marketing Research: Planning, Methodology and Evaluation*, Sumit Enterprises, Delhi, 2007.

Nigel Bradley.: *Marketing Research Tools and Techniques*, Oxford University Press, Jaipur, 2007.

P Kameswara Rao, N R V Prabhu: *International Marketing Research*, Excel Books, Delhi, 2007.

P. Arunachalam.: *Marketing Management and Trade Policy*, Serials Publications, Delhi, 2010.

P. K. Chopra, Bhawna Mehra: *Marketing Management*, Dreamtech Publications, Delhi, 2010.

Pallavi Bahuguna.: *Marketing Research*, Centrum Press, Delhi, 2011.

Pankaj Madan, Amit Mittal, Hemraj Verma: *Marketing Management*, Global Vision Publications, Delhi, 2010.

Parag Diwan & L N Aggarwal: *Marketing Management*, Vanity Books, Delhi, 2001.

Pingali Venugopal: *Marketing Management: A Decision-making Approach*, Response Books, Delhi, 2010.

Priyank Azad: *Marketing Management*, APH Publications, Delhi, 2012.

S H H Kazmi.: *Marketing Management: Text and Cases*, Excel Books, Delhi, 2000.

S.K. Bhatia: *Case Studies in Marketing Management and Research*, Deep and Deep Publications, Delhi, 2010.

S.K. Singh: *Marketing Research: Measurement and Method*, Anmol Publications, Delhi, 2010.

Saransh Pandit: *Modern Marketing Research*, Arise Publications, Delhi, 2007.

Sunanda Easwaran, Sharmila J. Singh: *Marketing Research : Concepts, Practices and Cases*, Oxford University Press, Delhi, 2006.

Index